Edge of the Orison

In the traces of John Clare's 'Journey out of Essex'

IAIN SINCLAIR

PENGUIN BOOKS

PENGUIN BOOKS

Published by the Penguin Group
Penguin Books Ltd, 80 Strand, London WC2R ORL, England
Penguin Group (USA) Inc., 375 Hudson Street, New York, New York 10014, USA
Penguin Group (Canada), 90 Eglinton Avenue East, Suite 700, Toronto, Ontario, Canada M4P 2Y3
(a division of Pearson Penguin Canada Inc.)
Penguin Ireland, 25 St Stephen's Green, Dublin 2, Ireland
(a division of Penguin Books Ltd)
Penguin Group (Australia), 250 Camberwell Road, Camberwell, Victoria 3124, Australia
(a division of Pearson Australia Group Pty Ltd)
Penguin Books India Pvt Ltd, 11 Community Centre, Panchsheel Park, New Delhi – 110 017, India
Penguin Group (NZ), 67 Apollo Drive, Mairangi Bay, Auckland 1310, New Zealand
(a division of Pearson New Zealand Ltd)
Penguin Books (South Africa) (Pty) Ltd, 24 Sturdee Avenue, Rosebank, Johannesburg 2196, South Africa

Penguin Books Ltd, Registered Offices: 80 Strand, London WC2R ORL, England

www.penguin.com

First published by Hamish Hamilton 2005
Published in Penguin Books 2006
1

Typeset by Rowland Phototypesetting Ltd, Bury St Edmunds, Suffolk
Printed in England by Clays Ltd, St Ives plc

ISBN-13: 978-0-141-01275-9
ISBN-10: 0-141-01275-7

To Anna

I had imagind that the worlds end was at the edge of the orison & that a days journey was able to find it so I went on with my heart full of hopes pleasures & discoverys expecting when I got to the brink of the world that I could look down like looking into a large pit & see into is secrets the same as I believd I could see heaven by looking into the water.

John Clare

Contents

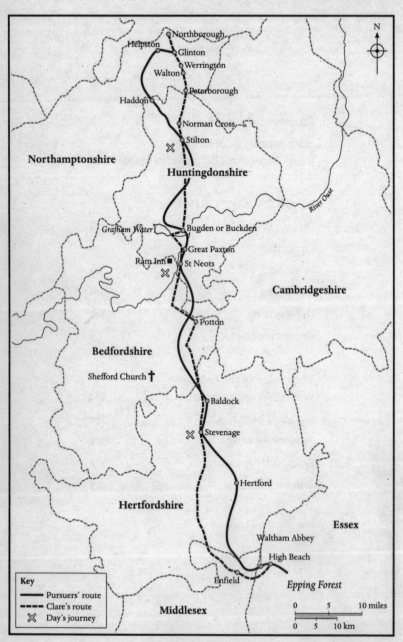

Journeys out of Essex: John Clare (1841) his pursuers (2000)

FLYING

The bulk of mankind is as well qualified for *flying* as *thinking*.

Jonathan Swift

Eighty Miles Out

It is a sleeping country, unpeopled and overlit. The sky cloudless. Horizon soft as milk in a contact lens. We wade, knuckling irritated eyes, through golden cereal fields, missing the familiar sound of the road. This is the conclusion, so we hope, of a walk from Epping Forest to Glinton (once of Northamptonshire, then Huntingdon, now Peterborough). Fifteen or so miles, a literal last leg, after three days shadowing the A1, the Great North Road, dawn to dusk and beyond: in the traces of the mad poet John Clare. Mad to be out of it, mad to chivvy the story along to a predestined conclusion, the reunion with his phantom wife, burnt Mary. Mad to shrug off the poultice of identity, to be everyone. Borderless as an inland sea.

You might think a circuit of London, twelve walks, inside and outside the orbital motorway, the M25, would have cured me of this neurosis: the compulsion to be on the hoof, burdened with packs, sketchbooks, cameras. Future memories. There was unfinished business. The gravity of London had to be escaped by a final, unwritten chapter, a shaky attempt to place my boots in John Clare's hobbled footsteps ('foot foundered and broken down' by the time he reached Stilton). The pain of Clare's journey ameliorated by the ecstasy of this achieved thing, a letter, never sent, to a dead woman. Mary Joyce of Glinton. Reluctant muse. Mother of invisible children.

I have written an account of my journey or rather escape from Essex for your amusement & hope it may divert your leisure hours – I would have told you before now that I got here to Northborough last friday night but not being able to see you or to hear where you was I soon began to feel homeless at home & shall bye & bye feel nearly hopeless but not so lonely as I did in Essex – for here I can see Glinton church & feeling that

Mary is safe if not happy & I am gratified though my home is no home to me my hopes are not entirely hopeless while even the memory of Mary lives so near me   God bless you My dear Mary   Give my love to your dear beautifull family & to your Mother

Renchi Bicknell, my companion on the orbital walks, a painter coming back to his practice after years running a bookshop in a small Hampshire town, had moved further west, to try a bed-and-breakfast place (fine view over the Somerset levels) in Glastonbury. His morning circuits, every day the same route, skirted the Tor, until this landscape, from which so many anxious seekers had squeezed the last drop of meaning, lost its novelty and became a part of him. He walked with his wife, plotting other excursions, the Clare hike, a heightened sense of vision. And then, motorway dust shaken off, an expedition with his son to Nepal.

Who you walk with alters what you see: the view, the prospect. With Renchi, circumnavigating London, rivers, concrete bridges over streams of blind traffic, we were conscious, above everything else, of doing a job: logging evidence, disturbing secure buildings, churches, bunkers, labouring at a narrative that was being shaped by our progress (the lack of it). Renchi's motorway paintings were obliged to perform as diaries, topographical records of simultaneity, like those pre-Giotto lives of Italian saints, where everything happens at once: temptation, triumph, torture, death. Resurrection. The soul, a golden kite, lifted into heaven by a flock of doves.

London's fringes, motorway 'edge lands', were infected by nightmares in asylums and hospitals, by the pressure of our nervous attention, worrying at the fabric, promoting a thesis: the M25 is more than a road, a misconceived one hundred and twenty miles of tarmac, uncivil engineering. It *means*. Our walk made something happen, happen to us. Nothing changed out there, in the drift of the motorists and their suspended lives; in my conceit, we were transformed. On a molecular level. Very gradually, and with considerable reluctance (on their part), forgotten ancestors acknowledged our feeble interventions. We re-lived their histories and remade our own. The noise of the motorway changed from nuisance to a chorus of oracular whispers, prompts, mangled information. Which we had volunteered to transcribe and interpret.

Walking with my wife, with Anna, the accident of our forty-year association having passed in an imploding instant of work, children, meals, holidays, bills, urgent inessentials and accidental epiphanies, was different. Very different. We started on the South Coast, the wind at our backs, a stroll to the pier; then the fishing huts, up the steps to the country park. A steady pace, no problems on the flat. But no detours, no church towers, those were Anna's conditions: no museums, book pits, interrogations of eccentrics met along the way.

We ambled, by gentle stages, from Hackney to Hastings, through a benign September; scarlet windfall orchards, the country estates of Russian oligarchs, golf courses where footpath signs had been destroyed and forest exits blocked by burnt-out cars. My perceptions were changed by the person who walked by my side. Some of the ground had been crossed, in the other direction, on the M25 expedition; but even the Darent Valley, Dartford to Shoreham, seemed new, quieter, less eager to pitch a yarn. A drowsy benevolence of climate and landscape. Dried hops were tucked under the straps of my rucksack to promote sleep. I didn't have to fix the details in my mind. I could draw them back, whatever I needed, from Anna. Our walk wasn't strategic. It marked a sea change, a shift in our lives. The slightly dazed second courtship of that time, after the children have left home, when we sleepwalk between what is lost and what we are learning to recover.

On a long straight road, coming out of Kent, there is a disconcerting incident. A stranger, dressed in the clothes Anna is wearing, a person of the same height, same length of stride, passes her, walking north. I'm slightly ahead, marching uphill towards a road sign, wanting to check if we're in the right place. I lift the camera, catch the moment. Anna split, travelling both ways at once; south towards the coast and back, alone, to London.

I remembered John Clare and his wife, the church-married one, mother of his children, Martha 'Patty' Turner, walking out near her father's cottage at Casterton: 'We both looked on the self-same thing/ Till both became as one.'

I imagined that stretching the length of the orbital circuit of the M25 into the English countryside, into somewhere as obscure (to me) as the territory between Peterborough, Market Deeping, Stamford and the A1, would complete that episode, bury it. But that's never how it works. My attempted divorce only confirmed the road as another ring, another shackle. London, better known, less understood, was more London than it had ever been; a monster greedy for expansion, eager to swallow underexploited ground and to bury it in satellite development.

Writers begin with discovery, discovering their subject matter, marking out their turf. And finish with dissolution. Learning how to suppress conditioned reflexes. Learning to forget. Arranging for their own disappearance. John Clare, hyped 'peasant poet', arriving by coach, a rattling, thirteen-hour journey from the George Hotel at Stamford to the Blue Boar in Holborn, saw the metropolis with clear, unskinned eyes: a city of ghosts, a dull river less impressive than Whittlesea Mere. His world had been stood on its head. By night, prostitutes promenaded the town, dressed like ladies. Resurrectionists lurked in the shadows. There were labyrinths beneath every loose paving stone.

If you are fortunate enough to start from London, the goal of every aspiring economic or cultural migrant, then any outward expedition becomes a flight. Heading up the Great North Road, we were not advancing into a fresh narrative, a novel set of coordinates, we were running away – like all those others who lost their nerve. The infant Pepys taken from the purlieus of St Bride's Church, off Fleet Street, to salubrious Dalston, haunt of milkmaids and agriculturalists. Daniel Defoe, the intelligencer, on the road: government agent, documentarist, contriver of myths and fictions. You can't just walk off, one fine summer morning, hands in pockets, and expect to get away, clear, scot free. You will be pursued: like debtors, subversives, those who adhere to the wrong religion.

Quit London and you will be trampled in the stampede. Plaguedodgers. Hunted criminals (like the Essex man, Richard Turpin). Property-hungry urbanites prospecting for unconverted cottages. The exhausted, the timid. The burgled, raped, assaulted. Overtaxed. Under-rewarded. Choked on thin air. Allergic to everything. Year-long hay fever. Summer colds that mutate into winter shivers. The sweaty heat of packed public transport, somebody hacking, coughing, spraying a fine mist down the back of your neck. The city is sick. The city is people. The city is watching you. It doesn't care. You don't register (until you transgress).

Eyes.

Lit from both sides. Memory and darkness.

A visiting poet, a hayseed, following the London mob, witnesses the funeral procession of Lord Byron; heading north, like the dead Princess Diana, away from town. A container of gritty ash in a carriage with an heraldic shield: the aristocrat's heart and brain removed for autopsy.

When, the walk from Epping Forest completed, John Clare lost himself in the long exile of Northampton General Lunatic Asylum, his eyes were smooth as stones. 'I have lost the irises,' he said.

Stilton

Clare arrived at Stilton, as we did, on the evening of his third day of walking; lamed, filthy, hallucinating. He starved, tearing handfuls of grass from the side of the road. We breakfasted, full English. He chewed tobacco. I worked moisture into a dry mouth, cleaned out pub lunches, reluctantly ceded, with wads of flavourless gum. He slept in a 'dyke bottom', outside town, where we booked ourselves into a decent pub. His memories, forged in a phantom letter (or confession) to his vanished muse, are one of the wonders of English prose. My notes, mere scribbles, are strategic prompts for some unresolved future project; more labour and sweat than anything our circumnavigation of the blight that is Peterborough could offer.

Major schlep from Alconbury up Ermine Street . . . old North Road to Stilton: abandoned cafés, petrol stations denuded of pumps . . . an industrial ice-cream bought from one of the last survivors, a filling station/ motel . . . you can see the destination signs bridging the parallel stream of the A1 like a set of gallows . . . Feet bad . . . hard to contemplate the final day, the day ahead. Bridge over A1 & into long thin stretch of the village of Stilton. Renchi dives into a bush to change his clothes, before the Bell Hotel. Chris Petit has driven up from London & is in the bath. We eat in the courtyard, with attendant Morris dancers. I don't have the haunted room, a small single looking out on the street. Dreamless sleep with no Anna to remember my dreams for me.

The journey from Epping, re-experienced in his detested Northborough cottage, undid Clare. He lived it through his notebook. He saw himself, once again, on the treadmill of the road: incidents from a fading fiction, the escape from Essex. An uncorroborated account of the last walk he would ever take, through summer countryside, one village to the next. Would he, in those asylum years in Northampton, travel more than five miles from his bedroom? A feared future in dispute with an ebbing past, events that might or might not have happened, makes sensory experience more acute, more painful. Journey as metaphor. Betrayed by the inadequacy of language. *Pilgrim's Progress* revamped, by the dispirited Clare, as a single, breathless sentence. A scream. The nib of his pen navigating a cluttered journal, before the doctors come for him, Fenwick Skrimshire and William Page. The poet's home-brewed ink, brown as a blood stain, eats through the surface of the precious paper. Word-marks too strong for the page to contain them.

but I dont reccolect the name of any place untill I came to stilton where I was compleatly foot foundered & broken down when I had got about half way through the town a gravel causeway invited me to rest myself so I lay down & nearly went sleep a young woman (so I guessed by the voice) came out of a house & said "poor creature" & another more elderly said "O he shams" but when I got up the latter said "o no he don't" as I hobbled along very lame

By the end of that third day, Clare was too tired to distinguish one hamlet from another, to copy names into his notebook. 'I have but slight recollection of the journey between here and Stilton for I was knocked up and noticed little or nothing.' The walker, early optimism dispersed, withdraws into himself. He sits under a hedge. He sleeps in a sodden ditch. He hears voices. He talks to strangers as if they were living and he, already, one of the dead.

Stilton, deprived of females to remark on the authenticity of our collapse, feels much as it did: limestone-golden in the twilight. The Bell is a coaching inn at which coaches no longer stop; it caters to a new clientele of wedding parties, shiny reps. Suits who have business with airfields. Awkward lovers in a black-beamed dining room. Travellers breaking their journey north.

Our overnight hotel is very much in the book, but the surrounding countryside is ex-directory, its history occulted; no suitable myths have, as yet, been discovered by the local heritage industry. Staying here, on a subsequent occasion, I set out for an evening walk: the village soon gives up the ghost. A sanctioned path rubs against the motorway, before twisting back among fields and ponds, rising gently towards the erased settlements of Caldecote and Washingley. Being allowed, even encouraged, to move in a particular direction kills the desire. Wildlife on its best behaviour. Muted squawks, strategic feather-ruffling. Cuteness as a plea against extinction (by gun, poison or lack of a well-connected pressure group).

There were no supplementary expeditions this time. Chris Petit was fresh. He'd strolled with us, on the first morning, from Epping Forest to the River Lea, then hopped a train at Broxbourne, pleading an afternoon appointment on the other side of town. Now he was back, with his video camera, personal bottle of Evian, selection of dark glasses: no unsightly rucksack. The camera slipped neatly into the pocket of his not-quite-distressed-but-ever-so-slightly-discommoded denim jacket. Discommoded to be in company with rough walkers, volunteer vagrants. With Renchi in his blue bandanna (adapted T-shirt). His shorts, ankle socks, sturdy calves. A Sherpa-sized pack leaking maps and grubby rags from every orifice. The badge of the sahib, Petit understood, was to carry nothing more than a splash of cologne.

Begin walking and reality kicks in. Inch by inch, through the heat of the day, this painful realisation: you are where you are. And you will stay there until you summon the energy to put one foot in front of the other. Petit has calculated the look perfectly: writer/director on sabbatical, a location scouting trip that might, though he won't admit as much, turn out to be an entry in his video diary. Ribbed, mid-calf socks of some non-synthetic material, enough tone in them to pick up naturally bleached desert-issue shorts. Tank commander's round, anti-glare lenses clipped over austere spectacles: he is prepared to take on Rommel. (James Mason as directed by Henry Hathaway.) Brown shoes, laced and gleaming, bulled overnight by an invisible batman.

Petit's status is ambiguous, he wasn't a party to the full Clare walk, but is willing to take a day out of town, as uncredited participant. The material might fit somewhere, a future documentary, part of an expanding catalogue of English landscape footage.

TO LONDON 74, it says, on the arch above the glass door of the Bell Hotel (with its three stars). Much further, the way we did it. With another fifteen miles to the finish. Maps examined, blisters pampered, we're ready to hazard a path across green-gold fields, across the A1 and the River Nene. The major decision is to avoid Peterborough (breaking faith with Clare, the town bridge, his meeting with Helpston neighbours, coins thrown from the cart). Peterborough has spun from its entrails a network of ring roads, roundabouts, underpasses and retail parks designed to confuse motorists (and pedestrians, vagrant folk); keep them, at all costs, away from the prolapsed centre. Cathedral, river meadows, arcaded mall complex. Newspaper headlines, signboarded in outlying villages, warn of a plague of rough sleepers, dispersed from Cambridge, and gifted with rail tickets to somewhere else, to Peterborough.

When we interrogated relevant OS maps, on the kitchen table in Hackney, the night before we set out, Anna argued that Clare's Helpston was closer to Stamford than to Peterborough. She had connections, a generation back, with that part of the world. With Glinton and the Fens. What did I know? One funeral service attended in St Benedict's Church? A couple of family visits? A swim in a gravel pit? No contest. Pan lids banged. Knives sharpened with intent.

She was right and she was wrong. Emotionally, Stamford is much closer. The Lincolnshire market town, a cluster of wool churches with fierce spires, was the destination of choice: grammar school, pubs, shops, narrow alleys, auction house. Peterborough, which threatened to swallow Glinton, as it had already devoured the villages of Easton and Werrington, was an invader, privileged by successive governments. A railway town. The town where Clare's madness was publicly demonstrated during a performance of *The Merchant of Venice*. 'We never went there.'

The discussion was heated. Enough to confirm my instinct to avoid the place entirely, to skirt its western flank, picking up on a long straight road from Castor to Helpston; a Roman road that marked one of the boundaries of Clare's childhood world. Peterborough suffered from another disability: its outline on the town guide was the twin of Hackney (pretty much England with Scotland bitten off). Hackney cut loose, transported into a planners' wilderness, with no proximate boroughs, no Islington or Bethnal Green, to temper its supernatural malignancy.

After a traditional hearty breakfast, on the morning of 20 July 2000, we crossed the wide Stilton street and headed off in search of a footpath to Folksworth. The idea was to work our way through the fields in the direction of Haddon, then towards the A1 as it pulled to the west. Haddon echoed my wife's maiden name, Hadman. Haddenham, Hadham, Hadun: dictionaries of place names concede that the root is probably manorial. Hadmans, if you find them, come from this part of the world. A relative, conducting a computer search, showed Anna a faded print-out: 'The German surname Hadman would appear to be a variant of the more numerous Handman and it is occupational in origin.' Hadmans belong near the base of the medieval social pyramid: 'Above the serfs were the peasants who worked the land in royal manors.' Anna's family were on the land, of the land, and in the land. Buried, forgotten.

My wife grew up in Lancashire, a suburb of Blackpool, but her father had a deep attachment to the place where he had lived until he went up to St John's College, Oxford. He bought a manor house in Rutland for his retirement. He wrote verse, in traditional forms, which he published – in an edition of one; a single, handsomely bound copy, now lost. Anna remembers a poem set in Market Deeping, bells heard across the Fens. From his home village? A redbrick house, close to the village green. Geoffrey Hadman was born in Glinton, the younger son of a farmer. He didn't tell her much about his parents, Anna said. And nothing about his other relatives. But he laid claim to kinship with a neighbouring celebrity, the unfashionable Helpston poet, John Clare. No details of this connection were revealed.

I liked the idea and it stayed with me. Clare's walk, out of Matthew Allen's Epping Forest refuge, High Beach, was one of my obsessions. I'd seen drawings of Clare on the road by the Leicester artist Rigby Graham in the collection of a dealer in Peterborough. Another dealer, Mike Goldmark, had shown me the tape of a television film made by Charles Mapleston, in which Graham (driven, not walking) recreates Clare's drudge up the Great North Road. Graham rather specialises in drudge, Neo-Romanticism with tractors and pylons. And the occasional disgruntled owl. Nothing suits him better than dabbing at a dissolving watercolour in a torrential rainstorm, while he confronts a Little Chef on the busiest section of the A1.

There was one other troubling detail: John Clare, through his rogue of a grandfather, John Donald Parker, the itinerant school-teacher/fiddler who abandoned his pregnant sweetheart, shared my provisional Scottishness. Highland blood, lost to both of us, affected him most as he slid into a confused plurality of identities in the dreary Northampton years. John Clare was the Anglicised version of the name on my birth certificate. My wife, like Clare's first love, Mary Joyce, attended a village school in Glinton. Anna was descended from tenant farmers who, like the Joyces, acquired land in the aftermath of the enclosures.

I was nervous enough of genealogy to re-read *Tess of the D'Urbervilles*. This business of manor houses on hills, perhaps connected to my wife's family, struck the wrong note. Beware, I reminded myself, of Hardy's Angel Clare; that character's priggish self-absorption, the furtive relish of his spurned wife's ancient blood.

Angel Clare rises out of the past not altogether as a distinct figure, but as an appreciative voice, a long regard of fixed, abstracted eyes, and a mobility of mouth somewhat too small and delicately lined for a man's.

Was Hardy reading the Northamptonshire poet? Did he adopt the Clare surname by accident, a half-memory of the peasant versifier grafted on to the evangelical parson's son?

Tess speaks:

'Because what's the use of learning that I am one of a long row only – finding out that there is set down in some old book somebody just like me, and to know that I shall only act her part; making me sad, that's all. The best is not to remember that your nature and your past doings have been just like thousands' and thousands', and that your coming life and doings'll be like thousands' and thousands'.'

Not to remember, that's the key. (Especially when your version of the past never happened.) Let family disappear, as our path through this wide field, parting waves of cereal crops, vanishes without warning. It was too good to be true, a track scythed for the benefit of hikers: hardtrodden, red-brown earth. There are attractions that we don't have time to investigate, earthworks, ponds, the remains of a motte and bailey castle – and then, a couple of miles to the south, Little Gidding. We'd planned, coming to Stilton from St Neots, before we found ourselves on that ghost road, Ermine Street, to detour in the direction of Little Gidding. But it didn't happen.

T. S. Eliot arrived there, the chapel, the site of Nicholas Ferrar's seventeenth-century Anglican community, in May 1937. The community gives its name to the last of his *Four Quartets*. Eliot sees this visit, unwalked, as a pilgrimage, resolution forced on an unshaped life. Either there is 'no purpose' or that purpose is shaped by a journey. 'Beyond the end you figured . . . altered in fulfilment.'

In August 1937, Eliot travelled to Somerset, to East Coker: another church, more graves. The desire, as the gravity of life pulls harder towards the earth, to locate and pay homage to his ancestors. To shrug off solitude. To belong. 'The future is before us.' He speaks in quotation marks. Concealed memory was always his method, his mask. Now, fearing war and the end of a cycle of civilisation, the mask bit into bone. His ashes would be buried in the parish church of St Michael, East Coker, where the first recorded 'Elliot', Katherine, was baptised in July 1563.

We are, this bright morning, pleased with ourselves, having come so far, and pleased with this land – in which nobody moves or stirs, no woodsmoke, no barking dogs. Our beacon is a mast on the horizon, the hill crest, a booster or photovoltaic scanner. Middle England, as we have discovered in the last few days, is stitched together from active or abandoned airfields, unpeopled farms, drowned villages and uncertain tracks that are visible only if you insist on them. You see the empty quarter, hedges cropped, absence of rubbish, middens, burnt-out shells of cars, and you sense: money. The lush chlorophyll of liquidity.

After the Enclosure Acts, Clare felt uncomfortable in newly ordered fields; he was watched, spied on, he had much better find himself a road.

> I dread walking where there was no path
> And prest with cautious tread the meadow swath
> And always turned to look with wary eye
> And always feared the farmer coming by

We don't crack along. Because Petit and his camera have a different eye on landscape. Renchi, by this time, had abandoned the detailed logging of the M25 project, snapshots, sketches. He had equipped himself with a cheap plastic prism and a Sherlock Holmes magnifying glass; he was shooting from the hip. The format of his prints was larger, rectangles busy with plant life, surreal close-ups or tilted expressionist skies. There were many versions of his red-faced companion with his Bunyan burden. Wattled neck-folds. Tight eyes. The eternal track. This happened. This is what I saw. I don't need to tell you everything. Spidery curtains, in a hotel bedroom, bunched in lazy folds. Sun splintering the breakfast window. Two walkers, monkishly tonsured, captured mid-stride, as they escape from Stilton, lurching towards furled cypress trees. Vision is also a form of narrative.

John Barrell, in the sharpest book on the subject, *The Idea of Landscape and the Sense of Place (1730–1840): An Approach to the Poetry of John Clare*, explains how the system works, this reading of view. There is, as eighteenth-century poets who learnt from the painter Claude understood, a 'circling landscape' – which, in obedience to accepted rules, can be projected on to canvas or given structure in verse. First, you require a proper elevation, a hill overlooking the *campagna* (the model is Roman). Then a soft blue horizon: how gratefully the eye leaps towards it, this hint of the celestial, before tracking back across an arrangement of parallel bands, towers, ruins, trees, peasants at work, groups standing around the entrance to a cave. There is a nice tension, Barrell suggests, between the 'prospect' and the properly schooled viewer. Otherwise, landscape is chaos: the busy particulars that overwhelmed John Clare. Everything happening at once and all of it with an equal claim on the observer's attention.

The horizon, according to Barrell, is 'at once the climax and the starting-point of the composition'. Dutifully, beyond Stilton, we search for it, this ambiguity; we tramp through fields marked off with bushes, thorn clumps, stands of trees. We're not excursionists, pastoral aesthetes; we're stalkers of the middle ground, reading contours, observed and observing. We must reach that radio mast, those pylons, to understand where we are; to appreciate everything we fail to notice when we pass through here, foot down, in our cars.

It's Barrell's fugue of 'roaming reassessment' that Petit is struggling to accomplish: where to point the camera, how to subvert the mechanics of exposure and focus. When to switch off. Naturally, this takes time. But Renchi doesn't do pauses. There is a rhythm to these walks that has to be maintained. My photographs show Chris, lagging way behind, gazing without conviction at a splash of Monet flora, poppies among the white, struggling to force nature to conform to the miniaturist proportions of his camera's touchscreen.

Duration is truth. The prospect, the 'circling landscape', is permanently out of the reach of duty-free technology. A panning shot would be an intolerable vulgarity. Petit pretends that he isn't here; he is an anonymous spy, hell-bent on erasing authorial signature. Tomorrow he'll be back in town, at his desk. That's what it says on the contract. Another thriller overdue, global conspiracies to unravel. 'The problem with my books,' he confesses, 'is that all the characters are dead.'

Two dogs appear. One is black and glossy, a labrador/retriever compromise with a savagely docked tail (which it attempts to wag). The other is, loosely, of the collie, German shepherd, wolf breed: amiable, to excess. They were hanging around, waiting for us, by a sign which said: 'Trespassers & Exercising of Dogs STRICTLY PROHIBITED'. These animals couldn't function without human company, a role to perform. Failing that, we will serve. At worst, they seemed to know which direction to take. I had the feeling they'd done this before. Walked out in company, returned alone.

Lurid sunshine on a red-grey road. No cars, no delivery vans, no people. Welcome to Middle England. Xanaxshire, in the wake of the Lloyds fiasco, the debt mountain, the Blairite establishment of urban fixers and spinners (no fox-hunting, acres of GM crops), is the home of dolour. State-sponsored clinical depression. Valium villages under the ever-present threat of imported sex criminals and Balkan bandits; human landfill dumped in an off-highway nowhere, an uneconomic airship hangar, a reclaimed bunker. Enclosure, suddenly, is a personal matter: you have been shrink-wrapped in your own skin and you can't get out. That's when the blameless horizon, that wood, those hills, begins to hurt. Immaculate properties from catalogue. New furniture under plastic sheeting. Television sets murmuring softly in empty rooms.

Faux-rustics in monster vehicles are servicing the USAAF base at Alconbury, or starting early for their circumnavigation of Peterborough (it would be quicker and less bothersome to commute to London). Those who are left are invisible, facing up to the consequences of the good life, the glutinous subsoil of somebody-else's labour; rituals of service and of release, drink, madness, suicide. Don't watch property programmes and buy into the conversion lottery for a barn you don't need and can't afford. Because at the end of it, you are misplaced. The heat of you, the immortal soul, is left behind. It looks comfortable, drifting through on a July morning, but living, off-road, in this summer country, is as hard as it gets.

The dogs, more by accident than intent, have put us on the right track, a drovers' path between rough hedges. Old-man's beard (also known as traveller's joy) hangs in a shaggy fringe, masking the pollen varnish of the fields. Bright colour in the abundant verges. Juicy air with a hit of toxic crop sprays. Our canine chums are panting, heavy-tongued, ahead of us, waiting by a gate; moving when we move. The novelty of their guidance has become a nuisance, a responsibility. They don't know anything more about the route than we do. They're faking it, in the hope that we won't turn them off, send them back to the misery of hanging about a farm gate, barking at delivery vans and the shadows of low-flying crows.

In truth, we're too lazy to dig the OS maps out of the rucksack. Petit, with his military background, barrack life, combined cadet force, does the business. We're going wrong, he says, slanting through unnecessary landscape, rippled hills. Country stuff. We must realign ourselves by the one constant, the song of the motorway, the whippy, many-laned A1 (very different from the sullen whine of the M25). Clare navigated, until he strayed out of his knowledge, by bird song. Petit does roads, Eddie Stobart lorries, dirty-white Transits, repmobiles, refrigerated carcasses swinging like a syncopated chorus line.

The fording of the A1 is a big moment. Out of the sleeping country around Stilton and into the Nene Valley, the beginnings of the true John Clare mapping. His circle of memory. Eight-mile walks (from his Helpston cottage) that defined his heart-place and sense of identity. The birds, animals, stones, clods, knew him. They confirmed, on a daily basis, the quick of his existence.

Our dogs crossed the A605, beyond Haddon, but the A1 was a

barrier they were forced to acknowledge. They stood together on the verge, surfing diesel fumes, as we dodged traffic, made our suicide runs. Getting over the road was easier than finding a way across the Nene; motorways are democratic, they'll splatter any life form, deranged pedestrian, badger or pecking crow. Water Newton, the village that guards the river crossing, is fastidious and unwelcoming. Museum-quality slate and stone, East German security. We skulk past 'Private Ground', skirt properties that back on to this desirable stretch of water.

On a bridge over the Back Dike of the Nene, the morning closes. Meadows threaded by a permitted footpath, the Nene Way. We locate the village of Castor, the unconvinced expectation of a pub lunch. A break before the walk up the road to Helpston and Clare's heritage-plaque, whitewash-and-thatch cottage.

The river pulls us to the east, but it remains our duty, fixed on Clare, to head north. We must respect that diagonal, the lie of the Jurassic, as exposed by another serial pedestrian, William Smith. Renchi, pockets heavy with chalk, limestone chippings, pebbles, brick, is big on geology. The colours of Smith's pioneering 1815 map are fixed in his head. Everything leads out of his West Country base, beyond Bath, to the Wash. Layer upon layer, fold upon fold. (Like my unorthodox vision of London as a conglomerate of pains and memories.) We chase the grain of limestone, slabs quarried and ferried down the Nene to Peterborough, a cathedral teased out of the ground.

We are on the outer rim of an eccentric saucer, the petri dish on which Clare fed, and out of which he was formed. Language predated poet, I have no doubt of that. It comes rough and fast, articulation is painful. Punctuation is superfluous when you transcribe the dictation of a multitude of dumb things. You suffer an atemporal otherness. The half-soul of a twin who got it wrong and survived, the weaker vessel. Bessy Clare was gone. Her womb-partner, poor John, lived. And lived with loss. Shame. Doubled consciousness, doubled guilt.

In the buffer zone, between A1 and A47, float the elements of our story. It's like marching through a theatrical costumier, trying on wigs, hats, boots. So many well-intentioned explainers busk different versions of the tale. 'Clare country' is marked by two spheres of influence, two great landlords (sources of patronage): Lord Milton (Whig) in Milton Park, now a golf course, and the Earl of Exeter (Tory) at Burghley, outside Stamford. Anything left over will be swallowed up by land-hungry bishops or Cambridge colleges.

It was Clare's associate, E. T. Artis, steward to Lord Milton, who unearthed the Roman settlement of Durobrivae (featured on our Landranger OS map as: 'Roman Town'). Artis came over from Milton Park, crossing the Nene, to pursue his hobby: scratching, digging out shards and artefacts. He conjured a Roman city from these bland meadows, a bow in the river. A collection of engraved plates, offered by subscription between 1823 and 1828, was published as *The Durobrivae of Antoninus*. Artis was made a Fellow of both the Geological Society and the Society of Antiquaries. And 'Friend Clare' was kept informed of his progress.

Jonathan Bate (in his Clare biography) explains how Artis took a life mask of the poet. Thereby inducting him into the panoply of Roman gods and champions. He drained colour, blood, to produce a simulacrum of rigidity and death. A mask without expression. Like the stiffened rictus on the face of a suicided farm-labourer fished from the Nene. The antiquarian steward, with his interest in genealogies, categories and subcategories, was attempting to make art from a living spirit. The process was uncomfortable. 'Clare,' Bate writes, 'did not enjoy the experience of having his head covered in plaster, and he opened his eyes before the oil was removed, causing them to smart and go bloodshot . . . Artis's handiwork fell to pieces after eighteen months.'

It is the river that fixes Petit. Minutes stretch into hours. He found his subject, dark water. He allows the camera to run with Warholite insouciance, until the battery gives out. Underwater clouds. Shrouded sun. Chris has more enthusiasm for rivers seen from a solid structure, such as this bridge, than for shorelines viewed from boats: those are a recurring nightmare, as I discovered on the Thames, when he fell asleep and woke with a start to the horror of Coryton oil refinery smokestacks. The same hellish fires that had been burning when he crashed out; our small craft making no headway against a running tide. This was a man haunted by drownings.

I kept myself busy while I waited. A repainted milestone: TO LONDON 81 STAMFORD 8. A restored millhouse. THIS EQUIPMENT OPERATES AUTOMATICALLY AND WITH-OUT WARNING. Water meadow, cows. Renchi lies flat on the river bank, ironed into the turf by his enormous pack. He hangs over the bank to photograph quietly flowing water, lilies as yolky and luscious as orchids. Focus is wilfully blown for a wider prospect, the broad river with its reflected clouds, Ophelia thickets of waver-ing reeds.

When we return, stomachs rumbling, Petit is still hooked over the rail, watching his camera do its work. Mesmerising abstraction. The Nene, with its arbitrary shifts and patterns, is cinema: as Petit recognises it. An occasion for tense watchfulness. He jabs a thick finger at the touchscreen, smearing any version that is too obvious.

The sun vanishes. We cross the bridge and march into Castor. Another hour or two should bring us to Helpston. To the meeting with Clare that we have been soliciting for three days, but which we have done everything in our power to postpone.

Hopes and Ashes

Something unexpected in an English churchyard: 'A poet is born not made.' Translated tag from the Latin poet Horace. Words cut by shallow strokes into John Clare's weathered tomb-lid: BORN NOT MAD. The E being lost, lichen-blotted. Pinkish-grey stone acts like an ornamental stopper on a perfume bottle. No fuss, no rhetoric. A slimline burial. The remains of a dead poet, his venom neutralised, posted into the ground like a tax return. Other Clares (not his wife or children) are scattered around, lolling with Stanley Spencer abandon, blithely awaiting the day of judgement. Open for inspection. The south-east corner of the burial ground of St Botolph's Church, Helpston. Helpston-next-to-Heaven. Next to nothing. These days, if you commission the monumental mason in Crowland, it will cost you £1 a letter. A good way to learn concision. E is the missing letter from the name of the village in which Clare was born: Helpstone, removed from Northamptonshire and given to the Soke of Peterborough. Made, mad. Helpstone, Helpston.

SACRED TO THE MEMORY OF
JOHN CLARE
THE NORTHAMPTONSHIRE PEASANT POET
BORN JULY 13 1793 DIED MAY 20 1864

Peasants were already, post enclosure, a diminishing resource. As were poets after the boom years of those death-courting Romantics. Keats, Shelley, Byron: all gone between 1821–4. Coughing, spitting blood, bitten by foreign bugs. Drowning in salt, drowning in earth. The grim reaper scoured the Mediterranean, the Grave Tour. Lay down your markers, boys, wherever you find a flat surface.

Body brought back from Northampton by railway, the only

journey Clare ever took in such comfort. In 1864 there was a functioning station in Helpston, opening the village to the wider world, making it ready to receive the remains of this exiled native. (He was laid out, overnight, at the Exeter Arms. And would have enjoyed that, a final jolly: suffering the foolish babble of the clowns, his neighbours. Clare's face was visible to the curious, a rosy death mask. Respects paid through glass. Pub breath clouding the porthole, the small Nautilus window in his oak submersible.)

Years before, in the fields, he had seen men out by Royce wood with poles, chains, measuring instruments, surveying his secret country for the coming railway. This island, edged against water, the huge skies of the Fens, was about to be breached. Its integrity ruptured: wetlands drained, open fields organised into new geometries – which called for new roads (Helpston to Glinton), for iron ladders to let the world in. The hidden places among woods and copses and beneath bridges, the trees into which he climbed, would no longer be secure.

There is no advantage in any man authoring his own life, predicting his future; it has already been told, warped, misappropriated by future biographers, special-interest pleaders, eco-romantics and fellow poets. Men such as Edmund Blunden, who used the intensity and detail of Clare's verse as a way of distancing the noise of the First War. Awkward memorials in every English village. Sculpted anthologies of sentiment. All these 'rescuers' of reputation would fix Clare to one place on earth: Helpston. Village as eye. Farms and cottages form a cluster like a ring of covered wagons, a focal point around which open fields spread. Roads were Roman, or they were drovers' tracks, footpaths, green ways flattened by habit.

Clare tried to be the architect of his funerary monument, but it didn't happen. BORN NOT MAD. Horace revised by harsh winds, soft stone. Directing his obsequies, ahead of the event, Clare asked to be put to earth on the 'North side of the Church yard just about the middle of the ground where the Morning and the Evening sun can linger longest on my grave'. At other times, brooding as poets will on his necessary end, he fancied the shade of a sycamore tree.

That position was taken. He was interred on the south side, returned to his parents, the sympathetic claustrophobia of cottage life. Returned to a period when he read his first poems out loud and pretended that they came from printed books. Death's narrow chamber was as busy and close as the smoky birthroom at the dreamlike border of his memory.

The epitaph that Clare composed was posthumously edited (yet again) into silence: 'HERE Rest the HOPES & Ashes of JOHN CLARE.' No takers for that one. Forget it. 'A poet is born not made.' Helpston gets its retaliation in early, the triumph of environment over visionary experience. Letters cut in stone like a copyright notice.

In St Botolph's churchyard you'll discover no sorcerer's grave warmed by morning and evening sun, no comfortable sycamore, but a granite jewellery box exposed to respectful eyes; a sharply angled roof, a set of dim symmetries endstopped by triangles and matching trapezoid panels. In life as in death, Clare fell victim to self-serving Victorian patronage. Tab picked up, so it is rumoured, by Earl Fitzwilliam. The grey village of Helpston, despite the Clare memorial paid for by public subscription, the poet's grave, plaque on cottage, never became a theme park. The Soke of Peterborough is not America, not yet. There is history enough to spare without pantomiming one sorry life. Nobody has the energy to work up the franchise. Nothing disturbs that sense of torpid, Middle English amnesia, thatched lives, the slow rotation of heavenly bodies: a place where it is hard to stop yourself floating outwards towards a hazy horizon, the hum of distant traffic on the dual carriageway.

Four years after his marriage to Martha Turner, just as the world began to know him, on the cusp of fame, visits to London, interested parties arriving with unwonted gifts, Clare saw himself, as Ronald Blythe reports, 'leaden with anxiety and thinking of death'. In his journal he issued instructions for his tomb.

I wish to have a rough unhewn stone something in the form of a mile Stone so that the playing boys may not break it in their heedless pastimes with nothing more on it then this Inscription

HERE Rest the HOPES & Ashes of JOHN CLARE I desire that no date be inserted there on as I wish to live or dye with my poems & other writings

Milestones stayed on the Great North Road, honouring the ghost walk, his true memorial, while the furniture of Clare's grave was invested with proper decorum. The peasant poet was wrapped in a paper shroud, thousands of lines of unpublished verse; hundreds of others emerged in 'improved' or bowdlerised revisions by well-meaning meddlers and promoters.

In 1820, on his first expedition to London, that primary disorientation, Clare did the tourist circuit and visited Poets' Corner in Westminster Abbey. On 13 June 1989, Ted Hughes unveiled a Clare memorial, and Ronald Blythe, President of the John Clare Society, gave an address. He said that Clare's 'enthralment by Helpston presents the indigenous eye at its purest'. The village, a bright lens in a circuit of fields, heathland, ponds, woods, had nominated its ideal viewer, its chosen voice. 'By his thrilling ability to see furthest when the view is parochial,' Blythe claimed, 'he was able to produce a range of perceptions which outstripped in their accuracy and authority all the literary attitudes to the countryside current in his day.'

The poet was the one chosen out of all past and future generations of Clares, labourers, parish clerks, railwaymen, to forge the memory system known as poetry; a refinement or written version of the folk songs his father knew and played. The gift for fiddling at wakes or weddings, for cash, was inherited from John Donald Parker, the itinerant Scotsman. And remained an important element in Clare's character, an excuse for sitting in the corner, playing for the company: rescuing songs, rather than inventing them.

The facts of such a life, exposed, teased out, become myth: a myth interwoven with the history of place. John Clare, the feebler of a pair of twins, was born in a heatwave (the weather we experienced on our walk from Epping Forest; green shade recklessly squandered for open roads and empty fields). In July 1793, the thermometer stayed in the eighties for ten or eleven days. A twin sister, Bessy, potential muse, the poet's 'lost half', dooms John to his quest; his guilt at surviving, at being male. Curses him with the impossible burden of explaining and justifying his presence on earth. Bessy's firmer resolution took her out early. The male twin, the survivor, fitted into a pint pot. 'What years of sorrow I had never seen,' Clare wrote. Wishing he had been spared that bruising passage, from salt to light.

'A gloomy village,' he characterised Helpston, 'on the brink of the fens.'

Parents: illiterate 'to the last degree'.

Cottage: a thatched loaf, close, cramped.

Father: Parker Clare, proud possessor of a first name given in memory of the absconding John Donald Parker. A bastardy without shame. 'My father was one of fates chancelings who drop into the world without the honour of matrimony.' The Clare grandmother, daughter of the Parish Clerk, untroubled and unhusbanded, lived to the age of eighty-six.

Mother: Ann Stimson. Eight years older than her husband, daughter of the town shepherd from Castor, Ann had four children, two living beyond infancy. Clare considered the lack of siblings, at a time when families of ten to fifteen were common, a blessing. More space, fewer mouths to feed: less suffering. Castor and its common land, running towards Marholm and Werrington, was another country. Six miles off.

Parker Clare laboured, peasant for hire, with a shared dwelling and shared garden (productive of Golden Russet apples). He was established in his place, status somewhere below that of 'cottager' (keeper of cow or pig, cultivator of vegetables). A noted local wrestler, strongman. When he began to fail, bent with rheumatism, Fenland damp eating into his bones, Lord Milton sent him to Scarborough, the Sea-Bathing Infirmary, for rest and recuperation. Trying to save on expenses, Parker walked part of the way home: exposure to English weather brought back the pains and 'reduced him to a more deplorable state than ever'.

Husband and wife: their affections, their troubles. Her sharpness, his mulish strength. They appear, now, to a reader of my prejudices and enthusiasms, as emblematic figures from a Beckett play, harshly sentimentalised, short on text: the Nagg and Nell (of *Endgame*) confronted by the wonder of this weak and willing child. His gifts, his differences. They are timid of exploitation. Of standing out. Ann Clare, when coins can be found, secures an education at the church school in Glinton, for both children, John and his sister, Sophy.

John Clare is hungry for it, books, the knowledge his mother believes to be a kind of witchcraft. Clare meets the children of tenant farmers. He meets Mary Joyce, daughter of James. He flings an unripe walnut in the churchyard, strikes Mary in the eye: myth. As in folk legends, the bond is made and the long price will have to be paid. Memory, highlighting such fantastic episodes, shorthanding the complex excitements and longueurs of childhood, inclines towards fiction: metaphor. Walnut, eye. Initials carved in soft stone above the church door. Walks to a bridge, the limits of knowledge, the beginning of the drowned lands.

Figures silhouetted and seen from behind. Childhood sweethearts. Mother at the cottage door. Father and son. A broad-shouldered, sturdy labouring man and his short, slight son (who would gain weight, bulk, ruddy cheeks in the asylum years). John Clare works at threshing in the winter barn with his child's flail. He works in the fields. Parker Clare, broken down, on parish relief, hobbles out to fill holes in the road. John looks for hedges to hide behind, somewhere in which to breathe without others hearing the sound.

By routine, small joys, a circuit of walks, the horizon is fixed. If a child died, another in the family would inherit its name. The poet's sister, Sophy, married William Kettle, and gave birth to two Johns. Clare's great-grandfather, the Parish Clerk, another John, fathered four sons with the same name. Three dead Johns who failed to reach their fourth birthday, before the last of them lived out a reasonable span of twenty-eight years, and married another Mary. It's not a failure of imagination: think of Helpston as a village in a wooden box, thatched cottages, church, public house, cows, sheep, and enough figures to dress the set, act out dramas of rural life. Johns and Marys, all of them. The chain stretches back, before enclosure, for centuries, with just enough fresh blood, if you're lucky, to avoid inbreeding and idiocy. Scroll through the census entries for the nineteenth century, somewhere to the east of Peterborough (say, Whittlesey), and check that final column: a deluge of ticks in the space left for the dumb, halt, lame, mad.

Clare's vision, the stages of enlightenment and self-knowledge, opens with journeys on foot (later by coach) that carry him away from his heart-place, the village of Helpston.

Childhood: a day's excursion, 'out of his knowledge', to Emmonsales Heath. A missing village lad, before the time of tabloid sex monsters, whipped on his return.

Early adolescence: confused, passions too large for his small frame. 'Gloves to hide my coarse hands . . . out grown my coat and almost left the sleeves at the elbows.' Travelling down the Nene to Wisbech. Failed audition as lawyer's clerk. Overprepared, awkward in kitchens. Wandering free, while he waits for the return trip, in a foreign town: bookshops, faces.

Late adolescence: unconvinced rebel, docile runaway. Escaped gardener. Over the wall at Burghley, hiking to Grantham and Newark-on-Trent. Disorientation: 'I became so ignorant in this far land that I could not tell what quarter the wind blew from & I even was foolish enough to think the suns course was alterd & that it rose in the west & set in the east.'

Hangdog return, stealing away in the night, 'ninepence half penny in debt'. A hard trudge back to Stamford, rough sleeping under the trees. 'The rhyme fell thick in the night & we was coverd as white as a sheet when we got up.'

Young married man: drawn by the gravity of future fame to London. A cure for all ills. Four trips to the city he would never learn to love. Theatres, drink, prostitutes, society. Ghosts, demons. Literary ladies and admirals. Possession by the spirit of Lord Byron.

A final road: High Beach to Northborough. Wiping memory,

putting London in its place: as a remote and cruel abstraction. Tramping instead of riding. The solitary figure on the endless road, sleeping with his head to the north, is a provocation for future walkers. Those who, hearing footsteps, cannot leave them alone. The ones who think that tracing a sleepwalker's journey will show them how to write.

Then it struck me. 'A poet is born . . .', the pious tag on Clare's gravestone, echoed a passage in his work. Trapped in the claustro-phobic regime of Epping Forest, in that great year, 1841, before the horror overwhelmed him, he moved from witness to visionary. He affected, and was affected by, place and weather. He registered a violent storm on 15 July, five days before he started walking: 'Roll on, ye wrath of thunders, peal on peal/ Till worlds are ruins and myself alone.' The fool becomes Lear. The road, if he can find it, now that those tricksters, the gypsies, have gone, will lead him back to an earlier self. To his wasted paradise. Possessed by Byron, or playing that game, he launched the satire of *Don Juan*. Corrupt politicians, unfaithful wives, addled eggs. 'I would MP's would spin less yarn.' Wellington, Melbourne. Hot little Vicky and her German husband. The poem of the world, cooked in the madhouse, begins with a stark declaration.

'Poets are born' – and so are whores – the trade is
Grown universal: in these canting days

Helpston

The publican's face in Castor, it was just what we expected: ginger eyebrows, broken veins in ruddy cheeks, unsubstantiated grin. He leans over the slatted table, resting his weight on powerful arms, ice-blue shirt, sleeves rolled to the elbow. 'Sorry, gentlemen.'

No food, no kitchen: an eccentric request, in the middle of the day, off-highway in England. Can't be done, but – seeing as how we've walked here from London – we can take a pint, outside, before we move on. So long as it's not – tough luck, Chris – the black stuff. Guinness pump is down.

I like this yard with its limestone discriminations, ancient wall of trapped sunshine, yellow slabs underfoot. Tokenist dressing of wallflowers. I like the publican. You could transpose him, with a dirtier shirt, straight into the Clare story. Seen it, done most of it, heard some tales in his time (he's paid to listen). Want to walk from Epping Forest to Glinton, gents? Fine with me. Swim, against the tide, down the Nene to Wisbech? Takes all sorts. Put your coins on the table, drink up, and don't piss in the terracotta.

A Peterborough face recovered from Clare's walk, from his life. They don't migrate these natives, they've been hanging around the same eight-mile circuit, good rich ground, since the Middle Ages. Sometimes farmer, sometimes butcher, sometimes publican: the expression of the man who slides your money into his pocket never changes. Country fatalism. It's bad, gentlemen, but it could be worse. When Clare, thrown fivepence from the cart of Helpston neighbours, demanded 'two half pints of ale and twopenn'oth of bread and cheese', that was perfectly acceptable. His pennies were as good as any other man's. Three and a half days of road dirt, gravel rattling in the shoe, dried sweat, the odour of a runaway; these things can be ignored as long as your equity holds out. The

Castor publican who pocketed our change had a professionally disinterested way of not-listening to a tall tale: strong teeth, weather in his face. A man who has come across from his fields to concede the obligatory show of hospitality. For a consideration.

Without funds, Clare wouldn't approach a public house. He knew from experience what would happen. Crippled foot, darkness falling, 'very uncomfortable and wretched'. Towards evening, after a long day, he located the Ram, lights in the window, countrymen drinking: 'I had no money and did not like to go in . . . so I travelled on.'

Beyond Castor, it's a great road for walking (if the cars don't get you). A classic straight track (on the Roman model), shaded by poplars or solitary hawthorn bushes, diminishing into hazy distance, between yellow fields, clumps of woodland. Warm pinkness in the cambered surface along which we progress, the last men in England. Heat rising from tarmac, drugged flies.

Once you cross the A47 (four lanes, all empty), and acknowledge the torched car in the cornfield, you discover that commonplace traffic, the swinish rush of metal, is happening somewhere else (probably Peterborough). If we don't meet Clare on this stretch, we'll never find him. Shimmering afternoon country, the thirsty pints at Castor, encourages the shamanic sense, it's not an illusion, that Hardy describes in *Tess*; we are flying, hovering a few inches above the road's sticky surface. Being carried forward without physical effort. Tess and her companions, drink taken, return to their chicken farm:

They followed the road with a sensation that they were soaring along in a supporting medium, possessed of original and profound thoughts, themselves and surrounding nature forming an organism of which all the parts harmoniously and joyously interpenetrated each other.

Chris deals with the burnt car, patterns of rust and scorch, gaping jaw. He comes as close to contentment as he ever will in this vale of tears. He has noticed a chain of polished repmobiles, in puddles of cool shadow, spread at regular intervals along the road, between Castor and Helpston. A sleep-therapy zone: men in striped shirts and loosened ties, necks twisted, cheeks against glass, mouths agape. Electric windows buzzed down. Sandwich wraps, burger cartons, cigarette packets. Mobiles switched off. The zizz. The throb of cooling engines. Slurry-eros of liquid shit, wild flowers, honeyed air. An ecstatic escape from Peterborough and its crackskull motorway system. They smile in sleep. Within the pod of the complimentary motor, the boxes of stock, lightweight jackets on hangers, they lay their urgent spiels to rest. A phantom babble of soft sell, unrepeatable offers, like wind in electricity cables.

Petit has located a definitive image of Blair's England. A best-value use of countryside. Every drowsy copse an oasis, every shady space pre-booked. Clare's mistake was in not travelling this road; he laboured through Peterborough, aiming for the Beehive at Werrington. Then rode the last miles in a cart, a Tyburn tumbrel, in the company of a stranger, his wife. A woman who 'caught fast my hands & wished me to get into the cart but I refused & thought her either drunk or mad'.

Meadowsweet, cow parsley, hairy verges: our road dips and climbs, one of us strides ahead to the brow of the next moderate hill, the point where overreaching branches meet and mesh. The Clare we searched for was the Helpston child, coming towards us, on that mythic expedition to Emmonsales Heath. The heath skirted Castor Hanglands Woods – formerly, Castor Anglings Woods – which we were now passing. We stayed alert for John Clare's first steps in his willed disorientation.

I had imagind that the worlds end was at the edge of the orison & that a days journey was able to find it so I went on with my heart full of hopes pleasures & discoverys expecting when I got to the brink of the world that I coud look down like looking into a large pit & see into its secrets the same as I believed I coud see heaven by looking into water

Searching for heaven, as Petit had done on the bridge over the Nene, is an initiation of gazing, losing yourself. Flowing water is a magician's hinge, the passage between worlds. John Clare's mother was absolutely right, book-learning is a kind of witchcraft, letters of the alphabet are instruments of intent. Like the coded language Clare noticed in the sky above flat fields. 'Wild geese scudding along and making all the letters of the Alphabet as they flew.'

The childhood walk to Emmonsales Heath, remembered, re-experienced as one of Clare's 'Autobiographical Fragments', was an announcement of difference, separation from the clods and clowns of Helpston.

I was finding new wonders every minute & was walking in a new world often wondering to my self that I had not found the end of the old one the sky still touchd the ground in the distance as usual & my childish wisdoms was puzzld in perplexitys

A sickness vocation: poetry. The poet's response to the privilege of place, the numinous road. To languages he would learn, of birds, snakes, foxes. Snail shells he would collect. Orchids. Difference was expressed as a fit, a throw of light: the way sorcerers feel each stage of their initiation as a physical blow, drowning in air, breathing in water, lifting from the ground. Elective epilepsy: plant-induced or resulting from trauma, a car crash, a street assault. The walker overwhelmed by the walk.

Edward Storey in his Clare biography, *The Right to Song*, describes 'fainting fits which [Clare] imagined owed their origin to the accident he had seen a few years earlier'. A man called Thomas Drake who 'fell off a load of hay and broke his neck'.

The accident happened in 1811, at harvest time. Clare was eighteen years old. Looking at something cold and empty, he knew the fear of being possessed by another man's spirit. Witnessing the chill of death. Light gone from the eyes.

The ghastly paleness of death struck such a terror on me that I could not forget for years & my dreams were constantly wanderings in churchyards digging graves seeing spirits in charnel houses etc etc In my fits I swooned away without a struggle . . . but I was always warned of their coming by a chillness & dithering that seemed to creep from ones toes ends till it got up to ones head when I turned senseless & fell Sparks of fire often flashed from my eyes

As a child, Clare solicited dramas that would bring about the necessary fracture in consciousness; make him a poet by default. He fell from a tree: 'I lay for a long time and knew nothing.' He slid into a gravel pit: 'I felt the water choke me and thunder in my ears.' A makeshift raft of bulrushes sank beneath his weight: 'I made shift to struggle to a shallow bush & catching hold of the branches I got out but how I did it I know not.'

Crossroads: Castor 3, Helpston 1¾. Barnack 4, Marholm 2. Puff-ball blisters cushion my tread, the cheapest form of inflatable trainer. Are we on time? I haven't looked at my watch in days: the pubs are all shut, we start walking as soon as it's light. I said to Anna, when she dropped us in Epping Forest, see you in Glinton at four o'clock on Thursday.

In response to a show he's seen at Tate Britain, a list of names painted on the wall, everyone the artist ever met, Petit amuses us by excavating celebrities of his own. He's fond of lists. And would write, if commissioners went for it, all his books that way. Favourite sounds from films: the whispering leaves of Maryon Park (*Blow-Up*), airport footsteps from *Point Blank*. Memorable meals. Much-loved cars. Coats, hairstyles, shoes, cigars. Recalling his time drifting around the Euro festivals as film critic (or film-maker), adventures as freelance essayist and thriller writer, Chris assembles an impress-ive (and ironically delivered) troop: the cocktail party from hell. Flesh pressed. Bottles shared.

J. G. Ballard. Warren Beatty. Robbie Coltrane. Richard Condon. Eddie Constantine. James Crumley: 'Montana man, drinker, very chippy.' Catherine Deneuve: 'Shared joke about *Repulsion*.' Ed

Dorn. Manny Farber. Fassbinder: 'Sat at the same table a couple of times, he was sweating in a heavy leather coat, wouldn't talk.' David Gascoyne. Annie Giradot. Lord Gowrie. Gloria Grahame. Monte Hellman: 'Played back a blank tape.' Werner Herzog. Patricia Highsmith. Bo Hopkins: 'Met him in a bar in LA, on his way to a wedding.' Geoffrey Household. Anna Karina. Harvey Keitel. Kraftwerk. Howard Marks. Lee Marvin: 'Interesting man, knew where he was, flat overlooking some stables.' Ed McBain. Michael Moorcock. Robert Mitchum. Jack Nicholson. Jack Palance. George Pelecanos. Donald Pleasence. Derek Raymond. Nic Roeg. James Sallis. Martin Scorsese. Andrew Sinclair. Steven Spielberg: 'Devouring a hamburger at ten in the morning.' Terence Stamp. Sting. Francis Stuart: 'That's right.' Donald Sutherland: 'Least actorly of actors, on his way to see Fellini.' François Truffaut. Christopher Walken: 'Strangest of them all by a country mile.' Wim Wenders. Donald Westlake: 'Can't see where those early books came from.' Billie Whitelaw. Shelley Winters. Rudy Wurlitzer.

Enough. The road is too crowded now, city noises, dry hum of air conditioning in generic hotel suites: Petit waiting for Scorsese in the wrong room. Cold coffee, remains of breakfast on a tray. Ghosts weary of playing themselves. Writers caught on the hop, terrified of giving the game away. Francis Stuart, toothless, bulb-nosed, admitting to everything: Yeats, Joyce, Beckett. The particular sound of white tyres splashing through puddles outside a restaurant in Berlin. Great days being wiped, inch by inch, as he stares, with no sign of recognition, at a dull landscape, a wet road.

As we approached Helpston, coming out of the woods, we spotted our first vehicle: a police car with a red stripe, parked, waiting. To warn off the unwary. Clare left here four times for London, days, weeks, mere excursions, but his list of celebrities could trump Petit, quality if not quantity.

Samuel Taylor Coleridge: 'His words hung in their places at a quiet pace from a drawl in good set marching order, so that you would suppose he had learnt what he intended to say before he came.' Thomas De Quincey: 'Something of a child overgrown, in a blue coat and black neckerchief.' Charles Lamb. William Hazlitt: 'For the blood of me I could not find him out.' John Taylor (the publisher Clare shared with Keats). Henry Cary, Dante translator. J. H. Reynolds. Thomas Hood. Lord Radstock. Lord Milton. The Marquess of Exeter. Painters of the day: Peter de Wint, Rippingille, Sir Thomas Lawrence. Thomas Wainewright, forger and poisoner: 'A very comical sort of chap.' Scottish poet Allan Cunningham. And, unconfirmed, Alfred Tennyson (visitor to High Beach, Dr Allen's Epping Forest retreat). Plus those with whom he conversed in secret, the ones he would become in the asylum years: Lord Byron, Lord Nelson, Jack Randall the prizefighter. And Victoria's mother too, it must be assumed, when Clare announced himself the spiritual father of the young queen.

The poet's Helpston cottage is endlessly reproduced in engravings, postcards, watercolours, but it's not here. This whitewashed replica is an occupied home, a desirable property (convenient for Peterborough). The Clareness of the thing is an act of faith.

IN THIS COTTAGE JOHN CLARE
THE POET WAS BORN
JULY 13: 1793
THIS TABLET IS ERECTED BY THE
PETERBOROUGH MUSEUM SOCIETY
1921

What is it about dead poets, their huts and gravestones? What are we looking for? Sombre enthusiasts, joiners of literary societies, guided tourists: what do you want? The superstition of touch. Affection without responsibility. We dowse with slim pamphlets handed out by museums, special-interest maps. We've walked all these miles for a shrine we are barely capable of recording.

With his magnifying glass, Renchi examines the grain in the stone, the Clare plaque – and the face of the young man in the William Hilton portrait of 1820, reproduced on the cover of my paperback edition of the poems. Hilton's Clare is a PR cameo, a lollipop of delight. A noble peasant in autumn's country casuals. (Down the street is Helpston's Gothic memorial with its grudging quote: 'THE GRAVE ITS MORTAL DUST MAY KEEP.') What happened? This can't be the same person as the old gentleman with the high forehead and bushy eyebrows, the private patient photographed in Northampton General Lunatic Asylum. The post-card with its oversize facsimile signature. The madhouse worthy looks towards us with narrowed eyes. Hilton's young man, pink in his cheeks, ignores our impertinent curiosity. He stares, unblinking, at an imaginary window.

I braved London's bright new National Portrait Gallery to witness the original Hilton painting, proudly hung with other Romantics of the 'Late 18th and Early 19th' centuries: Keats, Shelley, Byron, stern Wordsworth, Coleridge. High-toned company. William Blake. Cockneys and mountain men. Poets of family, education, private means: with access (when required) to conversation, credit at the chemist's shop.

Portraiture is the harbinger of mortality: if you are willing to be painted, you are willing to die. The Hilton Clare, full-lipped, fine-featured, has something of the contemporary poet Lee Harwood: clear eyes set on a horizon we can't bring into focus. Harwood's work, from whatever era, twenty years old to sixty, is youthful and optimistic: open. Darkness, at the point in Clare's career when Hilton caught him, stays in the background, bistre and lampblack. The artificial night of the studio. He's proud of the long coat (so green that it's brown), the high, soft collar and that astonishing necktie or cravat, a de Kooning spasm of yellow and green and gold. An oily river leaking from his throat.

The Hilton image, computer enhanced, is everywhere. A slice of it dresses Jonathan Bate's definitive biography. This is the Clare so many readers want to know, the country boy in town, on the cusp of fame. Helpston, once indifferent or antagonistic to the Clare project, now searches for ways to exploit the memory. Poet and village, so they think, are indivisible.

Combing the attic for family material, clues to her father's boasted connection to Clare, Anna found an envelope addressed in her mother's hand to '63 de Beauvoir Road'. This was our first experience of Hackney, a communal house on the west side of Kingsland Road. A mid-Victorian speculation with ambitions to infiltrate Islington. 'Special envelope – keep!' That was the extent of Mrs Hadman's message. The envelope was the point of the communication. It must have been 1968, the year before we took the fatal step and moved east, never to move again.

175TH ANNIVERSARY

OF BIRTH OF

JOHN CLARE

13 JULY 1988

HELPSTON PETERBOROUGH

The post office franking machine got the date wrong by twenty years. And offered, as compensation, a grey-on-grey version of the Hilton portrait, cropped and reversed: Clare spun deliriously, defined by dates he didn't want cut into his memorial slab. My mother-in-law, for whatever reason, was in Helpston on the day, 13 July, of the Clare anniversary. She may have been visiting the family grave in Glinton.

As the Hilton portrait flatters our notion of what a poet should be, imperfections smoothed, so Clare's Helpston cottage has shaken off its menial status, its smoky, small-windowed darkness. It stands back from the road as an extended white block, hung with flower baskets like a Routier-recommended restaurant. Roses climb the walls. Additional bedrooms, eyelashes of a Dusty Springfield luxuriance, bulge from crisp thatch above twinkling glass. The milestone Clare fancied for his grave decorates a welcoming mat of close-cropped grass, set in a bed of gaudy, freshly watered busy Lizzies.

In his book, *Literary Britain*, originally published in 1951, the photographer Bill Brandt swooped on 'Clare's Birthplace'. The idea of this project was: characteristic scrap of verse on the left-hand page, place associated with poet on the right.

> But painful memory's banish'd thoughts in view
> Remind him, when 'twas young, what happy days he knew.

Punctuation and sentiment are over-refined: Brandt (secretive, self-inventing, perverse) contrives a theatrical composition to counter the upbeat message with Fenland gloom. Graded monochrome doctored in the darkroom. A creeping miasma of sullen harm. A low stone wall where the driveway now runs down the east side of the cottage. Absence of TV aerials and masts. No milestones set in flowerbeds, no winking bedroom windows in pristine thatch. The rear of the cottage, back then, suggested a turfcutter's shack. Clare remained in the limbo of libraries, his books carted off to Northampton, his snuffboxes to Peterborough. The shoes with the flapping soles were not yet holy relics.

Brandt's vision of literary England is: absence. Classical statuary in sombrous gardens, rocks in operatic slap, lowering clouds, effigies – scarcely a human figure in the entire collection. A water-reflected stickman represents Parson Crabbe. (Clare mistrusted parsons. Crabbe, he reckoned, wrote about the peasantry 'as much like the Magistrate as the poet'.) England as a park from which poets have been permanently banished, leaving behind some very nasty weather and enough architectural salvage to fill a Hoxton builder's yard.

Morning mist over warming ground is typical of Huntingdonshire, Lincolnshire, Northampton: wretched conditions for airfields and motorways, a boon to photographers with a preordained vision. Brandt's suggestion is that the poet has just this moment stepped out. Clare, the peasant verse-maker, is never allowed to move beyond the Helpston perspective. The cottage looks on to a village green. The village is an island in a system of open fields, bordered on one side by low, wooded hills, the quarries of Barnack – and, on the other, by dark Fens, from which invaders, hobgoblins and Molly Gangs, will come.

In the afterburn of the Sixties, Clare's cottage was noticed by mid-Atlantic modernists: its potential as real estate was exposed. The poet Tom Raworth, acknowledged by his peers for his speed and sharpness of eye, had been packaged with the Clare lookalike, Lee Harwood. One of those three-poets-for-the-price-of-one Penguins. We all had the book, Liberal Studies would have collapsed without this convenient prompt. Harwood had contacts with the New York school (Ashbery, Koch) and Raworth was perpetually touring the States or signing in at some writers' punishment colony. Now, in the way of these things, the freelance life, he was at Essex University, outside Colchester. A friend and colleague of John Barrell, who published his Clare study, *The Idea of Landscape and the Sense of Place*, in 1972.

Raworth remembers Barrell investigating original Clare manuscripts, pouring over enclosure maps for Helpston. The poet Donald Davie's influence was still felt in Colchester (an active Essex/Cambridge nexus): Thomas Hardy, Pound, the landscape-architecture of poetry. Primary research was back in favour: examination of documents, land registers, meditations on painters and paintings. Along with, in the case of the modernist poets, scavenging of cultural ephemera: Hollywood clips, vintage postcards, kids' crayon drawings, French dialogue overheard and misreported. The dominant theory, adopted from a reading of the Black Mountain poet Charles Olson, promoted 'open field' poetics. A system which sat nicely alongside Barrell's work on Helpston and enclosures. 'The eye, snatched to the horizon, roams,' Barrell said. Clare's work belonged in the closed system of traditional forms. When the circle of Helpston landscape, once open and common to all, was hedged and divided into a complex jigsaw, John Clare was one of the hedgers. He needed the work. The rest of his life would be a series of personal enclosures, from London drawing rooms to Epping Forest, to the imposed restrictions of the Northampton years.

Moving, Raworth's 1971 publication, opens with a quote from Clare (placed against a page of coloured Camel cigarette packets by Joe Brainard). Icons of mass production find themselves in the company of lines from a famously grim asylum poem by John Clare: 'I am'.

> Into the nothingness of scorn and noise,
>   Into the living sea of waking dreams,
> Where there is neither sense of life or joys,
>   But the vast shipwreck of my lifes esteems;
> Even the dearest that I love the best
>   Are strange – nay, rather – stranger than the rest.

I'm not sure how many readers, at that time, picked up on Raworth's choice of epigraph; Jonathan Bate in his chapter on Clare as 'The Poet's Poet' doesn't find room for it. He traces an orthodox anthology of influence: Norman Gale, Arthur Symons, Edward Thomas, Edmund Blunden, Geoffrey Grigson, Robert Graves, Sidney Keyes, John Ashbery, Patrick Kavanagh, Tom Paulin, R. S. Thomas. Poets needing compensatory values in time of war, damaged rhymers and soil worshippers, thick in the tongue.

Raworth's 'HELPSTON £9,850. STONE BUILT RESI-DENCE' takes an oblique, 'open field' approach. Snippet from newspaper. John Barrell's eighteenth-century notion of 'view' acknowledged but found to be out of service: 'the view is again unapproachable'. The Helpston cottage has become an illustration in an estate agent's window. Clare's father trying to make the rent from the sale of apples, years of debt, fear of eviction, has now been translated into an aspirational lifestyle. Brandt's Gothic shipwreck, submerged in fog (but solid, rooted in melancholy), becomes a colour print, a development opportunity. A Victorian terraced house in Hackney, at the time of Raworth's quoted price, would sell for around £4,000. Large properties in squares approved by John Betjeman could be found for £7,000. And Helpston's once-spurned peasant cottage, with 'unapproachable' views, commands almost £10,000.

'The surface mysticism of the rich,' Raworth writes, 'which has eaten our country boys.' The functioning village, dependent on the benevolence of landowners, the patronage of parsons, the social ambitions of tenant farmers, has dissolved. Expensive properties and nobody at home. 'You change constantly/ a dog : a clown,' Raworth continues. 'Clown' being one of Clare's favourite ways of describing his neighbours, or indeed himself (when he ventured into polite company, mud of the fields on his boots). The clowns have ambled off into Fenland murk. The village is deserted. And betrayed. Clare is nostalgic about nostalgia, the old wound, the site from which he has been expelled – but where he still lives. Lost muse (two miles down the road in Glinton). Lost childhood (always present but out of reach). A cliff at the end of the world. The pit beyond the horizon out of which all evil things come.

Our weary trio, the latest cultural pirates, attempting to force meaning from the standing monuments of a future suburb, abandon the cottage and move away down the village street, Woodgate, past the Blue Bell (where young Clare worked and later drank), towards St Botolph's Church. We are conscious of trespassing in a heritage zone: the Clare memorial with its dates and anodyne verse, the Market Cross, the road out.

We try a little unconvinced sitting around on a bench under the trees, celebrating the fact of our walk's conclusion, then we creak to our feet. There's a lovely passage towards Glinton spire, a post-enclosure road that wasn't there in the days of Clare's schooling. The old track meandered through the fields towards Etton. Nothing is resolved and not much has been learnt. The four-day walk, pushing us hard, has been one of the best. With luck, Anna will be waiting with the car. Otherwise, we'll have to carry on to Crowland, Boston. The wind at your back, there is nothing to stop you, this side of the North Sea.

Glinton Spire

Glinton spire serves a double function. It reminds us of Clare and it reminds us that, as a fixed point on a flat plain, it helped him to organise the circuit of memory; a needle in the compass rose of childhood's mapping. The poem he wrote, with that title, 'Glinton Spire', came when he felt the need to reconfirm the markers in a threatened landscape. It was written at Northborough, in the suspended months between the escape from Epping Forest and the admission to Northampton General Lunatic Asylum. The period when he was 'tried' and found wanting by his wife.

> I love the slender spire to see,
> For there the maid of beauty dwells,
> I think she hears the sound with me
> And love to listen to Glinton Bells.

I came to St Benedict's Church once: for a funeral service, Mary Sugden, my wife's much-loved aunt, her father's sister. But I remember, before that, meals at Balcony House, prodigiously English, meat that *tasted*, that offered up the beast's biography as you chewed, platters of vegetables from the kitchen garden, summer puddings: which way to shove the port? How to trowel crusty, green-veined Stilton without destroying the integrity of the sweating brick? Elderflower wine with a lift in it, afterburn of brandy, so that, emerging into the damp afternoon air, the village is on the tilt, nothing anchored.

It's been a long time. My notion of how the road works when you drive here, coming from London, has gone entirely. (Walks are ways of remembering, drives wipe the slate.) Come off the A1 at Stamford – and after that? Stone walls of the Burghley House estate, anonymous hamlets, a railway crossing which is always against you; so crank down the window, listen for the train. Taste a different air. A flatironed land: stippled yellow fields burning out of a grey-blue haze. Tree-blots on a soft horizon and, behind those, Glinton spire.

I remember this point in our drive to Glinton, suit and black tie, scrubbed children, as we wait, on our Clare walk, at the same barrier. Red eyes of warning lights blink on the railway-crossing gate. There's a signal box with the Helpston name but no station, nowhere to offload a coffin. A wide road runs through wheatfields (huts, low barns, hangars); our shadows lead us eastwards. Now, for the first time, traffic sweeps past; frantic for mid-afternoon access to the Peterborough vortex. Clare's field path, his mazy journey to school in Glinton Church vestry, is discontinued.

> And when I gained the road where all are free
> I fancied every stranger frowned at me

All day, since we walked out of Stilton, we've been invisible (except to dogs); a freak of nature that allows us to move with liberty, naming names, looking without being looked at (the illusion). We experience a certain lightheadedness, the hollow aftermath of the lunch we haven't had, the anticipation of this evening's celebratory food and wine. The road from Helpston to Glinton purifies an overcomplex narrative, carrying us away from the intimate particulars of John Clare's writing. Helpston is family and blood. Glinton is Mary. A thing remembered and a thing that never happened. Wisps of cloud. The spire. A village whose potentialities are unsullied, until we arrive to find them mute, morose. Or not in the mood, that day, to give up their mysteries.

Anna's first cousin, Gini Dearden, a child in the early Fifties, remembers jumping over Glinton weathercock as it lay in the churchyard. Brought down for cleaning and restoration, it was found to be short of a few feathers, holed and peppered by some undiscovered assailant. The *Peterborough Standard* attributed this outrage to aerial combat: shrapnel, tracer or training stunt. The apparent emptiness of the landscape through which we had walked was an illusion, I knew that; behind perimeter fences, bunkers disguised as unlikely mounds, were active and decommissioned air bases. Fighters screeched across the sky, using cereal fields as virtual deserts. War rehearsals. The East of England Tourist Board peddles an 'official' map of USAAF airfields: Alconbury, Molesworth, Polebrook, Glatton, Wittering. Around twenty of them in the area we travelled, Bedford to Stamford. A major cluster of scarlet blisters disclosed between the M1 and the A1. With more ceded, barbed wire and CCTV, in the witch-country around Chelmsford, Bury St Edmunds and Norwich. Secrecy begets secrecy begets conspiracy theories. Whispers of rapes and child killings pinned on some local fall guy, lowlife, instead of the guilty American airman. Spiteful village gossip. It's nonsense, it doesn't stand up, but it shows how covert colonialism, misappropriation of land, affects our morality, our sense of what is just and visible.

The weathercock on the spire of St Benedict's is a true rooster, not a dragon or flying lizard. A cockscombed strutter. This is what makes the cloud-skimming attack *personal*: the crowing cock ('Commit thy works to God') is the totem of the Sinclair clan. Very appropriate, my wife thinks. An early-rising, puffed-up bunch, deficient in modesty. Treating the world as its farmyard. The borrowed Sinclair cock was an obvious target for bored pilots, pipe-chewing Battle of Britain aces.

The spire is taller than the tower of the church; you can't photograph it and fit the full span into your composition, unless you stand back, at a respectful distance, to admire its elegance. At first acquaintance – parish church, well-kept green, Sikh gentleman in charge of general store (branded pharmaceuticals, cigarettes, local newspapers, cellophane packets of crusty things that aren't quite cakes or biscuits) – Glinton is unexceptional. Then you notice the push towards clinical tidiness, competitive flora: the rural psychoses that keep the Miss Marple franchise in business. It's not enough to have church bells, comparing bells is a macho stunt, a testosterone trial. A pissing contest. Northborough and Peakirk have two apiece. Helpston has four. So Glinton has six.

Nothing is quite what it seems. The famous spire, thin as a radio mast, relies on entasis. Architectural trickery. A slight convexity has been given to the structure to correct the evidence of your eyes, the optical illusion that would leave the spire looking like a naked kebab skewer.

As we come on it, over the hump of the pedestrian bridge, over mini-roundabouts like tyres from gigantic tractors, earthed and planted, my faulty memories of the old road, Helpston to Glinton, straight as an arrow, have to be reconfigured. What has happened, in essence, is that an orbital motorway, shaped more like a Grand Prix circuit than the M25 oval, has been engineered around Peterborough. With the village of Glinton, not quite, not yet, inducted as the northerly pit stop. New estates, sports centres, captured hamlets: they are kept within the loop. Leaving industrialised farmland as an ill-defined outer limit, a dressing of countrystuff, fields, ponds, sponsored paths into reclaimed Fens (compulsory leisure). The spiritual desolation of a landscape where Clare, claggy-footed, watched for coded patterns of bird flight, migrations and roostings. A short, slight man, on the leash, in thrall to the gravity of the known, questing for cover. Walking out.

Survive the road system that cuts Glinton off from the old westward drift and everything lines up: spire, our path in – and a distant figure coming slowly towards us. The geometry is simple, a triangle: vertical stroke of St Benedict's spire, straight road to church, and imaginary dotted line darting from my eye to the restored weathercock.

That private family legend, I believe it now. Anna's father, Geoffrey Hadman, a young man of the village, used the weathercock as a target. Even with a sporting rifle, it's a magnificent shot. (As children, Anna and her brothers were put to target shooting, across a valley in the Lake District. 'Between one-fifty and two hundred yards,' she thinks. 'We were taught to line up the sights, be very still, squeeze gently. We were lying down.') Geoffrey rested his gun on the sill of an upstairs window at the Red House, the family farm in Rectory Lane, and made the cock spin. A metal bird shifting in the wind. This is a Lee Harvey Oswald moment in the catalogue of poultry assassination.

There is a wintry monochrome postcard of Rectory Lane, featuring the Red House and St Benedict's spire (as if produced to commemorate the sportsman's triumph). I tried to estimate the distance: several hundred yards down the lane, past another house, over the green, the road, across the churchyard – and then the

2322   Rectory Lane, Glinton

tower, spire, weathercock on its spike. Give Mr Hadman the prize. Give him James Stewart's 1873 Winchester from the Anthony Mann western. (The shots that missed, I wondered about those. Spent bullets falling from a great height, where did they land?)

In postcard memory, the single bowed window of the Red House is gleaming, bedroom windows too. A solitary figure stands outside, in pinafore, a maid. Her face is gone, a blotch of grey dots. No name. She stands square to the house, facing the camera, persuaded to come out, in order to give scale to the spire – which rises like a periscope of vanity from the squared church tower. Tenant farmers in Clare's day were the coming class. James Joyce, father of Mary, had Manor Farm, a substantial property on the other, Peakirk side of the green. The buildings that grew up, post-enclosure, around the heart of the old settlements were built, so Clare wrote (in 'The Parish'), 'by those whose clownish taste aspires/ To hate their farms and ape the country squires.'

Village pursuits haven't changed. Ronald Blythe, in *Talking about John Clare*, lists them: 'Boys stripping off to jump over a cat gallows. The pleasures of schoolboys climbing the leads of the church to cut their names there. The pleasure of pelting at a weather cock.' John Clare, like Geoffrey Hadman, honoured local custom. The boys of Helpston tried to throw stones over their weathercock. 'He who pelted o'er/ was reckoned on a mighty man.'

The linked initials – 'J.C. 1808 Mary' – that Clare is supposed to have cut into, variously, 'the school-room wall', an arch, a pillar, the frame of a door, have faded into oblivion. As moveable as the grave of Mary Joyce, who died, unmarried, at the age of forty-one, and who was buried in St Benedict's churchyard. The grave, pointed out to visitors by well-meaning church folk, is another Mary, daughter of William Joyce, not James. Not Clare's childhood love. Who is close at hand, under a cherry tree. A premature cremation. She died of burns sustained in a domestic accident.

Those Joyces, their daughters: James and Mary, James and Lucia Anna. Fictional projections and real myths. Names haunt me, asserting a presence when memorial slabs are erased and pillars scratched with a lattice of unreadable marks; when vulgar curiosity leaves us fumbling for any trace of the poet's cold touch.

Will we make it? The four-o'clock deadline. I haven't admitted that there is one, but, privately, I'm a time freak. I want to be there, Anna with me, as the hands of the clock take up their position and the clock face freezes in a cinematic insert. So, without making it too obvious, I step it out, stretch my stride. Glinton has some part of Anna that I don't know. She'd like to live in this territory, so she says, drawn back; a modest period house in Stamford would be ideal. The ones she marks up in the property pages look like variants of the original Hadman home, the Red House, nice proportions,

local stone or brick, Virginia creeper optional. This is desire on a molecular level, an instinct she has allowed to lie in abeyance. Her thirty-six-year captivity in low-lying Hackney, with occasional excursions to the seaside (my ideal), has been stoically endured, if not yet accepted: fate. My guilt at putting her through this exile is tempered by seeing, today, what Lesser Peterborough actually is: ribbon estates, self-regarding display, disputes with the vicar on points of doctrine (happy-clappy, lord-of-the-dance against hoary standards bellowed out by a diminishing congregation of Agatha Christie stereotypes).

Where did the Hadman house get its name? From the bricks, obviously, rosy and warm. I think we can discount William Morris and his National Trust stopover in Bexleyheath, too suburban. Too arty-crafty socialist. But I can't help thinking of A. A. Milne's one and only detective novel, published in 1922, *The Red House Mystery*. Julian Symons placed this bonbon in the tradition of Ronald Knox, an amusing yarn in which 'the amateur investigator gets everything wrong'. The dead stage their own disappearances. Raymond Chandler had no truck with Milne's gentility, the flaws in his plotting. The detective's sidekick from *The Red House Mystery* is given clear warning of his place in the scheme of things, the required level of masochism. He knows what he's signing on for: a narrative with good manners – followed by the temporary immortality of instant reprints and cheap paperbacks with gaudy covers.

The problem for our pedestrian trio (one of the problems) is that there are no sidekicks: or, we're all sidekicks but we won't admit it. Petit, drifting off the pace, hoovering up representations of the empty road, a second Nene, is jogging over the pedestrian bridge as I find (and photograph) a pair of oversized, handpainted roosters with fire-engine cockscombs: symbols of the new Glinton. Renchi's photographs are more like film, in terms of their narrative, than Petit's consoling video-meditations on distance: clouds, soft-focus traffic (moving through, moving on). Flip the pages of Renchi's album and the story of the walk flickers into life: my rear-view baldness, peeling ear-rims (disconcertingly like my father, returned and on the lurch). You can see the white shirt, the scarlet rucksack, the camera in my hand; Anna approaching. Broad grin. Grey top. White sunhat. She might be a villager, trowel at the ready, weeding the grave. Four o'clock. At Glinton. Just as I said.

AV TITMAN, FAMILY BUTCHER.

Anna is alongside the butcher's shop, this butcher of families, when we coincide, manoeuvre, embrace. The others, following discreetly behind, embrace her too. Grateful to come out of my fiction, always unpredictable, and back into something real and earthed and ticking in sunlight: the car.

From the boot, I fetch out sandals, a fresh shirt. And then we return to St Benedict's (church locked, stone effigies in the porch, man and woman, fabulously weathered), and to the Hadman family grave. This is prominently positioned, at the south-east corner, close to the gravel path. The lettering is fresh and black (restored in 1995, when Anna's mother died). Clare's inscription might have

Edge of the Orison

faded – NOT MAD – while the gravestones of his wife and children, in Northborough, need to be traced by finger like Braille, but this part of the Hadman story is fresher than newsprint.

TO THE MEMORY OF
WILLIAM HADMAN
CHURCHWARDEN OF GLINTON CHURCH 1921–1943
WHO DIED JULY 28th 1943
AGED 70 YEARS
ALSO OF FLORENCE HIS BELOVED WIFE
WHO DIED FEB. 4TH 1944
AGED 71 YEARS.
"HOME ART GONE AND TA EN THY WAGES"

Anna's grandfather. A farmer. Occupier of the Red House. Founder of the dynasty. That's as far back as we can go. Old William died a month after Anna was born. To be tagged with a quotation from Shakespeare. Chosen, so we assume, by Geoffrey Hadman, a once-a-year C of E man, dubious of the small print: so get what you can out of this life, every last drop, then invoice for everlasting bliss. A proposition vigorously contradicted by this landscape. Wages in hand, dues paid. No white mansions (like the Brighton seafront), no reserved clouds. Which play?

The golden lads and girls who come to dust. Anna gets it: *Cymbeline.* An unexpected retrieval. On her journeys to school, an hour's ride across town, Anna was instructed by her father to crunch her way through Shakespeare – which, obediently, even though it gave her a pounding headache and left her queasy, she did: a brown book with minuscule print. This ten-year-old girl, pale, rather grave, travelling across Blackpool, from Poulton-le-Fylde to Lytham St Anne's. (When I went to Blackpool, once, with my parents, it was an outing: the Pleasure Beach, sideshows, candy floss, waxworks of Stanley Matthews and Stan Mortensen with their cup-winners' medals.)

54

> Fear no more the heat o'th' sun,
>   Nor the furious winter's rages;
> Thou thy worldly task hast done,
>   Home art gone and ta'en thy wages:
> Golden lads and girls all must,
>   As chimney-sweepers, come to dust.

Legend has it that when Tennyson died, a copy of *Cymbeline* dropped from his lifeless hand. There was a spine-tingling moment at the memorial service of a later laureate, Ted Hughes, on 13 May 1999, in Westminster Abbey. A pre-recorded message. 'Ted's rich, quiet voice,' as Elaine Feinstein reports, spoke the first lines of the 'Song' from *Cymbeline*. A passage which includes the words on William Hadman's grave, sentiments respected by men who work the land.

The plot of *Cymbeline* is impossible to summarise: multiple identities, runaway daughters, 'clownish' sons, Cambrian caves, the dead returning to life. The *Oxford Companion to English Literature* has a brave stab at it:

Under the name Fidele Imogen becomes a page to Bellarius and the two lost sons of Cymbeline, Guiderius and Aviragus, living in a cave in Wales. Fidele sickens and is found as dead by the brothers, who speak the dirge 'Fear no more the heat o'th' sun'. Left alone she revives, only to discover at her side the headless corpse of Cloten which she believes, because of his borrowed garments, to be that of her husband Posthumus. A Roman army invades . . .

It probably plays better than it reads. Brothers lamenting an apparently dead girl, Welsh weather: waiting on an invading army. Some bright spark will set a revival in Afghanistan (clever use of monitor screens).

Florence Hadman (née Rose) was too ill to attend the funeral. She watched the procession from the bowed window of the Red House, but she never recovered her strength and died within seven months of her husband. There were substantial obituaries for William in several of the local papers, with smaller notices for Florence, commending her for rearing turkeys and taking prizes for her butter at the Peterborough Summer Show.

Anna spent an hour in Glinton before we arrived, enough time to weed the family plot, to plant salvias in the gravel (they failed). There was an additional plaque for her father and mother, though their ashes had been scattered in the north, Thornton (she thought) and Ullswater. With a second plaque for her father's sister, Mary, whose urn – when the stone, with some difficulty, had been taken up – was placed at the foot of the grave. This day, 20 July, was her father's birthday.

Next, Anna tried the pub – in case we had sneaked in while she was labouring. Renchi's wife, Vanessa, was also expected: she had a Glinton aunt. All the bloodlines of our story were converging on this village. The Blue Bell, astonishingly, was open. It was almost four o'clock. Anna walked towards the Helpston road, past the Titmans' butcher shop. (The graveyard was packed with legible Titmans.) Figures were advancing, from the Helpston haze, at a gallop; she recognised them. One in particular.

After a subdued session, sitting outside at green tables, slow pints and no Vanessa, we climbed into the car, leaving Renchi in the pub. Chris, returned to Stilton, left immediately for London. Vanessa, stuck on the road, was delayed – but arrived, with Renchi, in time for another courtyard meal (without Morris men) at the Bell.

At breakfast, next morning, I asked Anna about the haunted room. She said it was nothing like the one in Whitby. That attic, though busy, shapes pressing against her bare legs, was benevolent, 'filled with children'. As were her dreams: a nursery of spirits, active and warm-breathed. Curious little things. Stilton was very different, the proportions, the weight of the furniture. Nothing floated, it dragged. A sufficiency of brandy took care of sleep, pushed the dreams too deep for retrieval. But they were still there, unappeased. Living faces in an album of cancelled topography. Backgrounds fade, gardens disappear, the eyes of those who have once been photographed continue to search out an audience. The ceiling of the disturbed bedroom was so low, she felt, that the plaster took an imprint of your sleeping face.

Flying

Wrapped like something precious, a bundle that might shatter, the feverish child was taken from her bed and driven to the airfield. Not quite seven years old, she thinks. All the details are still there, vividly so. The emphasis in her voice when I question her. 'The back seat was round, like a bucket.' Arms thrown wide – 'so' – as she enfolds an imagined space. No smell of fuel in the cockpit. The leathery closeness of a borrowed coat. The plane lurches into the air, wind pushing against the perspex bubble.

Anna frowns, the sequence of events is vague. It was so long ago. She is careful not to betray her own memories or the memories of those who were with her.

Three children, Anna the eldest. Her brothers, William and Robert. They were born, one after the other, at yearly intervals. And they were all sick: whooping cough. Has it gone out of fashion? Not much in evidence when our own children were young, but making a comeback, I'm sure. The name fits the period: postwar, National Health Service ready with corked medicine bottles of sweet orange juice, a sticky spoon of Radio Malt, liberty bodices, kaolin poultices for mumps (cooked and hot). Nasty business, whooping cough, acutely contagious. Bouts of paroxysmal coughing followed by the involuntary drag and scrape of breath (the whoop): a feeling of helplessness on the part of parents, listening from another room, or fussing at the bedside.

Mr Geoffrey Hadman, industrial chemist, lateral-thinking businessman, occasional artist, had a theory: on everything. Assembly-line chickens in a shed at the bottom of the garden. Indoor mushroom plantations. Asbestos insulation. A central heating system that, like the footballer Martin Peters, was years ahead of its time. Outboard motors were tested (and failed) on the deeps of Ullswater. Money-making schemes of great ingenuity (and lethal consequence) imported Fenland self-sufficiency into the refined suburbs of Blackpool. A gardener from the works took care of the lawn and tennis court. Works' plumbers installed car radiators throughout the house. Copper pipes, heated from a coal-fired stove, passed through the children's bedrooms.

Anna woke to a 'sweet smell' and had the wit to rouse her father. Who sprung from his bed. 'Robert was nearly dead.' Fumes. Father, faced blackened, was not discouraged: teething faults, nothing wrong with the theory. Pipes were re-routed to an exterior wall. 'The house was still freezing.'

Two of the coughing children, William beside his father, Anna in the green leather seat at the rear, were placed in the Auster. Squire's Gate Aerodrome, Blackpool. Or they might have been taken up one at a time. Mother waiting in the clubhouse. The idea was: altitude. Fly as high over the sea as the small plane would go. Relieve pressure on the lungs. Relieve? Some version of the bends, knowingly induced? A struggle for breath to punish infection? There is a primitive magic to it, energetically homoeopathic. Let the bacteria in the air passages fight for life. The shock, looking down on white-capped waves, would kill or cure.

Austers were most frequently used in aerial surveys, for reconnaissance; skimming telegraph wires, hedge-hopping. I've seen photographs in reference books. I've seen Austers, blue-painted, dressing Miss Marple costume dramas, swooping over Gothic turrets; ex-Battle of Britain chap, goggled, flinging open the door, hopping out in time for the final act. (The slightly blunted young blade fulfilling this function in the TV adaptation of *4.50 from Paddington* was David Beames. An actor who played the lead in Chris Petit's first feature, *Radio On*, and never quite recovered.) I've seen larger planes, assembled from kit, hanging in juvenile bedrooms.

The adventures of childhood seem reasonable at the time. Somebody is in charge, this is how they behave; we lived to tell the tale. An Auster, co-owned in the era of photo albums featuring motorbikes (racing circuits, golf courses, ski slopes, punts, picnics), is itself a statement. Another theory: of private enterprise, freedom to travel, faith in the machine (cavalier disregard for diminishing fossil fuel reserves). Pipes, cigarettes, cigars. Hats, furs, car coats. German cameras to record (and retain) English scenes. Memory is competitive, siblings play back the same events in different ways. Robert Hadman calls up flights to northern France, casino towns, jollies. Anna associates the Auster with holidays in Cap d'Antibes: 1947 and the next five summers, two months at a time, rented villa in a discontinued resort (the ghosts of Scott and Zelda had decamped). Disputes with Madame the landlord. Swimming trials for ice-cream rewards. Morning lessons and the confinement of afternoon rests. Bill Hadman remembers the short, homemade boleros the children wore and the blocks of ice he had to carry from a flatbed truck into the cool room. There were no fridges. Now Anna understands the peculiar odour in the next property, the two Dutch women and their little weakness, opium. The family (absent father) might be accompanied by a BBC man, rather fey, who penned silly-season detective novels. In scrub woods, on a slope behind the villa, the

children discovered an unexploded shell (as tall as they were) and rolled it down the ramp towards their horrified parents. It was placed in an earthenware pot to await the police.

The highlight was always the gathering on the terrace – mother and children having driven down, the long haul, camping on farms – searching the sky for a first sight of the circling plane, the Auster. You heard the characteristic sound, this lawnmower of the clouds. A tip of the wing. A wiggle of the pipe clenched between the pilot's teeth. Mrs Hadman was off to collect her husband from Nice airport, leaving the kids with a helper, a woman friend. And the detective-story writer who had excellent French.

Cloudless skies, blue water. Bougainvillea, pine resin. It doesn't fade: that colour. Warmth in the blood after seven years of Lancashire monochrome, shivering on windblown beaches, being asked to carry out impossible exercises from their father's cramped script. Schooled at home on scraps of unrelated information: foreign capitals, distance to Jupiter, king lists, vocabulary to be learnt by rote. The horror of struggling with Archimedes' principle. Powers of ten. Periodic tables learnt by mnemonics. 'Little bees beat count-less numbers of flies.' Lithium, beryllium, boron . . . 'Nations migrate always, sick people seek climbs.' (You needed lithium to survive the experience.) Anna can never forget the terrifying squeak of chalk on the blackboard in the schoolroom. The challenge that would be sprung, months later, when the list was entirely forgotten. 'Sick bees migrate always.' Fear was the contract, the price of this privilege, French beach, rundown villa, coastal strip with its fascinating detritus of war.

On the day of their departure, bags packed, the children were marched to the beach to dive from a raft and collect weed from the seabed. Previous attempts had failed. Another spluttering return, empty-handed to the surface, and they'd be abandoned in France. Refusal was never an option. Pleasure was programmatic. A solitary dish of ice-cream you taste for the rest of your life. The triumphant child licks and luxuriates, the others are confined to quarters.

But they look happy in the yellowing photographs, the sexagen-arian Hadmans who were naked kids on the French Riviera (pro-tected from the sun by a quick dab of Nivea on the shoulders). Photographs have wrinkled, taking the blight that should have distressed their overexposed subjects. Older prints trap the family dead in eternal wedding parties. They grin or frown from sidecars and wingless planes. Large adults clambering into the scaled-down transport of Blackpool's Pleasure Beach. Revellers with drunken hats on flights that never leave the ground.

Black albums, interleaved with grey tissue, have a potent smell: sometimes camphor and closed bedrooms, sometimes a bonfire of autumn leaves. Dust of pressed flowers. Pages marked with faded ribbons. Sticky corners that have worked loose. Inscriptions in

white ink on brown paper. Anna in Antibes. Sitting on the sand, clutching her knees. Salt-sticky hair curled to the scalp. She is glossy and dark; a grave child with a private agenda (the look of Evonne Goolagong). Whooping cough defeated. Unexploded shells planted in terracotta pots. Beakers of pink Grenadine waiting on the terrace.

Around this time, before school or knowing children other than her immediate family, Anna flew with her father from Squire's

Gate, across England, to the Hadman farm in Glinton: a summer field, a bumpy landing like one of those French Resistance films with Virginia McKenna. Wings on struts; single prop loud enough to leave passengers, shaky from vibrations, deaf. 'Everyone who talked to you was very far away.' The soothing cup of tea on arrival rattles in your hand. Lips move but you can't hear what they say. Is this the same country? No passport control. No radio. Register your flight plan, follow major roads; when in doubt drop down to read the signs.

A flight recovered from a child's dream. Memories retained by a woman revisiting a place that is no longer there. She is confused, not by the parts that have disappeared, but by the buildings that are *almost* as they were: Auntie Mary's Balcony House, Uncle Lawrie's Red House, the post office, the school. Anna wants this to be what she wants, a slow life under pressing skies, a village organised around church and the passage of the seasons. Paths walked with cousins and aunts. With dogs.

Her father flew back. She stayed in Glinton. She wrote a letter to her brother William. 'I am going to treasure island on Saterday, it is a play . . . You will be able to rite in ink one day . . . With very much love, Anna.' Now she understands the distance between Blackpool and Glinton, she has witnessed it. The lurch, the vibration, the forward momentum of the Auster hauling itself over hedges and huts. She has never been on a commercial flight. Fields, she remembers, the pattern of them. But it's not the landscape, looking out on miniature farms and cars, it's reverie. Infiltrating that old dream of a life that is always there. Roads are white arms, rivers glitter. She is with her father, they can't speak. She's too deep in the seat, the leathery smell, to see out. It's not alarming. It takes a few days for the noise to fade.

She finds herself in a mirror country where, for the first time, other girls have her colouring, shape of eyes, generous mouth; sweet natures that snap, on the instant, flare and forgive. Photographs. Anna and her cousin Judy as children, on the farm: they could be sisters. Kittens. A keeshond called Woolfy. A strange, floppy, hairless doll sagging from her grip: more like a thing used for practice by expectant mothers. A hooded and mittened child in the leafy lane outside the Red House. If Anna was lost and I had to search for a duplicate, I'd launch my quest in Peterborough. They are there still, in arcades, by the river, the ones with that Glinton look. Dark eyes that put the beam right through you. The Hadmans have stayed in one place for a long time.

After the Clare walk, our night in the Bell, we came back to Glinton. We had to do a last section to Clare's cottage in Northborough, the site of his discomfort, disorientation after the family's removal from Helpston. That short distance, three miles or so, undid the poet: from the circle of land edged by hills to the damp clutch of the Fens. A pull towards Market Deeping, Deeping St James and Crowland, instead of Stamford, with its bookshops, lively pubs, radical newspaper. Its mail coach connection to London. Northborough was a blot on the wrong side of the Maxey Cut. The wrong side of Glinton spire.

Edward Storey describes Northborough:

The darker, brooding, lonelier landscape was to be a fitting scene for his darker poems . . . The soil was different. The air was different. The sun appeared in a different quarter of the sky. It was a world which, deprived of limestone, could not grow many of his favourite wild-flowers, especially the orchis he loved to study. There were fewer trees and fewer birds. The hedges were, he tells us, 'a deader green', the sun was like 'a homeless ranger'. Even the clouds and water lost their poetry, their deceptive innocence.

Glinton graves are scoured by wind and weather. Mary Joyce can be found, though we don't find her, not that day. But tucked in, sheltered at the west end of the church, is a fenced enclosure, teddy bears and flowers, kept up, dedicated to the memory of a dead child. A loud splash against the local bias towards grey, rain-coloured limestone.

Village history is summarised on a board: 'Since 1900 the most prominent farming families in Glinton have been the Hadmans, Holmes, Neaversons, Reeds, Rollings, Sharpes, Titmans, Vergettes and the Websters.' Vergettes and Titmans are well represented in the graveyard; lichen-licked to the colour and texture of dried mustard. Clustering together, they dominate this ground as, once, they dominated the surrounding fields. Grotesque stone heads rim the church. Overseers or magistrates watching for unseemly behaviour down below.

The fenced schoolyard brings it all back. After the original excursion, the Auster flight, Anna returned to Glinton, to Balcony House, in 1951. To stay with her father's sister, Mary Sugden. She found a letter to confirm the story that I was inviting her to tell.

I am havin a lovelly time. In the afternoon Antie Mary lets us take our shoes of. On the road the tar squeezes up. When I had my shoes, we were by the road and hapened to sit on some of the tar. Uncle Hubert got it of with some stuff out of a bottle.

Last night we had Judy to tea, after tea we all went for a walk with Judy's dog Chuffy. We had a long walk over fields and along the River far towards North Fen brige. We went through a field with very LUMPEY soil. The soil got into our sandals. Robert got left a very long way behind. He got nettle stings. I went back and tried to help him. He wouldnt come back for me but Judy gave him a piggiback. Some cows chased Chuffy and we all ran. Then a lady told us we were not supposed to be in those fields so we came back the way we came. Uncle Hubert met us on the way back and gave Robert a ride on his bike. I heard the clock in the tower strike eight when I got into bed.

My diary is packed every day.

Eight years old: Anna's first experience of being taught with other children. Her father had been sent to Mexico by ICI. Some woman was making her presence felt and Joan Hadman was required to fly out immediately. The three older children were dispatched to Glinton, while the youngest girl, Susa, was left for three months with the gardener and his family.

School involved certain difficulties, such as religious knowledge: shades of St Benedict's vestry, John Clare and Mary Joyce. Mrs Rawsthorne, the school mistress, was tall, thin, grey; feared and respected in the village, lovely to the children. Anna's father, Geoffrey, had been one of her favourites: a person of character from the start (bane of future headmasters, inadequate instructors and minders). Anna had no experience of the Old Testament, unforgiving prophets who set bears on children. Beards who rode to heaven in fiery chariots. She remembers how prayers had to be copied out, with the threat of your books being taken in and inspected. Playtime was a relief: her younger brother, Robert, banished to the infants' enclosure, pressed a round red face against the fence, watching her. Mute and accusing.

The summer of 1951 is replayed as Anna watches current Glinton children moving around the yard. She had an affection, undeclared, for a boy called Maurice Waghorn. Another classmate, a 'rough, rangy, village boy' with red hair, Roy Garrett, pursued her with dogged intensity. The other kids chorused news of this infatuation. 'Roy Garrett loves you.' Heady times: the bruising dramas of village life, after fear-inducing lessons at home. Latin grammar, French verbs, lists of rivers in places she had never been.

Mary Annabel Rose Hadman: 'Anna'. Three shots at fixing her, all wrong. The Mary part came from the Glinton aunt at whose house she was now staying. The Annabel sounds aspirational: tennis, riding, a Betjeman role that never took and was soon abbreviated. (William Hadman, her brother, named after his Glinton grandfather, would be sent to Marlborough, Betjeman's cordially loathed public school.) Because Mary comes first in the list it's the name on the cheque book; the unknown person asked for when the phone rings with official requests. Anna never understood the late Rose addition. Her father returned from registering the birth to inform his wife that he'd decided, on the spur, to make an adjustment. ('rose : as you grow i weaken', wrote Tom Raworth in his Helpston poem.)

And what of Clare's mysterious poem, 'A Moment's Rapture While Bearing the Lovely Weight of A.S'?

> Now lovely Anna in her Sunday dress
> In softest pressure sits upon my knee

This young woman, whoever she was, gives her name to Clare's first child, born in 1820.

Anna belonged to Glinton in a way that her mother, a Lancastrian, never did. The awkwardness for Joan Hadman, her first visit after marriage, of those farmers' meals, quantities she couldn't manage, green bacon with ruffs of heavy fat. The slithery weight of it, food too close to source, pigs in the orchard; the decorative pattern on the plate buried under layers of freshly killed meat. 'She's pleasant,' her mother-in-law reported, 'but unfinished.'

We never hear what Mary Joyce, the tenant farmer's daughter, thought of John Clare. It's always his side of the story, the walnut thrown in the schoolyard, the walks to North Fen bridge, yards of poetry (attempts to trap her in a mythic past). There is no written account of Mary's time in that Lady Chapel school, her afterlife, post Clare. Young woman, social being. Spinster living at home. It's a harsh destiny: muse by appointment. Heritage pests paying their respects at the wrong grave.

Anna locked her cousin Virginia (Gini) in the empty pig sheds and left her there. She remembers where the sheds were, on the far side of the lane. Ground that is built over, new houses. Discovered, she was imprisoned in that concrete box as a suitable punishment.

On later visits to Glinton, Anna was putting on time, slightly melancholy (as it might appear), but generally content, waiting for something: an operation, entrance to university. Auntie Mary to the rescue. Inflamed appendix. Taken out of school. Three weeks in hospital. Then, as the rest of the family went on holiday, Anna was left behind. The operation would be performed in September, when her parents returned. Meanwhile, a warm, dusty August, forbidden to swim, she hung about with her aunt. She did swim (permission granted by local doctor) in the gravel pits, deep cold, clear water: out at Tallington, beyond Lolham Bridges, where Clare cut his initials into stone, and where he fished.

Before Dublin, her start at Trinity College (where, at last, our paths cross), Anna was back at Glinton. An August like one of those French novels told in letters, solitary bicycle rides through flat country, heat haze, lazy rivers. Law books piled up, unread, beside a deckchair: seasonal lethargy. She'd been working as a receptionist at a hotel in Blackpool, the big one, the Imperial; catching the eye (tall, dark, dramatic) of businessmen and French waiters, but still living at home. This was a different movie. English rite of passage at the seaside (social surrealism), Blackpool always obliging to location scouts. Her father walked into the Imperial with a party of colleagues and pretended to flirt. He made her write a poem a day, every day, no nonsense about inspiration, a poetry notebook. The Clare inheritance (with chasers of Rupert Brooke): approved subjects in established forms. Prize-winning sonnets.

Myron Nutting's 1923 sketch of Lucia Anna Joyce (daughter of notorious Paris-domiciled novelist, James) replicates Anna Hadman's Glinton interlude. Weight of hair, tilted head, eyes closed in concentration, pen in hand: the duty of composition. Winning paternal approval. Task set, with good intentions, by a troubled father: be what you are, my daughter. Demonstrate the gifts I gave you. Geoffrey Hadman made family sketches. He worked in pencil, chalk, crayon; portraits of his children, of the gardener, craggy work folk. Portraits of Anna. Sitting, as ordered, unoccupied; inventing herself, slowly.

We followed the North Fen path Clare is supposed to have taken with Mary Joyce, out towards the trysting bridge. It was a walk Anna often took with her aunt and the golden Labradors. Balcony House had long since been sold, the garden pebbled and planted in a Jacobean style that played up to the unusual balcony addition. The weather was kind; our path soon escaped the village. But it was not the path Anna remembered. The high, wild hedges were gone, fields were exposed. This landscape, evidently, had come full cycle: the hedges and odd-shaped strips of enclosure returned to the wide horizons of Clare's childhood. William Hadman, before moving to the Red House, had his farm out here: ground once occupied by James Joyce, Mary's father. William rented his property to the eccentric Mrs Benson, who ran it as a home for children, which she later moved to another gloomy property in Rectory Lane.

Thorny copses offer good cover as we approach the bridge and its heritage prompts. A humped silver car squeezes past and is later discovered, parked on the verge, dos-à-dos to a muddy hatchback. (Number plates blanked to protect the guilty.)

I notice a bush that has been dressed, country fashion, with a limp crop of grapeskin condoms. Over a mulch of crumpled cigarette packets. Pie wrappings. Discarded tights.

Beyond Car Dyke and the Welland, the half-hidden Paradise Lane leads straight to Northborough and the poet's cottage; which is now in the keeping, so we discover, of a dealer in teddy bears. Northborough is heavy with absence; of all the cemetery villages encountered on our walk out of Essex, this is the paradigm. Internal exile as a prelude to the Big Sleep.

We confront the bridge. Three bands of human affection can be felt: the romance of those youthful lovers, John Clare and Mary Joyce, given emphasis by our demand that it should be so, innocence before the fall; then illicit conjugations, off-road couplings authorised by the signboard broadcasting Clare's passion; and, finally, a stolen time with Anna, triggering memories of all our earlier walks. Embraces. Collusion. Private interludes rescued from domestic routine. The knowledge that you may be watched is both exciting and inhibiting: in a landscape shaped for ambiguity. Assignations, close talk in parked cars. A line of furled poplars diminishing into a blue distance.

I draw from Anna an account of her Glinton holidays, village school, appendix operation, forbidden swim – and, most vividly, that period before we met, before she came to Dublin, the afternoons cycling down these lanes, sitting on the lawn, in her bedroom with the window open: a compulsion, lightly held, to remake the past, mend a fractured narrative.

Her father had friends in Germany, student years, late Twenties, early Thirties, everybody went there. Auden, Isherwood, Spender. University men, gays. Left and right, all persuasions. Samuel Beckett. The friendship with his cousin, Peggy Sinclair. Geoffrey Hadman, returned from Oxford, poses against a tall hedge in the garden of the Red House. 'What a handsome man,' my daughter said. Blazer and flannels, heavy brows, off-centre parting, frowning at the camera: clenched left hand. A moment of consequence. Excellent degree (1932). Newspaper cuttings of his performance in the 'half-mile handicap'. Scrapbook thick with young women, rivers, parties, snow. Big coats, arrogant hats. The women are laughing. The men are pleased.

GLINTON SCHOLAR'S SUCCESS

Mr. Geoffrey Hadman, youngest son of Mr. and Mrs. Hadman, of the Red House, Glinton, has gained first-class honours and his B.Sc. degree at Oxford University.

Mr. Hadman is an Old Boy of Stamford School, to which he won a scholarship from Glinton School at the age of 10. Whilst at Stamford he became head boy and captain of the Rugby Team. He was also prominent in running and swimming, winning many honours in both . . .

After spending a well-earned holiday with his parents, in September Mr. Hadman takes up a post with Imperial Chemical Industries.

Among Anna's files is a letter from Imperial Chemical Industries to the headmaster of Stamford School.

Subject to the fulfilment of these conditions, the commencing salary to be not less than £350 per annum. If Hadman should prove satisfactory he would be continued in our employment and would be given an agreement for a period of years, with every prospect of advancement.

  Might I ask you to be good enough to communicate this decision to the boy . . .

Anna bribed £10 to cram five hundred words of German vocabulary (never used). That climate of cultural seriousness combined with physical exercise, nude bathing, mountain walks (Leni Riefenstahl): a firm grip on social problems, the mob. Students in college scarves driving buses and ambulances at the time of the General Strike. Now it was spoilt, Germany. Painfully so. Friendships suspended.

From Oxford, the best of times, into digs in Thornton Cleveleys, north of Blackpool. According to family legend, Geoffrey Hadman

was the youngest works' manager ever appointed by ICI, that global power. Mercurial, he challenged received notions: premature free marketeer. He was elected as a Conservative (for want of a stronger word) to the local council, but couldn't stick the addle-brained bureaucracy. Lancastrian committee men brokering deals on a nod and a wink. Debate not decision.

There was to be no advance within the corporate structure. No invitation to join the main board. An early ceiling. Too bright, too singular: too bloody-minded. Team captain, not team player: action in place of consensus politics and spin.

He brooded on radio news: Germany and England, the breaking of that bond. The splitting of the atom: Anna remembers her father, alone in a darkened room, knowing immediately what the announcement meant. 'It's the end.' The children talked in whispers. Her mother stayed out of the way. Anna was the one deputed to sit with him, keeping him company.

Something happened. Something that is hard to appreciate: a brain tumour, one son says. An episode nobody but a man as driven as Geoffrey Hadman would interpret as a sign of weakness. Anna thinks it was more probably a stroke, requiring weeks, months, in hospital. Out of circulation. 'We thought you were dead,' colleagues muttered when he reappeared.

Geoffrey didn't tell his parents. He wrote letters from his hospital bed without alluding to the drama. He let them think he was still at work. He ignored, as far as was possible, the partial paralysis in his left side, the clawed hand. He couldn't run, but he would walk, shoot, load the children into the Bedford van on cold Lancashire evenings, wind cutting off the Irish Sea, a compulsory dip in the murky waters. Poppa would set out from the house in a towelling robe, driving barefoot, stiff leg on pedal.

'I am a new man,' John Clare wrote to his Cambridge friend, Chauncy Hare Townsend, 'and have too many tongues.' The Helpston boy divorced himself from 'the old silence of rusticity'. For every social gain, there was private loss. He knew that he was no longer the subject of his own story. Succeed elsewhere and you can't go home again.

When Anna was flown across England, Blackpool to Glinton,

her father had suffered his stroke; loss of sensitivity in the left side, dragging leg. His fingers wouldn't open. In a car, he drove at speed, impatient with socialist regulations. Now, high over fields and roads and reservoirs, atrophied nerves tightened the grip on the joystick. The young girl in the bucket seat was unafraid.

DREAMING

Anxiety – ghosts, nothing specific.

Max Brod (on Kafka)

Poet in the Park

He had to learn the difficult thing, in different places we are different people. We live in one envelope with a multitude of voices, lulling them by regular habits, of rising, labouring, eating, taking pleasure and exercise: other selves, in suspension, slumber but remain wakeful. Walking confirms identity. We are never more than an extension of the ground on which we live.

The birds knew him, knew John Clare, a wanderer in fields and woods; they recognised him and he belonged. They proved his right to common air. He shared their heat. Twenty-three years fixed in Helpston, between limestone outcrop and Fen, flailing, herding, stalking the circle, minor expeditions, runs at the horizon. The child lost among the yellow furze of Emmonsales Heath. The crabbed adolescent on the barge, Peterborough to Wisbech. The hot young man tramping to Newark. The lime-burner landing himself with a wife. On an invisible leash, Clare was drawn back, always, to his 'hut', hovel, home.

Poetry is a form of going away. Of holding landscape, and its overwhelming, simultaneous particulars, in the float of memory. 'For Clare, as for all poets in the Romantic tradition,' wrote Jonathan Bate, 'writing was the place of remembering, of preserving what was lost: childhood, first love, moments of vision, glimpses of ordinary things made extraordinary by virtue of the attention bestowed upon them. Without loss, there would be no reason for the poetry.'

It arrived, this seizure, disturbing intimations of destiny, as Clare walked back from the market town of Stamford, towards Barnack and his cottage at Helpston. The first Clare biographer, Frederick W. Martin, publishing in the year after the poet's death, turns the documented materials of a life into romantic fiction; a fiction extracted from Clare's scribblings, his papers. Extracted from a single visit to Helpston, interrogation of unreliable witnesses. Everything folds back into Clare's own telling, his autobiographical 'sketches'. Freed from punctuation, memory flows, racing ahead of itself in accordance with the (future) Kerouacian recipe for spontaneous composition: first thought, best thought.

'I think I was 13,' Clare wrote. 'Trifling things are never pun[c]tually rememberd as their occurence is never strikingly impressed on the memory.'

An acquaintance, a Helpston weaver, owns a copy of James Thomson's poem, *The Seasons*. Young Clare's immediate and intense desire is to *possess* this wonder. Stamford on Sunday morning, bookseller's premises closed. He bribes a lad to mind the horses he has been paid to watch over. Dereliction of duty. Early return, before first light, to the market town, waiting for the shutters to be thrown open: book secured for a shilling. Clare, not wanting to be observed in the act of reading, unconcerned about trespass, climbs over the wall into Burghley Park.

Let future romancers retell the episode as they will, following Clare's template. His rapture.

Weather? 'Beautiful.' (As summer mornings, in memory, always are.)

Scenery? 'Uncommonly beautiful.'

Explainers improve on the poet's ravishment, his incident of unearnt bliss, the vagueness of light, setting, height of Burghley wall. The tree. Its welcome shade. 'The beautys of artful nature in the park.' Coming late, we want more. Who owned this park? Where were the gamekeepers? How did the canopy of leaves shimmer and dance? What were the smells and sounds? A callow youth hiding himself away while he allows the rhythms of Thomson's verse to affect his pattern of breath.

> Be gracious, Heaven! for now laborious man
> Has done his part. Ye fostering breezes, blow!
> Ye softening dews, ye tender showers, descend!

> And temper all, thou world-reviving sun,
> Into the perfect year! Nor ye who live
> In luxury and ease, in pomp and pride,
> Think these lost themes unworthy of your ear

Showers of exclamation marks. Insidious commas. Nature personified. Mannerly verse interceding between observer and place, a technique for healing the complexity of the world. The peasant in the park, unprotected by family, costume, education, is shown another method of disappearing: into thickets of nicely lubricated language. A memory system of regular and irregular stresses.

'I got into a strain of descriptive rhyming on my journey home,' Clare reported. 'This was "the morning walk" the first thing I commited to paper.'

And strain it was, agony. A colder sweat than his labours in the fields provoked. Grubbing at wrapping material, bills of sale, defacing paper with a slanting scrawl: the curse of poetry. Walking. To release the pressure. Inspiration arrived on the tramp, solitary expeditions. Frederick Martin has Clare appointing 'an old oak, on the borders of Helpston Heath' as his office. Caught short on some rough track, he would press his hat into service as a crude desk. 'Inspiration seldom came to him in-doors, within the walls of any dwelling; but descended upon his soul in abundant showers whenever he was roaming through the fields and meadows, the woods and heathery plains around Helpston.'

'Demons,' said Ingmar Bergman, 'don't like the open air.' Poetry is the absence of demons, a rapt cataloguing of the natural world. Clare's Northamptonshire verses are burdened, according to his contemporary critics, with excess of description. If Helpston and its walkable circumference, up to that point in its history, had been uncelebrated, without language, John Clare accepted the burden of authorship. He became a scribe to locality. A poet in a place that had never, previously, had any use for such a being.

He was seen as clown, a clod, an unholy innocent achieving inspiration through drink or derangement. A conceit that surfaced, once again, in Edward Bond's 1975 play, *The Fool*. Bond's Clare, a mummer, frolics at the gates of the great house, a beaten savage with a choke of song in him. A beggar on the stony road. A beggar who refuses to beg. A lumbering, undersized bear with memories of its abdicated humanity. 'I dreamt I saw bread spat on the ground.'

The season, the lull after the Napoleonic Wars, was ripe for it, a new peasant. Clare had taken the lure, his discounted copy of *The Seasons* (knocked down from 1s. 6d.); his first dealings with those vampires, the bookmen. Dust for blood. The addiction was on him, to the despair of Patty, his new wife: subscriptions to magazines, library debts, books gifted, books for study. Yards of poetry that would be heaped on a cart as soon as he was dead and gone.

In Burghley Park, 'excited beyond his capacity for explanation', young Clare plunged into Thomson (who made his verses for the favours of patronage, English landscapes dressed and flattered). Saccharine bites like acid into the enamel:

> Come gentle Spring, ethereal Mildness come;
> And from the bosom of yon dripping cloud,
> While music wakes around, veil'd in a shower
> Of shadowing roses, on our plains descend.

The form of the poem, Clare recognised, was epistolary; you learn to compose a letter in verse, a letter to yourself. Peasant poets were a commodity, living fossils, respectful toilers who filled out the middle distance in one of Thomson's conceptual landscapes. London shops were heaped with rhyming peasants. Robert Bloomfield, cobbler and agricultural labourer. Stephen Duck, author of *The Thresher's Labour*. Kirk White, a butcher's son. They were lionised for a season, then permitted to decline, by gentle increments, into poverty; verses unmanned by the attempt to strike a properly deferential note.

Clare was more awkward: clothes, stance, size. Attitude. Deficient in humility. Short stature, tall brow, hair hanging to the shoulder: a suitable case for flattery by the commissioned portraitist,

William Hilton. In his Napoleonic greatcoat (gift of the publisher John Taylor), Clare backed into a circle of candlelight. A countryman with stones under his tongue. Silent, often. And thirsty. When he talked, he talked; canny, discomforted, loud, shy, giving offence by accident or design. Custodian of the poetry that came to him by default. Covert things made public to his advancement, a handful of gold coins drawn from the deep pocket of Lord Milton. An investment fund subscribed by Prince Leopold of Saxe-Coburg (future King of the Belgians and father of another Leopold, the slave-master who ran the Congo as a private fiefdom). The double-edged sword of charity. A gesture that sets a royal name in the almanac of benevolence. Small change lobbed at an English peasant poet by a dynasty that enforced a barbarous regime on colonial Africa. Leopold II, according to *The Inheritors* (a novel composed in tandem by Joseph Conrad and Ford Madox Ford), was 'a philanthropist on megalomaniac lines'.

Clare saw workmen surveying ground for the railway that would revise Helpston and challenge the description he was trying to compose, the sounds, shapes, secrets. The railway from Matadi to Kinshasa that opened up the wealth of the Congo for Leopold was under construction when Conrad underwent his own heart of darkness, his trial as a riverboat captain for the Société Anonyme Belge pour le Commerce du Haut-Congo. The company agent at Stanley Falls, Georges Antoine Klein, feverish, sick with dysentery, was brought aboard Conrad's steamer, the *Roi des Belges*. He died on the voyage downstream and was buried at Tchumbiri Station.

Before the coming of the railway, before Clare's shortlived fame, few travellers made the journey from Helpston to London. Stamford, Market Deeping and Peterborough fulfilled the need for a market. If you required exotic produce, such as string, you walked to the convenient town. Clare's career turned on his desire for a blank ledger. A workbook produced to order by a local printer was a serious investment. A necessary first step in the poetry trade.

At the May Fair in Deeping, John's mother bought him a pocket handkerchief (the kind he would later employ as an auxiliary suitcase for his London visits). The handkerchief was embroidered with a portrait of Thomas Chatterton and a few lines of complimentary verse. Up from the provinces, adrift in London: Chatterton, the boy martyr, was an icon to be hawked at country fairs. A dangerous model. Clare mopped his sweat on the Bristol poet's glamorous profile: involuntary possession. Faces pressed together, Chatterton's verses printed (in reverse) across that high, smooth brow. Clare's poem, 'The Recognition', as Jonathan Bate recognised, was an imitation of Chatterton: 'written as if by the poet just before he poisoned himself with arsenic, at the age of seventeen, having been reduced to despair by poverty and neglect'.

The Deeping printer J. B. Henson offers a vanity deal: at a price. You pay, I publish. Flyers to distribute. The aspirant author is both excited and shamed; having to cobble together, stub of pencil, scrap of paper, an advertisement for himself. Frederick Martin appreciates Clare's native gift of poetry, but refuses to acknowledge the prose. It lacks structure, organisation of thought, he asserts. From another perspective, another time, I see those journals, letters, fragments of autobiography, as alert, fresh, sinewy. The best of their kind. They are the simplest way to catch Clare's voice, the modesty, the hesitation: the sudden rush of remembrance. It's a walking language, uncensored, immediate: going nakedly for what has to be said. Anecdote as essence.

I cannot say what led me to dabble in Rh[yme] or at what aged I began to write it but my first attempts was imitations of my fathers Songs for he knew & sung a great many & I made many things before I venturd to comit them to writing for I felt ashamd to expose them on paper & after I venturd to write them down my second thoughts blushd over them & [I] burnt them for a long while but as my feelings grew into song I felt a desire to preserve some & used to correct them over & over till the last copy had lost all kindred to the first even in the title

Such instincts were recognised, by villagers, as alien and unwholesome. Clare's mother would never, he says, have given him that handkerchief, with its melancholy token, if she had known that he would, one day, become a poet. Initiation begins as an urge to remake whatever is admired: 'I was fond of imitating every thing I met with and therefore it was impossible to resist the oppertunity which this beutiful poem gave me.'

Composition undertaken in the open fields, reading under hedges, publication in town. Stamford with its raft of newspapers (*Stamford Mercury*, *Stamford Champion*, *Stamford News*), its mercantile and political interests, was a significant provincial nexus. Here was the third medieval university, the one that didn't happen: Oxford, Cambridge ... Stamford. The right distance from London. The right geology: honeyed limestone. Cambridge colleges, like Ely Cathedral and Ramsey Abbey, emerged from Barnack quarries. Stamford was a once-wealthy wool town with a peculiar micro-climate of resentment: suppressed university, disenfranchised scholarship, news from elsewhere. Pride without visible means of support. Factions. Spheres of influence. Drinking schools that never ventured from their own pubs.

Taken by his father, apprenticed to the big house, Clare was never comfortable. With his fellow gardeners, he escaped at night from locked quarters, out of Burghley Park: they patronised a Stamford dive called the Hole in the Wall. The apprenticeship was in drinking and whoring. The foul-tempered Burghley garden-master favoured another establishment. Clare was frequently sent, by this man's wife, to fetch him home. He was coerced into epic sessions, subjected to a boozer's sentimental charity. Slurred monologues that turn on a beat into violence. Stamford majored in civic amnesia, private sleights remembered for generations.

I've always felt, even before Anna's advocacy, that Stamford was the model of an English provincial town: hill, river, labyrinthine passageways, bloody-minded inhabitants dozing away the centuries with no great interest in life beyond the eight miles that have to be walked to work up a thirst. Bookshops of every stamp. Dealers who came off the Great North Road and lacked the imagination to move on. In Stamford you are far enough from London to spurn the place as a creation of the Devil. (Even if you are one of the fortunate few who are aware of its existence. The rest devise their own pleasures: bull-baiting, Christian fundamentalist sects, fleecing tourists.)

The London coach departed from the George Hotel. We stayed there once. Anna was delighted with a group of beet-faced farmers, razor-raw and scrubbed, convened around a long table. They were worn by (as much as wearing) hairy tweed suits in various shades of yellow and green. The table sagged under the weight of food, their pewter pots. They ate, heads down, in silence. You could hear teeth snapping bone. And feel the cold rush of the beer going down, half-a-pint at a swallow. Pleasure for the fraternity of agriculturalists was a solemn business. They finished, spoons down, on the beat; they rose as one. Retired to the bar, drinks secured, they relaxed. Roared. The formality of the dinner over, they were allowed to enjoy themselves.

The farmers would have been perfectly recognisable to Clare. He was astonished when his old Stamford contact, Ned Drury, returned from Lincoln for the Mayor's Feast, which followed the traditional running of a bull through the streets. 'I would not go one Mile,' he wrote, 'to hear the din of knifes and forks and to see a throng of blank faces . . . that boast no more expression than a muffin.'

Stamford was always a town of books and booksellers. A newsagent with the usual clutter out front might carry, in his back room, a stock of miscellaneous secondhand volumes, a locked glass cabinet with pristine Sax Rohmer first editions in garish period jackets. A Vietnam War refusenik, veteran of New York's Peace Eye bookshop, could hide out, nurturing a massive De Quincey habit, in a stable yard by the river: Lucozade, ampoules and well-thumbed copies of Book Auction Records. Further up the hill, you would discover a long-established antiquarian dealer; the kind who might have patronised Clare – and then turned him away when he reappeared, hawking bundles of his own work, unwonted copies of that unwonted book, *The Shepherd's Calendar*. Visit the premises now, put the silver key to the lock of the private cabinet, and battered late editions of Clare's first book, odd volumes of the second ('with all faults'), are prized exhibits. Alongside the John Speed maps from 1610 (handcoloured, 2001), the Helpston poet gives credibility to an anachronistic enterprise.

When I was a jobbing dealer, hitting Stamford, Clare was out of my league. I couldn't afford the cabinet. I worked the shelves, just inside the door, paperbacks and fiction deemed cheap enough to take its chances with ram-raiders in anoraks, unselective klepto-maniacs. One morning, at the start of a day's book trawl, I found a run of Colin Watson novels, crisp and clean, unsullied by the fingers of previous owners. Watson's shtick was comedy and sudden death; mysteries set in the flatlands, bodies draped over electricity pylons. Tales he delivered with the verve of Tom Sharpe. At his best, he was almost as good as Jack Trevor Story. He factored a strain of cynical, corrupted Englishness that I admired without reservation. Born in Croydon, a journalist and leader-writer for Thomson News-papers, he knew where the bodies were buried and knew that life beyond the metropolis was still worth recording: ugly-lovely, lustful, ultimately absurd.

It turned out that the author had dumped the books, he was a friend of the proprietor. An action forged in the spirit of John Clare. The best writers, the ones with spiky independence and a voice of their own, finish up hawking unsold stock, discounted by bored publishers, door to door. I took everything by Colin Watson and arranged to visit him, out in Lincolnshire, on the road to Sleaford. West Street, Folkingham: the address. In the general direction Clare travelled, on foot, when he dragged himself and his bundle of books to Boston. Frederick Martin has the poet achieving this walk, Helpston to Boston, a distance of more than thirty miles, burdened with his sack, in a single day.

He walked all the way, and arriving in the evening of a beautiful day, ascended the steeple of the old church, just when the sun was sending his last rays over the surging billows of the North Sea. The view threw Clare into rapturous delight. He had never before seen the ocean, and felt completely overwhelmed at the majestic view which met his eyes. So deep was the impression left on his mind that it kept him awake allnight; and when he fell asleep, towards the morning, the white-crested waves of the sea, stretching away into infinite space, hovered in new images over his dreams.

Gaunt, sharp-featured, a little wary of the stranger on the step, Watson interrupted his work as a silversmith. Eyeglass. Tools in hand. He couldn't understand where it had gone wrong. His novels were well received – 'Watson's portrait of the tawdry side of English provincial life is saved from bitterness by something rare in detective novels: a dirty sense of humour' – and they'd even had a few moments of television time, with Anton Rogers (who used to come around my stall in Camden Passage, Islington, asking for books on fishing) as the detective.

The problem was that Watson, lese-majesty, had trashed Agatha Christie in an essay called 'The Little World of Mayhem Parva'. Big mistake. Watson's Flaxborough, a credible setting, packed with 'sentimental animal lovers, drunken journalists, randy aldermen, and corrupt doctors', was all too real. Stamford, Boston, Helpston, Glinton. Lesser Peterborough at the turn of the Millennium. Folkingham in 1985.

Watson put away his instruments, took me upstairs to the living room. He had a vision, Lincolnshire inspired it, of epic tank battles, an H. G. Wells Armageddon. Machines crushing humans for the benefit of remote viewers. The future, yet again, recovered from Victorian or Edwardian science fiction. The pain of it was in his face.

He signed my books, we parted. He was astonished that his early first editions were a desirable commodity, while his current publications, the boxes of Book Club editions, filled his shelves. He would have to let the writing game go, it didn't pay. Concentrate on silver rings and decorative trinkets. The Helpston villagers, according to Frederick Martin, had the same advice for Clare. Give up poetry, peddle jewellery, fancy handkerchiefs, patent medicines. And even then, they thought, he might be setting his cap too high. 'They looked upon a bagman as a person of superior rank – decidedly higher than a poet.'

Stamford businessmen with a weakness for literature took Clare up: Octavius Gilchrist, gentleman grocer, and Edward 'Ned' Drury, bookseller, proprietor of a circulating library, cousin to the London publisher John Taylor. They sniffed at his verses, but recognised that the vogue for peasant poetry was still in the air. Taylor agreed. Last season's new face, the Cockney Keats, wasn't making much of an impression: go pastoral. First the work, then the man. Bring him to London. The decision was made by those with his best interests at heart. Clare submitted. In March 1820, accompanied by Gilchrist, he took the Regent coach from the George Hotel in Stamford to the Blue Boar in Holborn. The city of ghosts. His dream, his undoing.

In Transit

A great year, 1820. Clare's first book, *Poems Descriptive of Rural Life and Scenery*, is published by John Taylor. He marries 'Patty of the Vale' (leaving her at home with her parents, near Pickworth). He makes his first visit to London.

A book cannot exist on its own, the author must also be published, brought to the place of publication, exhibited. Clare is puffed, patronised, dissected. Versions of his life are finessed into magazines. The poetry is a minor extension of personality: this season's wonder, a Northamptonshire Peasant (precursor of the Elephant Man). The process of splitting away from the generating landscape is begun. Octavius Gilchrist, Stamford grocer, contributor to London periodicals, is appointed his guide. Minder. Driver. Cultural pander.

Up before first light, Clare began his day with a tramp of six or seven miles, Helpston to Stamford. A walk he did not need to register, it was already imprinted; he had done it so many times. He overtook earlier selves, plodding ahead of him. The village boy, on his errands, seeing shapes in the dark, Fen spirits, soul-stealers. The drunken youth returning to Burghley with fellow labourers, wall at a tilt, to sleep under a tree. Waking dew-soaked, creaking like leather. Clare is the supreme articulator of the mundane. Self-appointed laureate of a corner of disputed land, sometimes in one county, sometimes in another. He is obliged to act as clerk to the specifics of place; at whatever cost, he must transcribe the natural history of nowhere. His accounts of Helpston's flora and fauna become a series of brief lives, genealogies of lichen, snail shells, stones. His separate existence, divorced from these things, is an unstable fiction.

Gilchrist accompanies the timid poet on his first expedition to the metropolis. He has arranged for Clare to lodge with his brother-in-law, 'a German called Burkhardt'. An economic migrant, who kept a jeweller's and watchmaker's shop in the Strand, Burk-hardt loved to astonish country folk with the sights of London. The greatest of them, happening on his doorstep, he missed entirely. An event too subtle to capture his attention.

William Blake's landlord in South Molton Street sold his business in the spring of 1820. The Blakes, William and Catherine, decamped – books, pictures, sheets, portfolios, tools – to Fountain Court. Their final marital home was hidden away at the back of the Fountain Tavern in the Strand. Close to the river. Strange to think of the two poets, seldom connected in critical discourse, living for one week in close proximity. William Blake wandering out to collect his jug of evening porter. And Clare, famously thirsty, shaking off his well-meaning minders. It didn't happen. Not in the only version of Clare's biography that we can assemble from accounts left by scholars and documented witnesses.

Writers are too deeply mired in fantasy to notice one another (except as rivals, caricatures, refractions of their own brilliance). Heads down, necks twisted: mud and stars. Two poets, in fortuitous conjunction, navigate trajectories through different cities that happen, just then, to be in one place. They are blind as comets.

London is voices. Clare does well to stop his ears, to assert his singularity: that is what publishers require of him. In 1820, by way of mail coach, correspondence (paid for by recipient), by newspapers and magazines, London extended its sphere of influence, sixty miles out and more. The market town of Stamford was as near to the capital as decent men wanted to come.

'Are you St Caroline or "George 4th"?' Clare wrote to his co-publisher Hessey. 'I am as far as my politics reaches "King & Country" no Inovations on Religion & government say I . . . Poor St Caroline she has seen much trouble & perplexity God for-give her.' Squabbles of distant royalty engage Northamptonshire labourers and village gossips. Like Princess Di and her stiff husband, the diminutive cuff-twitcher, German princelings of Clare's time were figures stuffed with straw. An excuse for rustic pantomime. Punch and Judy. Hanoverian snouts leaking blue blood.

Helpston pretends, for one night, to be London. 'This night is the grand illumination for our City in honour of St Caroline,' Clare asserts (in his letter to Hessey). 'The woman that is to personate her majesty is a deformed object who is to be dressed in white.' Clare's cottage window must be lit or it will be broken. Factions of court and city spill into dim countryside. Provincial centres channel hot news.

Poor Clare is dragged in the other direction, towards the centre, a rhyming clown. He will travel with Octavius Gilchrist, literary vendor of hams and cheeses. London 'held terrors he could not face', claimed Edward Storey. But face them he did; back to home, eyes to the south. Watchful, tense. Rattled, shaken, suspended above the road. Out of his knowledge. The Regent coach, boarded in Stamford, at first light. The reluctant voyager interpreted a rush of unfamiliar sensations in a rational way. 'The thoughts created such feelings in him,' Storey wrote, 'that he fancied he had changed his identity as well as his occupation, that he was not the same John Clare but some strange soul that had jumped into his skin.'

Burghley House. Those walls. He had been possessed, once, by the achievement of James Thomson (initiated into verse). Then the escape with the deserting foreman, a walk, twenty-one miles, north to Grantham. Now this: jolting through literary and historical associations. 'I have often read myself into a desire to see places which novelists and Essayists have rendered classical by their descriptions of th[eir] presence and other localitys rendered sacred by genius.' Oliver Cromwell and the poet Cowper at Huntingdon. Robert Bloomfield at Biggleswade. (Clare meant to visit him, on his return journey, but the cash was exhausted and he hurried home.)

Riding in comparative comfort as a paying passenger confers the responsibility of bearing witness. To a constantly shifting landscape. Clare, drawn out of Helpston, sonar echoes of wood and heath, mislaid his sense of self. New perceptions, a shift in the geology: a second soul gained entry. He impersonated the poet they expected him to be, his publishers, promoters, patrons. Before he had travelled forty miles, the sights and sounds that confirmed his former identity were dead to him.

Coming south, an excursion as mad as Clare's, a four-day book-hunting tour that took in Carlisle, Glasgow, Stirling, Edinburgh, Newcastle, Durham and many lesser pit stops, I recognised Stamford as the starting point for a shift of my own: into fiction. The thing had been cooking for a long time. My feeling for this territory was informed by my relationship with Anna. The country around Stamford was attractive in a perverse way: the contrary of everything I knew and understood. John Clare was part of that difference. I looked at books, birthday gifts to my wife, where they sat, top-dressed in dust, on a red shelf. The 1956 biography by John and Anne Tibble. A new edition of *The Shepherd's Calendar*, which had been inscribed by a Glinton uncle (aunt's second husband): 'For Anna, whose majority falls in the year of Clare's centenary.' Volumes opened at whim: 'His toil and shout and song is done.' This was the Clare I steered respectfully around. The rustic verse-maker associated with David Gentleman woodcuts and English Heritage gift shops. Editors boasted of their ambition to 'bring Clare back to the general reader'. To decent folk who join the society, do the walks and attend the lectures. The ones who plant midsummer cushions on a little-visited grave.

I enjoyed my lost years as a book scout, doubling through the East Midlands, Lincolnshire and East Anglia, air bases, dormitory villages, barns stacked with plunder. Being out on the road, red-eyed, buzzing with caffeine, hammered by monologues, the nervous occultism of fellow dealers, was an excellent preparation: for what? For defacing notebooks, formulating skewed theories, misreading signs. Pre-fictional chaos. I abandoned my attempts to construct pseudo-epics that mingled (without distinction) poetry and prose. Bookdealing, I consoled myself, was a form of authorship: my Thursday stall at Camden Passage Market could be viewed as an exhibition of chosen texts. A modernist collage of found objects. Perfect-bound quotations to take home for cash. Being on the road was a willed dreaming, very much like the dipping into random books, the brooding on sofas, that preceded the furtive announcement of a poem.

The town of Stamford was a portal. I kept coming back. It wasn't the bookshops, it was the setting. The desktop booklets I published, assembled from recovered jottings, were given away. There was, I knew very well, no other way of dealing with them. These effusions would rightly be called 'occasional'. Postcards sent from unfestive locations to mislaid friends. One poem is titled '6 February 1982: Beyond Stamford'. A section of it runs:

> one breath later, a roadside pub
> sunk in fens, where Gothick poverty
> fed the English opium crop:
> the moon-faced idiocy of dazed mechanicals
> watching their entrails turn to water, high
> on turnips rotted in black overloam'd earth

Lincolnshire reportage is extracted from a chapbook published in an edition of twenty-one copies. Sent free to unsuspecting colleagues. Sheer hubris on my part to produce so many. I knew all my readers. They had problems of their own. The next book ran to twelve copies. And the last, ten – with one extra made up for a new patron, Mike Goldmark of Uppingham, the madman who agreed to sponsor my first novel. A thin time, just then, for all of us. The Thatcher spectre had former poets cowering in their traps.

Fiction, for me, begins right here. Incidents, borrowed from book-hunting trips, pressured into another form, a sensationalist account of something that didn't happen: stalled car (Volvo), coke-crazed dealers, sleeping landscape. A sudden turn off the A1, coming south, left into Stamford.

A cheese-coloured town, slicked over with fen sleet, damp as an abattoir coldstore, distinguished by a profusion of moulting snail-horn churches, their steeples discouragingly set with sharks' teeth.

The chief book-hunter (real name, Martin, in unconscious homage to Clare's first biographer) suffers from stomach pains. Clare's distemper starts with heat in the belly. He complains (to Thomas Inskip, 10 August 1824):

an acking void at the pit of my stomach keeps sinking me away deeper and deeper . . . the next thing for me to try is salt water . . .

And again. To his publisher John Taylor (7 March 1831). Hopes (dashed) for a solution to the present crisis:

I was taken 3 weeks back or more – with a pain at the stomach which would not go off & as it affected my head very much I felt alarmed & took a part of Dr Ds last prescription . . . but whenever I attempted to walk friction brought it on as bad as ever & the pain at my stomach started again . . . I awoke this morning with a burning heat in my fundament where the humour again made its appearance . . . I got tollerable rest but the pain at my stomach was more frequent in its attacks & I awoke in dreadful irritation . . . my future prospects seem to be no sleep – a general debility – a stupid & stunning apathy or lingering madness & death . . .

I picked up on the tenor of Clare's correspondence, the packets sent to Taylor, by way of Stamford. Torrents of verse. Overdue bills. The early bounce gone from his language. A dead car. The Great North Road. Cold weather. So it begins, my introduction to fiction: *White Chappell, Scarlet Tracings*.

There is an interesting condition of the stomach where ulcers build like coral, fibrous tissue replacing musculature, cicatrix dividing that shady receptacle into two zones, with communication by means of a narrow isthmus: a condition spoken of, with some awe, by the connoisseurs of pathology as 'hour glass stomach'.

Waves of peristalsis may be felt as they pass visibly across the upper half of the abdomen . . . A boring pain recurs, beaks in the liver, even the thought of food becomes a torture; a description that starts at discomfort is refined with each meal taken until it colonises the entire consciousness, then copious vomiting, startling to casual observers, brings relief.

An oaty puddle shines at the roadside, the imposing gates of Burghley Park. Regurgitated bile hangs from tough spears of grass. No other passenger sees it: future vomit melting the snow of a parallel Stamford. The travelling poet, John Clare, is not himself. He is neurotically alert for portents of coming damage, romancers who will exploit his memory. The coach jolts towards the Great North Road. It overtakes a stalled Volvo in which reprints of his books are so much ballast, among sacks of provincial trufflings that will be traded in London markets.

Stamford, with its pretensions to society, its newspapers, its status as a spoilt university town, refused to appoint Clare as its salaried fool. Lord Exeter guided him, his muddy, creaking boots, down the endless corridors of Burghley House, making promises. But long before this, before London, Stamford had a mythic status, referred to in the ancient chronicles of Bladud of Bath, the English Icarus. Bladud was portrayed as the 'Ninth King of Britain'. Philosopher. Magician. Leper and pig-keeper.

Howard C. Levis published an account of *Bladud of Bath. The British King Who Tried to Fly* in 1919.

Not only did Bladud try to fly, but he is the traditional founder of Bath, and, practising magic, produced the hot springs . . .

He was sent by his father to Athens to be instructed in philosophy and the liberal sciences. Hearing of the death of his father, he returned home, bringing with him four philosophers, or, according to some authorities, teachers of the four principal sciences, and founded a university at Stamford in Lincolnshire, which was attended by a large number of students, and flourished until the coming of St Augustine, when it was suppressed by the Pope because of the heresies which were taught there.

Bladud practised necromancy or magic, and taught it throughout his kingdom . . . He was incessantly performing marvellous tricks, and, to keep up his reputation, made wings of feathers, with which he attempted to fly at Troja Nova (New Troy) or Trinavantum (now London), but he fell on the temple of Apollo (which had been founded by his ancestor, Brute, when he built New Troy), and was dashed to pieces . . .

Geoffrey Hadman's flight across England in the Auster was in keeping with local custom: heresy. Dream voyages. Mushroom-induced cloud visions. Stamford needs its spiked churches to keep out devils. The devils Clare knew and accommodated: Fen agues, heat in the stomach, sore fundament. Poor sleep. Walking early through wet fields, prospecting for language. 'Clare is constantly wandering, in his circumscribed domain,' said John Ashbery (in *Other Traditions*, his Norton lectures at Harvard), 'but there is not much to see.' Pinched reality is what Clare knows: flatness, huge skies, hidden streams. It is the going away, towards the overwhelming noise of London, that is the terrible thing.

Here is a common sensation: spirit quitting or entering the body. By nostril, eye, navel. Heel. Aura pierced, worn away. Flight. Derangement. Having begun my novel with a rude invasion of Stamford, I couldn't shake free of the figure of Clare on the road. Carried south in a coach. Walking home to recover himself, to prove his memories. Even when I was describing other characters, shifting around London, they behaved like avatars of Clare. The shamanic march out of Essex.

He is foaming, white spittle; he is chewing leaves torn from the roadside. He is talking in tongues, prophesying what has already passed. He is seeing nothing.

'I hate Stamford,' Clare wrote to Taylor (March 1821), 'but am dragged into it like a Bear & fidler to a wake.' He had seen London now, the experience had undone him. 'My vanity is wearied with satisfactional dissapointments.' Losing himself, the poet skulked among former drinking companions. A straw bear, out of season. Out of fashion. A fiddler waiting for the next funeral.

London

Early spring, season of Clare's recurrent unease. Madness did not come on him suddenly, out of nowhere. Fourteen hours, on a strange road, travelling towards London: first light to last. 'The road was lined with lamps that diminished in the distance into stars.'

He watched labourers in the fields, a disturbing change of angle: one Clare stooped over brown earth, picking out stones, while another, newly privileged, stares back from the window of a coach. 'I could almost fancy that my identity as well as my occupations had changed.'

But they had not changed. He would still work for day hire, setting hedges, harvesting. One foot in the ditch. Until he was fetched home, to play the poet. The freak of fame. Until he was dragged to the city and cut loose, a bear searching for its fiddler.

> Life to me a dream that never wakes:
> Night finds me on this lengthening road alone.

There were four visits to London and it was never the same place. Clare persuaded himself, as his acquaintance expanded, as he managed to walk between Fleet Street and Stratford Place (off Oxford Street), that the city absorbed him, tolerated his presence. Long before the steady stare of camera poles and CCTV monitors, he felt the prick of eyes on his skin. Watchers. Primed to spring trapdoors hidden in the narrows of Chancery Lane. Cannibal cellars. Blood drained from a wound in his throat. They left him dangling on a meat hook, a husk of dry paper. London was a scarlet nightmare.

When I used to go anywhere by myself especially Mrs Emmersons I used to sit at night till very late because I was loathe to start not for the sake of leaving the company but for fear of meeting with supernaturals even in the busy paths of London & tho I was a stubborn disbeliever of such things in the day time yet at night their terrors came upon me ten fold & my head was as full of the terribles as a gossips – thin death like shadows & goblings with soercer eyes were continually shaping in the darkness from my haunted imagination & when I saw any one of a spare figure in the dark passing or going on by my side my blood has curdled cold at the foolish apprehension of his being a supernatural agent whose errand might be to carry me away at the first dark alley we came too

His host, Burkhardt, led the poet to the river at Westminster Bridge, a hoped-for Wordsworthian epiphany. Clare's soul was resolutely dull; the nocturne, silver lights in liquid darkness, spurned. 'I was dissapointed thinking I should have seen a fresh water sea and when I saw it twas less than Whittlesea Meer.'

Women parading the streets were of greater interest. Perfumed exoticism. So many and so magnificent. Burkhardt shocked Clare by revealing their trade. The weary, befuddled tourist couldn't get his bearings. Nothing was as it appeared. The Helpston poet imposed a system of equivalents on London. The Thames becomes Whittlesey Mere. Westminster Abbey is Peterborough Cathedral. St Paul's stands for Glinton spire. One of the gorgeous nightwalkers might be Mary Joyce. He refuses to venture in high literary stocks: London reconstituted as a wild geology of cliffs, crags, cataracts. No laudanum, no lakes, for John. The murky expanse of Whittlesey Mere, witnessed during that long, dull voyage from Peterborough to Wisbech, stayed with him in a way the muddy Thames never would. Clare was impervious to German metaphysics. His romanticism consisted of viewing prostitutes, in their nocturnal perambulations, as grand and stately creatures. In acknowledging prizefighters as poets. Poets as labouring men.

In John Taylor's Fleet Street office, Keats used the back of a letter from Clare to his publisher (litany of ill health, underpayment, bores of verse) to tinker with a draft of *Lamia*. Clare was unsentimental about his Cockney colleague's damaged lungs, his voyage to Italy.

'I should like to see the fiz of the man,' he wrote to Hessey (29 June 1820), 'before he drops off and hope he will last till next winter when I shall hazard myself to town unaccompanied.'

Born in a Moorgate pub, Keats was the voice of London: and he had escaped. Broken away. Sickness. Foreign parts. The two poets never met. 'Give my respects to Keats and tell him I am a half mad melancholly dog in this moozy misty country he has latly cast behind him.'

When Keats died, unsold stock piled high, Taylor presented Clare with a copy of Chaucer that had once belonged to the London poet. Clare's library grew until it threatened to overwhelm the limits of his wife's tolerance. His tastes were orthodox, his reading wide. He valued books as objects. He solicited gifts from other writers, from patrons. Promised many, he received few. One complimentary volume of Keats, gifted by Taylor, he sent back: to demand the poet's inscription. He badgered Peter de Wint for a drawing:

The favour requested & the liberty taken to request it being neither more or less than a wish to possess a bit of your genius to hang up in a frame in my Cottage by the side of Friend Hiltons beautifull drawing which he had the kindness to give me when first in London what I mean is one of those scraps which you consider nothing after having used them & that lye littering about your study

To keep the incidents of the city fresh in his mind, for future exploitation, Clare made shorthand notes. 'Mem: ladys thronging the streets at night.' He worked hard to flesh out his self-portrait as a premature flâneur. 'One of my greatest amusements while in London was reading the booksellers windows,' he confessed. 'I was always fond of this from a boy and my next greatest amusement was the curiosity of seeing litterary men.'

Churches, theatres, the premises of John Murray (Lord Byron's publisher). Dues paid, Clare lost himself in the mob, the incessant scurrying of tradesmen, whores, beggars, loiterers. He was hustled from place to place, room to room, patron to patron. They tried his conversation, Lord Radstock and Mrs Emmerson; they were short of a biddable peasant, rough trade with a bundle of unedited manuscripts. A non-insurrectionary poet who knew how to be grateful. They set up funds, they badgered publishers.

The first London excursion: novelty. Muffled in a long green coat, Clare comes to terms with the conditions of notoriety: being watched, gossiped over, tested. Frederick Martin tells us that he was 'unwilling to play the part of a newly discovered monkey'. He remained unimpressed: by the tourist circuit, the gaudy of Vauxhall Pleasure Gardens. He dragged himself to one of Taylor's literary dinners. He met Hazlitt: 'A silent picture of severity.' J. H. Reynolds: 'He would punch you with his puns very keenly without ever hurting your feelings.' Henry Cary. Lord Radstock (admiral, Christian). And, by way of Radstock, the flutteringly determined poetess (and collector of poets), Mrs Eliza Emmerson. One empty chair: John Keats was ill.

The best of London was quitting it. A more comfortable coach ride. The Bull Inn at Ware. A serving girl who caught his eye. A sonnet. Clare's London poems, the residue of this visit, are prose. The notes of a survivor. Gossip, anecdote, confession. His new friends, concerned patrons, nudge him towards marriage with the definitively pregnant Patty Turner.

June 1822 brings Clare back to town: alone, unaccompanied, sensations sharper. Celebrity has curdled. His first book, *Poems Descriptive of Rural Life & Scenery*, has run through four editions. A second book is unpublished. The vogue for peasants is over, poetry is out of fashion. Clare sits in Taylor's window, in Fleet Street, and he watches. That property, on the south side of the street, to the east of St Bride's, is currently (2004) occupied by The Link, a mobile-phone franchise. '£20 off. Pay as you like.' Curved window, dirty red brick. Cheap novelties.

He perches, undisturbed, where so much business is transacted, a press of humanity streams below. He is positioned at one of the great crossing points of London. Fleet Street is the original connection, emphasised by Samuel Pepys (born alongside St Bride's, schooled at St Paul's), between the gated city and royal Westminster (king, parliament, court). Pepys, making his way home along this muddy highway, is tempted by a prostitute, a girl in the shadows. He goes with her, takes fright, says that he hasn't enough money, runs. (And records his humiliation. London insists on records being kept. The hot eyes of the future. I re-walk, compulsively, routes other men established.)

All of this, the cocktail of human dust and stone dust, is available to the seated poet. John Clare, breath stopped, coexists with the crumbling figurines, gods and mythological presences in alcoves above jewellery shops, tobacconists, legal stationers. The city is freighted with code, Coade stone imitations: Mercury, Neptune, Minerva, bulls, bears, griffins. (Coade, in later times, move their operation to Stamford.) Livery companies, trade associations, fraternities. Fleet Street, bridging the Fleet River, an enclosed sewage ditch, runs parallel to the Thames, that old brown god.

The Link: a window display of husks, bright plastic carapaces. Babble of electronic non-communication: so many of the walkers are not walking; they are muttering, mumbling, talking to themselves. Mad folk, pre-visioned by Clare. Hands against his ears to keep them stoppered. To hold the letters of the alphabet inside, in case they spill.

Watch a street and you become it. You construct, if so inclined, a narrative: but you are also part of the witnessed event. You shape what you see. Clare suffers futures, future suffering, displaced persons struggling to set themselves on the right road. The view from Fleet Street, looking east, so busy in engravings and photographs – railway, smoke, interlocking carts – is botched: penance not pilgrimage. (St Paul's, in the summer of 2004, is wrapped like a convalescent. Christopher Wren's Temple Bar will be removed from its present obscurity in Theobald's Park, out near the orbital circuit of the M25, and returned to captivity in Paternoster Square. A heritage trophy. A lifeless version of itself: no gate, no psychic marker, not even a folly in a rich brewer's park. A naked and all too pristine freak. London, once again, reduced to an exhibition of fraudulent symbols.)

Irritation of the eye. Clare is not used to sitting in windows, but he treats it like a job:

on my first visit to London I had a glimpse of things as they are & felt doubtful on my second I had more dissapointments & in my last I saw so much mistey shuffling that my faith of the world shrunk to a skeleton & would scarce fill a nutt shell or burthen a mouse to bear it

Pepys, Dr Johnson (stalking with the poet Savage), John Donne, Keats, Jack Kerouac (on his one recorded London hike), Edgar Wallace (whose plaque is across the busy traffic, at the corner of Fleet Street and Farringdon Street): they are there and not there. Voices. Threadlike entities. Supernatural agents as involuntary glimpses of future times. In years to come, watching the watcher, Clare fanatics will stare at the arched window of the publisher John Taylor and insist on a glimpse of the vanished poet.

Watching, walking, drowning. Clare couldn't delete what he knew, his seven-mile circuit of Northamptonshire countryside, by crouching at a Fleet Street window. The city would have to be mapped by a sequence of zigzag perambulations, mimicking a state of intoxication. That is how nineteenth-century London is to be understood: a town out of its head on drink. Resurrectionists and corpse-suppliers. Labourers who will push a body in a cart from Bethnal Green to Smithfield, to Southwark, to Soho. The hospital porter, the surgeon: falling down drunk. Gin, claret. Lawyers, judges, priests and hangmen: reeling, staggering, spitting red.

Clare's final visit, February to March 1828, took place three years before the murders by the 'London Burkers', John Bishop, Thomas Williams and James May. Easier to facilitate death's passage than to raid burial grounds. Less digging, more time to drink. To make a slow, wandering circuit of the pubs: while the victim (dosed with porter and laudanum) snores on the dirt floor of your kitchen. The orphans, street performers, vagrant children, who were murdered (made into art works, anatomical specimens), had no fixed abode: they were part of the drift of the city, the slipstream Clare now entered.

He ventured as far as St Paul's; he promised to find material for Patty and his sister, Sophy. Such change as he carried in his pocket, so Jonathan Bate tells us, was given to 'an African beggar' outside the cathedral. Stall-holders and shopkeepers fleece the countryman. He expects this and is not disappointed. It gets him out of further marketing. He acquires a guide, Thomas Bennion, Hessey's porter. Bennion is a Londoner. Bennion is at his shoulder. Bennion likes a drink. Clare likes Bennion, understands him. He manages a letter home, the confirmation that he is elsewhere:

My journey up ended very bad indeed – we went 20 miles and upwards in the most dreadfull thunder storm . . . but I am safe thats satisfaction enough – my respects to all and a kiss for Anna.

Anna is special: firstborn, daughter. Patty is pregnant again. Clare floats ('grass-green coat and yellow waistcoat') between the fixed point in Taylor's window and his rovings with Bennion. 'They went to raree-shows together,' records Jonathan Bate. Literary dinners for the *London Magazine* set. Clare slept in different houses: Mrs Emmerson's little room with the skylight, a few nights with Cary in Chiswick (Hogarth's old property). He visited the grave of James Thomson in Richmond. He met E. V. Rippingille, the painter whose work he had seen in a shop window on that stolen Saturday, wandering through Wisbech. A youth whose wrists poked out of his sleeves.

'Rip', now based in Bristol, came up to town at regular intervals, nudging his career, taking on projects such as the group scene *The Stage-Coach Before Breakfast*. A conversation piece loud with celebrity. A precursor of *The Colony Room* (1962) by Michael Andrews. Or rock-vampire Ronnie Wood's corralling of the ghosts of the Ivy; the presently notorious (in their own estimation) herded into improbable conjunctions. Rip was ahead of the game: future icons, at breakfast, waiting on the celestial coach. The Wordsworths (William and Dorothy). Samuel Taylor Coleridge. A man, in coat and hat, umbrella under arm, staring into a mirror and discovering that it is a clock. This obscure traveller, preparing himself for the road home, might be Clare.

Prizefighting. French actresses in Tottenham Court Road. Strategic retreats from soirées organised by Mrs Emmerson. Rip was Clare's boon companion, his agent of pleasure. He took the poet by the elbow and guided him into a different London. Another spiral of the labyrinth. Nights in Offley's tavern swilling Burton's Ale. Conversation among equals. No requirement to perform.

Hot-faced, the sturdy peasant poet is presented to his peers. As he sees, so he is seen. His trajectory intersects with those of other persons worthy of biography. He encounters De Quincey. Frederick Martin cooks the fable:

Mr. De Quincey being announced one day, just when they were sitting down to dinner, Clare quickly sprang to his feet to behold the extraordinary man; but was much astonished on seeing a little, dark, boyish figure, looking like an overgrown child, oddly dressed in a blue coat, with black necktie, and a small hat in his hand. Clare's astonishment became still greater when this singular-looking little man began to talk, not, as the listener innocently expected, of such abstruse subjects as he was wont to write on in the *London Magazine*, but in a banter about the most ludicrous and vulgar things.

Eccentrics were De Quincey's stock-in-trade. He collected Clare as he collected 'Walking Stewart', a man who had lost his wits in epic hikes across Europe and Asia. Stewart owned a house, he published. He was one of those creatures, unrecorded, who drive the secret generators of the city by congenital restlessness, long days on the treadmill of the pavements. Men with black bags (women too) moving slightly faster than the rest of us; stale odour, steady stare.

I met one such, as I was walking – I hadn't meant to take this route – from the Serpentine Gallery (Cy Twombly), through the park, Mall, Admiralty Arch, Trafalgar Square, Strand, Fleet Street. In search of Clare's window.

Into my stride, I overtake window-grazers, mobile-phone gabblers, and am overtaken, in my turn, by appointment-keepers, Anzacs with tight shorts and rucksack destinations. A comfortable momentum is achieved, at which certain details are registered, but the freewheeling mind doesn't drag like an anchor; you are not caught up in anticipations of arrival.

A gaunt man, respectably dressed (once, years ago), swept past me so effortlessly that I felt the breeze. He swung away towards the Embankment, the river. He had the black bags, as well as an ancient leather attaché case. I was tempted to pursue him, but understood that it was hopeless; he'd already gained a hundred yards, didn't concern himself with traffic, weaving through it, untouched. He might have been a lecturer, tenure not renewed. He touched things, railings, posts. He was weather-beaten; beneath the crust, fiercely pale. His path and my own (which contained unfulfilled projects, attempts to register John Clare's movements) were not complementary.

The displaced lecturer was another Walking Stewart. One of the brotherhood that De Quincey knew so well. De Quincey is a walking writer; his prose bustles, gasps for breath, edits itself as it races on. He might travel from Manchester to London, on foot, to the Lakes, but he failed to keep pace with Walking Stewart and the robotic, disenfranchised walkers who keep the arteries of the city open.

When De Quincey chanced on Stewart, near Somerset House (where I noticed my Quixotic pedestrian), the urban stalker told him that he was leaving that night for Westmorland.

Thence I went, by the very shortest road . . . towards a point which necessarily led me through Tottenham Court Road: I stopped nowhere, and walked fast; yet so it was that in Tottenham Court Road I was not overtaken by (*that* was comprehensible), but overtook Walking Stewart

. . . There must have been three Walking Stewarts in London. He seemed nowise surprised at this himself, but explained to me that somewhere or other in the neighbourhood of Tottenham Court Road there was a little theatre, at which there was dancing, and occasionally good singing.

The fraternity of walkers, having no obligation to remember (or record) their journeys, are everywhere at once. They are immortal. Faces rust but they don't change: clear, burning eyes. London offers them the anonymity Clare could never achieve. In Helpston, he struggled to disappear into the landscape. Moving through London, he was everybody. And nobody. He lacked the terminology to describe what he was seeing. What he felt was happening to him.

De Quincey places Clare, quite securely, in a cabinet of curiosities:

In 1824, perhaps upon some literary scheme, he came up to London, where, by a few noble families and by his liberal publishers, he was welcomed in a way that, I fear, from all I heard, would but too much embitter the contrast with his own humble opportunities of enjoyment in the country. The contrast of Lord Radstock's brilliant parties, and the glittering theatres of London, would have but a poor effect in training him to bear that want of excitement which even already, I had heard, made his rural life but too insupportable to his mind. It is singular that what most fascinated his rustic eye was not the gorgeous display of English beauty, but the French style of beauty, as he saw it amongst the French actresses in Tottenham Court Road. He seemed, however, oppressed by the glare and tumultuous existence of London; and, being ill at the time, from an affliction of the liver, which did not, of course, tend to improve his spirits, he threw a weight of languor upon any attempt to draw him out in conversation.

French actresses, bare-knuckle boxers. Fellow poets. Clare was supplied with images and fancies that made domestic life in North-amptonshire difficult to endure. 'I wish I could live nearer you,' he wrote to Taylor (February 1825); 'at least I wish London could be within twenty miles of Helpston. I live here among the ignorant like a lost man.'

The third visit to London, May 1824, was made on the excuse of consulting Dr Darling. The city tormented him. Night walks were an agony, shifting between Taylor and Mrs Emmerson, visiting Charles and Mary Lamb in Islington. He lived in fear of that ditch, Chancery Lane: law, bankruptcy, high red cliffs. The wigs, the black gowns, books from which words leak. He paid to be cheated. A watchman led him home the wrong way, confirming his opinion of London. In daylight, he wandered: 'trying to catch the eye of the most beautiful women'. Dr Darling advised: rest, not much reading, no excitement. Clare burnt, sweated. Rip was back in town. They visited the phrenologist Jean Deville. A cast was taken; Clare entombed in white plaster, breathing with straws up his nose like a parodic yokel. The bust was presented to Mrs Emmerson. It tumbled from its perch and was 'shivered to atoms by the fall'. Pieces of the poet covering the carpet like white sand, scouring powder.

A mania for prizefighting was the consequence of accompanying Rippingille to bouts in the Fives Court. Harry 'Sailor Boy' Jones took Clare's fancy. He fused notions of aristocratic patronage with fantasies of himself as an undefeated champion: 'Boxer Byron'. Jack Randall, the former pugilist, kept the Hole in the Wall in Chancery Lane. Clare, when the old boundaries of self wore away, would become Randall. Poetry was his challenge to the world of critics, explainers, newspaper readers.

Oxford Street. Walking towards Mrs Emmerson's house, a route that was grooved into his experience of London, Clare came upon a crowd, expectant, faces to the traffic. The funeral procession of Lord Byron:

I saw his remains born away out of the city on its last journey to that place where fame never comes ... I happened to see it by chance as I was wandering up Oxford street on my way to Mrs Emmersons when

my eye was suddenly arested by straggling gropes of the common people
collected together and talking about a funeral

He noticed a young girl, a figure borrowed from De Quincey:
the spectre of Ann, the child-prostitute of Oxford Street. ('Recoiling
from that unfathomed abyss in London into which I was now so
wilfully precipitating myself.') The portrait of the girl, her response
to the melancholy event, is Clare's attempt at public reportage.
This is how the city should receive a poet: with dignity and awe.
Empty carriages. Heraldic shields. Black drapes over the urn which
contains Byron's ashes (heart and brain removed at autopsy).

Monday, 12 July 1824: the fabulous hearse began its journey from
St George's Street (Westminster) to a village church in Nottingham-
shire. A bruising flash of recognition, poet to poet. Clare solicited
an immediate transference of spirit (as Blake accepted the task of
recomposing Milton, 'correcting' his errors). In the Epping Forest
madhouse, he re-remembered Byron's *Don Juan* and *Childe Harold*
and made them his own. Dr Darling, a well-intentioned man,
suggested an alternative career for the stressed author. Cottage
gardening? Orchard keeping?

Returned to wife and family, Clare wrote to his friend and
supporter, the Scottish poet Allan Cunningham: 'As for myself, I
am as dull as a fog in November, and as far removed from all news
of literary matters as the man in the moon.'

His last trip: 1828. A final consultation with Darling. Sickness was
already part of the landscape: belly, eyes, head. Little sleep, early
wanderings in the fields, prospecting for language that was no
longer to be found. 'Yet I know if I could reach London I should
be better,' Clare wrote to Taylor (his reluctant confessor), 'or else
get to salt water. Whatever Dr. Darling advises I will do it if I can.'

Too late. He is heavier now, body thickening, tongue too full
for his mouth. 'His forehead was so broad and high, as to have
bordered on deformity.'

Patty struggles with another difficult pregnancy. He tries sulphur baths, walks in Hyde Park (pretend country). He visits Cary in the British Museum and is 'overawed by the quantity of books'. Not knowing that one day they would be removed and the circuit of the Reading Room dressed with fakes. (Or so a used-bookdealer from Charing Cross Road told me, volumes as furniture. Truck them in: yards of dross, dead libraries. We can't disappoint the punters, they expect that shock: that there should be so many books in the world. In one building. And none of them by John Clare.)

Frederick Martin has the poet noticing spring violets on Hampstead Heath and deciding, on the instant, to return home. He would try fieldwork. The city was done with him. If he came south again, he would be accompanied by attendants, carrying him off to High Beach. London, from the ridge of the forest, was a mirage. Helpston felt closer.

Early on the morning of the 16th of July, 1837, Clare was led away from his wife and children, by two stern-looking men, who placed him in a small carriage and drove rapidly away southward. Late the same day, the poet found himself an inmate of Dr. Allen's private lunatic asylum, at Fair Mead House, High Beech, in the centre of Epping Forest.

WALKING

In the blue mist the orisons edge surrounds.

John Clare

Forest

You say 'High Beech' and I say 'High Beach', there is no correct answer to the riddle. Jonathan Bate favours 'Beech' (as he prefers 'Helpston' to Clare's 'Helpstone'). William Addison, author of *Epping Forest, Its Literary and Historical Associations* (1945), opts for 'High Beach'. Clare is an improvisatory, free-jazz speller. 'Leopards Hill' is his improvement on 'Leppit's Hill Lodge' (or 'Lippitts Hill', according to the OS map), the villa that housed the most troubled of Matthew Allen's patients, the 'incurables'. Period illustrations, offering a white house surrounded by lawns and shrubs, use the title: 'View of Leopard's Hill Lodge'. Authentic Lea Valley pastoral. Greenhouse, creepers, encroaching forest. English clouds. The only way Clare could gain access to such an estate was through the tradesman's entry: straight round to the potato beds, John. Moleskin trousers kneecapped with twine. Sharp thorns under blackened fingernails. Buttons struggling to confine a greasy leather waistcoat.

Leppit's Hill Lodge, photographed for the edition of *The Letters of John Clare* (1970 reprint), edited by J. W. and Anne Tibble, has a very different atmosphere. Dread. More Harry Price (ghost hunter) than M. R. James (connoisseur of mezzotints). James, scholar and establishment man, liked scaring the wits from his pupils with tales of demons, East Anglian entities summoned by whistle. He interrogated black-letter texts and woodblocks, waiting for that slender figure in the background, the man with the scythe, to slide forward. A dull print, examined with enough care, becomes a window into a discontinued narrative.

Harry Price, psychic investigator (Borley Rectory, talking mongoose), unloaded his kit and tapped the atmosphere for likely prospects. Leppit's Hill Lodge, as a monochrome print, is fearsome. Roof, position of door, brick porch: all wrong. Heaps of rubble in overgrown grounds. This is one of those buildings that hang on beyond their time; shuttered windows, dark interiors nobody wants to disturb. Asylum. Isolation hospital. Articulate ruin.

Clare writes home (23 November 1837):

> My Dear Wife
>   I write to tell you I am getting better I cant write a long letter but wish to know how you all are the place here is beautiful & I meet with great kindness the country is the finest I have seen write & tell me how you all are I cant write a long letter but I shall do better God bless you all kiss them all for me
>   Yours ever
>   my dear wife
>   John Clare

A brave, tremulous message dispatched by a boy who is away from home for the first time. Private school. Borstal. Contagious ward. National Service. Strange food, stranger company, not enough blankets. Cold showers, hikes in the forest. Putting a brave face on circumstances that are unlikely to improve.

Clare made a reasonable fist of his time with the Napoleonic War volunteers; comedy routines (like Justice Shallow's apple orchard troop), knockabout material for his journal. King's-shilling drunk (several times over). Obnoxious corporal punched on the nose. Oundle, where he was billeted in modest style, was on the clay, beyond Stilton; at the outer limits of known territory. He could walk home in a day.

When Anna's father, Geoffrey, was five years old, he disappeared from the farm: as Clare had done, when he set out to find the edge of the world. 1914: military bands were marching around the villages, accompanied by recruiting sergeants. Young Geoffrey Hadman followed them out of Glinton and was recaptured, hours later, on the road to Helpston: an underage volunteer for the trenches.

Epping Forest: new soil, new sounds. Special light. Clare perched on a high ridge that offered the classic James Thomson view: river, fields, small farms, tower of the church of Holy Cross and St Lawrence at Waltham Abbey. A relief from the crushing phobias of the Northborough cottage. The regime is benevolent, he will 'do better'.

He eats, grows sturdy. He potters in the kitchen garden, wanders through the forest. But he is still a prisoner. Constantly watched (even when the watchers hide behind trees). After the 'escape' Clare wrote to Matthew Allen, a courtesy, describing his walk out of Essex and asking for the return of books lent to women of the neighbourhood: 'I dont want any part of Essex in Northamptonshire agen I wish you would have the kindness to send a servant to get them for me.' A feigned passion for literature is a useful means of striking an acquaintance with the local author, the faded celebrity. Wives, and Essex women in general, were hereby forsworn: 'I should [like] to be to myself a few years and lead the life of a hermit.'

The fault lay with a system based on surveillance. The rhetoric of freedom, announced with breast-beating sincerity, is exposed as a politic lie. Of the kind we have come to know so well: Lea Valley estates thrown up on poisoned ground. Liberty under law. No healing of a spirit that remains in bondage, despite the boasts of the keepers. The ones who have invested in green-belt real estate.

I can be miserably happy in any situation and any place and could have staid in yours in the forest if any of my friends had noticed me or come to see me – but the greatest annoyance in such places as yours are those servants styled keepers who often assumed as much authority over me as if I had been their prisoner and not likeing to quarrel I put up with it till I was weary of the place altogether so I heard the voice of freedom

Matthew Allen's establishment was hierarchically organised (wards beyond wards): three properties. Controlled liberties for those responsive to the notion of cure. Seclusion and restraint for loose women and stubborn, dirty men. Leopards Hill was the worst, a hideaway for self-soilers, screamers, non-citizens. (The

madwoman-in-the-attic syndrome. Hogarthian torments under the
eaves of a white mansion. In brick outbuildings, styes.) Fair Mead
lived up to its name, a country house; a pond with lilies, resident
waterfowl. Springfield housed fifteen women. The local authorities
signed the relevant forms: care and comfort in retirement from the
world. A curtain of oak, elm, beech screening the worst of it. An
easy ride back to town for duty visitors.

Allen, who had worked with the Quakers in York, an institution
known as The Retreat, brought some of the patients south with
him. He was a man of schemes. The sort of character who looks
for property on the rim of London. Ethical front with aggressive
marketing strategy. Soft Buddhism. Trim lawns, bright windows.
Landscape prospects as the deal clincher. Fee-paying mad folk
busied into craftwork, supervised gardening, bullied back to health.
The uncooperative would be restrained, without malevolence, in
one of the mean back rooms.

The life, at first, suited Clare. The new horizon, if he sat on Fern
Hill, was seductive: 'At the back of the chapple a beautifull retreat
from a mad house.' This forest was as disconcerting as the Fens,
too much information rather than too little. Light filtered, ground
soft underfoot. Woodier smells: clay mulch, leaf-mould, deer drop-
pings. Sandy tracks throwing his compass out of alignment. He
could dress himself in other identities, let in Byron, double-voice
him, two sequences in parallel: 'Child Harold' and 'Don Juan'.
Letters to the outside world were capitalised. Sometimes he corresponded with his earthly wife, Patty. Sometimes with his spiritual
bride, Mary Joyce. Each sentence suggests the title of a new poem.
He is resolved, settled to his fate: 'The Spring Smile's & So Shall I.'
He is irked: 'For What Reason They Keep Me Here I Cannot Tell
For I Have Been No Otherways Than Well A Couple of Year's.'
Essex and Northamptonshire are fixed in perpetual conflict. Clare
labours. He grows plump and smooth, the docile rustic his patrons
expect. He enjoys the company of Thomas Campbell, another
inmate, son of the poet. He hoards rude fantasies about female
patients, their house is a brothel of the senses.

Alfred Tennyson, another man in the wrong place at the wrong season, postpones marriage, cultivates a beard, endures the yelping of dogs. He is domiciled in High Beach, a rented house. He visits Allen, ventures capital in a scheme to develop a steam-powered wood-carving machine. He loses everything. Jonathan Bate reminds us that Tennyson spent time at Fair Mead, 'occupying a status somewhere between patient and house-guest'. There is no hard evidence that he met Clare. The poets set their gaze on different Englands. If they coincided on forest walks, they kept their eyes down, scuttled for cover. Private language systems. A copyright on singularity.

Epping Forest was never a lucky place for authors. T. E. Lawrence acquired land on Pole Hill, a little to the south of High Beach, alongside the obelisk marking the line of zero longitude. He projected a retreat, a private press. In the dry summer of 1921, grass on Pole Hill was fired, the hut destroyed. A man called Vyvyan Richards, who taught at Bancroft's School in Woodford Green, stored Lawrence's books, his teak doors, shipped back from Jidda. Lawrence camped in the Pole Hill cloister but couldn't bring himself to live there. He preferred, like Clare, to slip identities. He tried 'Ross' for size, enlisting in the Royal Air Force. Then 'Shaw' for his move to the Tank Corps, the cottage at Clouds Hill in Dorset.

Writers kept coming, but rarely settled. Arthur Morrison, composing his *Tales of Mean Streets*, Jago warrens, riverside dens, tried High Beach as a necessary palliative. The poet Edward Thomas and his wife, Helen, rented a cottage near Paul's Nursery, between the Robin Hood pub and King's Oak. A winter interlude before his return to France, the trenches, death. He encountered Clare's work in the 1908 selection edited by Arthur Symons. He considered the process whereby the anima of Mary Joyce becomes the muse of the asylum poems. Mary died, unmarried, on 14 July 1838, the day after Clare's forty-fifth birthday. He had been at High Beach for exactly one year. Such anniversaries meant nothing. Clare's mind, according to Matthew Allen, 'did not appear so much lost as suspended in its movements by the oppressive and permanent state of anxiety and fear'.

He is comfortable, fed, supplied with books. He is removed from the burden of providing for his family and from the horror of love (children in sickness, ageing parents, unhappy wife). He works when he will, and is praised for it – but unpaid. He composes 1,600 lines of poetry and 1,500 lines of biblical paraphrase. Allen's asylum is a forcing house. Clare takes dictation from elsewhere. He makes few annotations on wild nature, electing to deal in topical satires and scatological barbs. Doctors, whores. Vulgar royalty. Newspaper scandals turned mad and loud. Poetry is a hot coal in the mouth. The *Athenaeum* publishes an appeal for funds: 'The malady by which the poet is lost to himself has caused him to pass from the memory of others.'

And from the memory of place. The circle of landscape in which he had once been anchored. As John Clare, he was unvoiced. One of the invisibles buried on the green perimeter of London. A living corpse. 'O would it were my lot,' he said (quoting Byron), 'To be forgetfull as I am forgot.'

After four years enclosed in the forest, he feels that it is time to escape, to return to Mary. His wife and children, settled in their Northborough cottage, have been erased. The imagined crime of bigamy purged by elective amnesia. A walk into the past is contemplated. (By suffering, he will revise errors of biography. Open an alternate life. Follow a different path.) Essex in Northampton is a collapsing topography. There is nowhere of any consequence between High Beach and Mary Joyce's Glinton. 'Yon spire that points to heaven . . . True as the needle to the pole.'

In April 1841, still writing in capitals, Clare describes an Easter Sunday visit to Buckhurst Hill Church:

Stood In The Church Yard – When A Very Interesting Boy Came Out While Organ Was Playing Dressed In A Slop Frock Like A Ploughboy & Seemingly About Nine Years Of Age – He Was Just Like My Son Bill

When He Was About The Same Age & As Stout Made – He Had A
Serious Interesting Face & Looked As Weary With The Working Days
As A Hard Working Man – I Was Sorry I Did Not Give Him The Last
Halfpenny I Had & Ask Him A Few Questions As To His Age & Name
& Parents But Perhaps I May See Him Again

There was also a young woman, dressed as milkmaid or farm
servant. 'I Did Not Speak To Her But I Now Wish I Had & Cannot
Forget Her.' The instant of composition keeps the memory alive,
raw. He will walk forward, with pain and difficulty, into the past
and make it cohere. The church spire is a needle to his pole.

Returned home, after his successful flight from Matthew Allen's
madhouse, 'where men close prisoners are & women are ravished',
Clare wrote a premature farewell to a fading landscape. His essay
on Autumn:

& there is the beautifull Spire of Glinton Church towering high over the
grey willows & dark wallnuts still lingering in the church yard like the
remains of a wreck telling where their fellows foundered in the ocean of
time – place of green Memorys & gloomy sorrows – even these meadows
arches seem to me to be something of the beautifull having been so long
a prisoner & shut up in confinement they appear something worthy of
notice

The pressure of revised history, a parallel life, was extreme. It
countered a shameful present, the forest confinement. The ever-
watchful eyes of Matthew Allen's servants. In the territory of the
mind, John Clare was no longer a peasant poet. He was a boxer:
Jack Randall, Champion of England. Establish a new identity and
the old Clare can float free. Other fools will accept his folly.

Jack Randall The Champion Of The Prize Ring Begs Leave To Inform
The Sporting World That He Is Ready To Meet Any Customer In The
Ring Or On The Stage To Fight For The Sum Of £500 He Is Not Particular
As To Weight Colour Or Country

Clare is Lord Byron in reduced circumstances, flaying 'Docter Bottle imp who deals in urine'. He witnesses deviants abusing prisoners: 'I have often seen such dirty sights.' He resurrects Mary Joyce, childhood sweetheart. The schoolroom in Glinton Church. The walks to North Fen.

The flight from High Beach can be seen as a shamanic voyage to a more persuasive reality. This dreaming between two worlds is sensible and practical. Clare never denies the existence of Allen's asylum, it was an obligatory trial. A test of his mettle: imprisonment in the dark forest of the grail quests. He has triumphed. From Northborough, he composes a letter of explanation to his former keeper.

Having left the Forest in a hurry I had not time to take leave of you & your family but I intended to write & that before now but dullness & dissapointment prevented me for I found your words true on my return here having neither friends or home left but as it is called "Poets cottage" I claimed a lodging in it where I now am – one of my fancys I found here with her family & all well

The walk, the frantic pilgrimage, was the last of it: sanity. High Beach, like Patty and the children (who are now hers alone), is a 'fancy'. A contract has been broken or a contract fulfilled. Clare tried London and was mocked by his success. (The fourth visit is always the killer. Dylan Thomas blustered across America, three tours, and returned to Laugharne with a few dollars and a criminal hangover. Trains and women. The fourth trip did for him.) The portraits and life masks of John Clare confirm an absence. They register a person who is no longer there. Travelling, tramping the Great North Road, he swims in his own shadow. He forgets where the sun rises.

On the cusp of a final exile, abdication of world and family, Clare analyses his own condition, the frail distinction between being forgotten and eradicated. Silenced.

A very good common place counsel is *Self Identity* to bid our own hearts not to forget our own selves & always to keep self in the first place lest all the world who always keeps us behind it should forget us all together – forget not thyself & the world will not forget thee – forget thyself & the world will willingly forget thee till thou art nothing but a living-dead man dwelling among shadows & falsehood

He talks to his old friends, the gypsies, at their forest camp. They offer, for a price, to smuggle him away. He returns, they are gone. He picks up a discarded 'wide awake' hat and puts it in his pocket. He plots his escape like a military campaign. There are provisions: notebook, chewing tobacco, hat.

I Led the way & my troops soon followed but being careless in mapping down the rout as the Gipsey told me I missed the lane to Enfield town & was going down Enfield highway till I passed "The Labour in vain" Public house where a person I knew comeing out of the door told me the way

John Clare was launched on one of the great English journeys, three and a half days, 20–24 July 1841. Hungry, hobbled, deluded. An expedition to recover a self he had no use for, a wife he didn't recognise, a cottage he loathed. He would confirm the validity of a double consciousness: London and Helpston, poet and labourer, Patty and Mary. A nest of earthly and spiritual children that had been fathered, mislaid. A text, already composed, to be justified by bitter experience.

High Beach

It's July, but not that July, the time of Clare's walk (1841), or the July (2000) when we tracked him, High Beach to Helpston. It is 2004 and I'm trying to remember the details of that evening, four years ago, when Renchi arrived and we spread competing OS maps on the kitchen table. Anna, as you will remember, lurked significantly, preparing dinner and making pointed remarks about comparative distances between Glinton and Peterborough, Glinton and Stamford. We were trespassing, heavy-footed, on her territory. If her memories were not entirely accurate, it wasn't our business to correct them.

The 'Journey out of Essex' as depicted on a map in *John Clare by Himself* (edited by Eric Robinson and David Powell) is admirably straightforward: a vertical line dangled between Northborough and Enfield with a kink snagged on High Beach. Around eighty miles: Essex, Hertfordshire, Bedfordshire, Huntingdonshire, Northamptonshire. Find the Great North Road and the rest is a dumb plod emptying heads of all previous convictions.

Clare slept, head to home, letting the true north of pain and loss act as his guide. He travelled towards the thing that troubled him most: memory. Robinson and Powell's map was arctic white, lacking hills, rivers, woods, farms, churches, airfields, concrete bunkers, Happy Eaters, ibis hotels. (The materials in which we dealt.) Factor in our preliminary stroll from Hackney, detours, digressions, and we should be able to stretch this excursion to the required length of 120 miles. Or: the distance around the M25, London's orbital motorway, drawn out like slack elastic.

It must be the season, old hurts return as I look at my original photographs, read the crabby journal of that walk. The flaw has a name: scoliosis. A lateral deviation of the backbone caused by congenital or acquired abnormalities of the vertebrae. One leg shorter than the other. With inevitable compensations: muscle strain, skewings of tissue. Enough miles on the clock, over the last half-century, to do real damage. In July 2000, I was a month beyond my fifty-seventh birthday. Clare, when he marched down the hill towards Enfield, was forty-eight. His life had been harder, much harder. Poor diet, nights sleeping under trees. Chemical imbalances, thin blood. Digestive problems untreated or made worse by quacks. There were physical (as well as geographical) elements in his supposed madness. Call it the Northampton Syndrome: incest, witchcraft, land too recently recovered from the water.

The prospect of repeating Clare's walk alarmed me. Piece by piece, I was wearing out; years of lugging boxes of books, packing a child under each arm, had taken its toll. I only visited doctors for inoculations. Other symptoms, I suspected, would cure themselves; more or less, eventually. Or not. Best advice: keep clear of hospitals, you'll catch something. Hospitals are future development opportunities living on borrowed time. Scandals waiting for available indignation.

Backs, at my age, are a given; bad ones. Our walk should have been sponsored by Mr Venus, the Clerkenwell taxidermist. Everybody on the Helpston excursion had temperamental spines, legs of different lengths, pains in the side. Would we make it? The *London Orbital* tour was easy; a day on the road, home to warm bath. This was more challenging, three and a half days, straight – following Clare's route or chasing rivers and footpaths. We couldn't decide.

I reconnoitred the forest. My sense of direction in London is adequate, even the bits I don't know; the base map is etched in my skull. The serpentine Thames. The pattern of churches. E. O. Gordon's sacred elevations (as described in *Prehistoric London, Its Mounds and Circles*). But Epping Forest, the Peterborough diaspora? I couldn't fix where the sun rose; shifty skies, vague horizons. Time, recycled, borrowed from another man, won't behave. It sticks or it races. Old heart beating like a pigeon trapped in a chimney.

I set out from High Beach in winter, logging contour lines of lager cans, burger cartons, cigarette packets, bits of cars. Cargo-trash getting denser as I approached the roundabout where four roads meet: A121, A104, B172, B1393. I found a silver Christmas watch, pressed into a muddy hoofprint, and left notices in huts and nature reserves. It was never claimed.

With Renchi in tow, I searched for Matthew Allen's three houses. Building work in progress, convenient footpaths and bridges across the Lea, from Enfield Lock to High Beach, were discontinued. Maps are so selective. They have no truck with the former Small Arms Factory or its abrupt translation into Enfield Island Village ('An Exciting New Village Community'). Rifles, the community pub, knows what kind of customers it wants: 'Over 21's Smart Dress Only. Travellers Not Welcome.' Thirsty, we wait for Turpin's Cave on the road to the forest.

Dick Turpin was an Essex boy who drifted north: York. A horse-trader brought to the rope, the triple tree. The custom then was that a felon who agreed to act as hangman, to stretch his fellows, would be set free. There was a price on Turpin's head, for the murder of Thomas Morris, servant to Henry Thompson, one of the Keepers of Epping Forest. Turpin's criminal history was traditional: family of publicans and butchers, membership of a gang raiding farmhouses and isolated properties on the fringes of London. Nothing out of the way. They only harmed their own. Born too soon to take advantage of the M25.

James Sharpe, examining the legend in a recent book, *Dick Turpin, The Myth of the English Highwayman*, traces the famous pantomime ride back to Defoe, *A Tour through the Whole Island of Great Britain* (first published in three volumes, 1824–6). A robbery at Gadshill in Kent, mariners paid off at Chatham. The former royalist officer, Richard Dudley, turns highwayman. He escapes across the Thames into Essex and rides up the Great North Road to York. Turpin's legend evolves from a careless reading of Dudley's career.

Turpin on the run, like Harry Roberts (the 1966 police killer), is supposed to have hidden in a cave in Epping Forest. Roberts, after a botched robbery in Shepherd's Bush, bought himself some camping kit in King's Cross and took to the forest. He had done his National Service in Malaya. He knew how to set up a number of camps and to keep moving. Despite the manhunt that was inevitable, given his crime, Roberts eluded capture – until he made the mistake of crossing a main road, carrying a blue holdall. 'No one in the country had a bag like that,' he said.

Numerous hotels on the Great North Road lay claim to Turpin's ghost. His spectral presence is felt at the George Hotel in Buckden. The Bell Inn at Stilton, according to Sharpe, was another 'regular haunt'. This phantom self, a creature of myth, travels the length of a route Turpin never took (preferring the back roads, the rivers of Fenland). It is the Great North Road that disappears, displaced by the impatient carriageways of the A1. Between Norman Cross and Alconbury, we will discover abandoned filling stations, tin huts and shacks that once offered all-day breakfasts to travellers and hauliers refused entry at Rifles in Enfield Island Village.

An Enfield publican put Clare straight, pointing out the shortest way. The contemporary version is less certain of local topography. An instruction has gone out from the brewers enforcing a total embargo on courtesy. This was one of those 'High Beach, John? If I wanted fuckin' High Beach, I wouldn't start from here' scenarios. All we learn, from another lunchtime casual, one-eyed and three pints in, is: 'There used to be a road. I think. Once.'

Perhaps the same road that rose out of nowhere to greet Clare's old friend Charles Lamb in his Enfield retirement? John Taylor wrote to Clare, one of those weary lectures about unsold stock, delays in publication, texts to be edited, censored, aborted. 'Poor Charles Lamb is dead – perhaps you had not heard of it before. He fell down and cut his face against the Gravel on the Turnpike Road, which brought on his Erysipelas, and in a few days carried him off.'

Premature road rage. The rage of the Turnpike against Islington travellers who don't know where they are going or why: remedial excursionists. A long-distance walk is a serious affair. You shake up every atom of your being. You arrive, footsore, at your destination: lighter, shorter, hungrier. A stranger to those who stayed at home. Head emptied of old fears. With room made for the new.

From High Beach, Clare contacted his medical adviser, Doctor Darling. 'Sounds affect me very much and things evil as well [as] good thoughts are continually rising in my mind. I cannot sleep, for I am asleep, as it were, with my eyes open, and I feel chills come over me and a sort of nightmare awake and I got no rest last night.'

What sounds oppressed him from under the duvet of the forest? Acoustic footprints of future roads? Chained patients in outhouses? The bells of Waltham Abbey? Sound is torture. Fish speared in the beaks of cormorants, herons. Owls swooping on field mice. Feet tramping gravel. Sound brings back memories. Doctor Skrimshire, in 1832, applying leeches to Clare's temples. Blistering glasses to the nape of his neck. Cold showerbaths, drenches. A cloth they wrapped around his head, its flabby slap. Grey bandages soaked in brandy vinegar and rainwater. Cutting off breath, squeezing the bone-armature of the skull. Something he can't see, but can hear, dripping slowly, so slowly, into a white bowl.

Swallowed in that verdigris coat, a grub in a cabbage leaf, Clare was the Green Man in London. A pub sign on the move. A drowned thing fished from Whittlesey Mere, mud and straw, limping down Chancery Lane, fending off soot demons. Yellow gash at throat, loose kerchief. At High Beach, he faded. Vanished into the dense foliage of summer trees. He spoke of John Clare as someone quite separate from his present identity. Which was? Unknown. Ahead of him on the road. An empty house waiting for someone to take possession.

Maps are thoughtfully provided by the developers, Fairview, to tell you where you can't go: PRIVATE PROPERTY, NO PUBLIC RIGHT OF WAY. Padlocked gates across ancient footpaths. Dry flowers woven into mesh fences. Rain-erased memorial labels. Smeared ink of lost names. WALTHAM POINT NEW 48 ACRE INDUSTRIAL PARK. Tolerated edge-land irrigated by a blurred section of orbital motorway. Low hills dressed with cemeteries, Jewish burial grounds. Limestone pebbles on granite lids.

As we climb, the forest enfolds us. Cars behave like interlopers, hiccupping over speed bumps. Drivers park and disappear. Empty vehicles, huddled together for reassurance, witness supposed beauty spots; sites neutralised by an excess of gazing. HIGH BEACH: (30).

We have only the feeblest notion of the whereabouts of Matthew Allen's asylums; images in a documentary film, drawings by Rigby Graham. A name on the OS map: Springfield Farm. So we begin at the Royal Oak pub and navigate, blind, from there. Until we achieve: 'Clare House'. Fancy lettering on a garden gate. A pale blue dish with flowery rim. Clare House is a lodge with mock-Tudor gables. The owner, interrogated, has no knowledge of the poet and seems unsure about the provenance of his home. The lady next door has lived in High Beach 'for forty-nine years', we're told, but she's not available. Doesn't answer the door. We try a younger couple, cycling, and get as deep into the forest as a sign for 'Lippitts Hill'. I'm sure we have the right pond, sluggish, green: Allen's Fair Mead. Or a first hint at the quiddity of the place: muffled sound, vibrations of the city felt through the soles of your feet.

It takes another excursion, accompanied by Anna, to identify the former asylums with any degree of certainty. We try Buckhurst Hill Church, where Clare noticed the boy in the slop frock, the young woman in 'Darkish Flowerd Cotton Gown'. 'Bucket Hill', Clare called it. 'A place of furze and clouds.' Another spire: poor substitute for wind-scoured Glinton. No humans on this damp afternoon. A stone angel with a missing head. Pink roses growing from a cracked grave: 'No Artificial Flowers Permitted.' Horned snail silver-scripting wet memorial slab.

Tracking Clare's 'brook without a bridge' back to forest, Fair-mead is revealed in its present disguise: The Suntrap Field Study Centre. Thicket, pool, notice forbidding unauthorised entry. We snoop, we pry. Rainwater drips from the collars of our raincoats: July as October. Nature studies (woodcraft for recidivists and malefactors) have replaced the trade in lunatics (returned to their communities). Clare's fascination with creepy-crawlies, fungi, ferns, is now proposed as therapy for a sick city. Revised asylum properties have a sorry atmosphere, the cures have curdled. Solutions are largely concerned with adequate security and raising funds. Business plans, sponsorship, limited opening hours. Placate bureaucracy. And keep a low profile.

Anna helps. She comes with less baggage and no obligation to tease out a narrative. She's perfectly happy to lean for a moment on a gate. Rain brings out the grassy sweetness of the forest. Curtains twitch in plasterboard bungalows, assembled from kit in the wrong place. In expectation of future marine invasion.

Leopards Hill. The Owl pub. Springfield Farm. Anna remembers: stables, a white building. Weatherboards. This was the asylum that housed fifteen females. Springfield, seraglio of forbidden and dangerous women, was a zone of peculiar fascination for Clare:

> Nigh Leopards Hill stand All-ns hells
> The public know the same
> Where lady sods & buggers dwell
> To play the dirty game

Three off-white enamel troughs, raised on bricks, in a stable yard. 'Butler's sinks', Anna calls them. Ripped from a cold pantry and deposited here. Refreshment for horses, returned from their forest rides. The sinks might be remnants of Allen's madhouse, water treatment in open air. To cool the heat of inappropriate lusts. Clare's fevered imagination.

A man emerges from the stables. He is interested in our interest. Like many who congratulate themselves on being out here, fifteen miles from London, cushioned by greenery, this person has a story to peddle. An incident to validate his tentative mortgage on history. (Thereby enhancing property values.)

The attic of Springfield Farm, creaking boards, warped window frame, is haunted. The women's dormitory, he calculates, of Allen's day. A 'very old' book is kept there. He doesn't recall its name. The book is open. It is not a bible, one of those family bibles, but it's just as thick. Although the open pages are secured with four black stones, it doesn't help. Every night, without fail, the pages turn. Every morning a new passage is revealed.

High Beach to Broxbourne

A green as dull as pewter: Epping Forest at first light. Stooped over dripping foliage, Renchi Bicknell uses a cheap magnifying glass, held at various experimental distances from the lens, to mess with the mindset of his camera. We're agreed: High Beach is bindweed, nettles, ankle-tangling fronds jewelled with overnight rain. A chill start. Sky like the skin on cold soup. Chris Petit picked us up in his current Mercedes at five-thirty on the morning of 17 July 2000.

It was decided, and rapidly undecided, to follow Clare as closely as we could, up the Great North Road. Or should we settle for starting with the Lea, then cutting across country, to rejoin the exhausted poet at Stevenage? We would sleep, if we could, in the same places. Our journey would be an approximation, in the spirit of the original 1841 walk, with several fixed points: a private hotel booked at Stevenage, a pub in St Neots, the Bell Inn at Stilton. Anna would be met, under Glinton spire, at four o'clock on the afternoon of the fourth day. No ditch bivouacs, too old for that. No trespassed barns. Renchi had walked, in his youth, from London to Swansea, to the west of Ireland, bedding down where he stopped, woodpiles by the Thames, hostels with vagrants and night-smokers, Welsh mountainsides. Without photographs, and with no companion to confirm a memory stitched from fading highlights, the journey was mythical. Now he discovered our lodgings through the Internet and secured them with credit cards. He was, after all, the co-proprietor of a vegetarian B&B with a panoramic view over the Somerset levels.

Obligatory male scratching and rucksack-shrugging and we move off, stopping every twenty or so paces to wrestle with oversized maps. Once exposed, that's it: the landscape in front of us, a sulkily permissive bridle path, bears no relation to the printed diagram.

We lack those clear pouches official hikers sling around their necks. Our maps, torn, smudged, swollen with rainwater, can never be refolded in the right sequence. Petit would rather have his arm amputated at the elbow, without anaesthetic, than appear in public with an unsightly plastic envelope dangling across his breast on coloured string.

Clare was alone. He cheered himself by treating this section of the walk like a military campaign. He was in the grip of a very convincing delusion: Mary Joyce, his waiting muse, would help him roll up the bad miles travelled on that first coach trip to London. His return would be an unwalking, a reforgetting. He would suffer enough to overlay the particulars of the fantastic London adventure. No more poetry, no more fame. The beginning was deceptively smooth: 'Down the lane gently . . . and bye and bye on the great York Road where it was all plain sailing.'

We share his difficulty in setting an orientation. There is no York Road for us, not yet; roads are barriers, the commuter blitzkrieg of the A1037, charging up the flank of King George's Reservoir, ignoring hand-painted signs for off-highway produce, Lea Valley fruit and flowers (imported by containerload from Holland). M25. A10. A hyperactive bifurcation of rivers, navigations and railways. You are meant to *use* these engineering marvels (with or without tickets) and not treat them as an obstacle course. London snorts human meat through metalled tubes. And later exhales the de-energised husks, its wage slaves.

Three men in a broken file, three projects under a single flag of convenience, complicates the first mile of the John Clare memorial tour. Renchi sees this walk as the validation of a shift from cataloguing into unifying vision. Clare's seizures, his mimetic fits, were emblems of integrity. Images derived from the journey, photographs or paintings, must subvert the taint of calculation, the obligation to record. There should be minimal intervention, Renchi announced, between walker and walk. His return to visionary art mirrors the shift in Clare's work, from modest epics of noticing, to troubled gazing, to possession by the unquiet spirits of Lord Byron and Jack Randall. 'I've stood and looked upon the place for hours,' he writes of the High Beach pond.

Petit, on the other hand, glances at his miniaturised screen, held out from the body, only to confirm the worst: tumbling cultural stocks, property market in freefall. He disdains *raw* imagery and requires every frame to look like a quotation, a retake. His task, as he sees it, is to eliminate any trace of human awkwardness, material that might be mistaken for the work of inferior or overpraised rivals. He stands, legs apart, struggling to devise a record of something tangential to the thrust of narrative. Exposure blown, focus twisted: a revenge on cinema. Another step towards relinquishing his iconic status as a film-maker who doesn't film. Movement, he decides, is the only solution: new location, new life. Art without the artist. Unmediated light: as witnessed, by preference, from a car window (the higher the better). River, sea. Desert, distant mountain. Fenland skies. Especially the area around Denver Sluice.

Recall his 1993 novel, *Robinson*:

I found a road. It was straight and flat, the unchanging landscape an endless grid of drainage canals and black fields. No cars passed. There was a line of trees on the edge of the mist and I counted them as a way of making progress. Sometimes the road disappeared under water, and the surrounding fields became lakes. Then the landscape was gone altogether, leaving me nothing except a feeling of acute physical discomfort. I was wet to the skin and shivering. Blisters grew on my heels.

The keynote for our walk had been established. Petit was reluctant to advance, unwilling to commit anything to tape. Renchi, preparing for the worst, crammed rainsuits into a bulging rucksack. He adjusted his piratical red bandanna: GENUINE/ U.S.C.L. AUTHENTIC/ (Est.1957). I relished the itch of future blisters. And anticipated a greasy spoon breakfast.

Setting off down the track that runs alongside the forest bungalows, our private methods of remembering where we are soon have us spread out like fastidious stalkers. We manage the first

Clare trope: getting ourselves lost. And before we have advanced a mile from the former asylum. The point is that the ground over which we walk has to concur with three very different points of view: the spiritual, the aesthetic – and the fetish for delayed narrative. For digression.

'This is a world,' Chris later reported (in a proposal for a triumphantly unmade film), 'in which meaning is subject to constant reinterpretation, where the conventional boundaries – most noticeably between fact and fiction – are questioned, as is the method, in a process which depends on a series of visual and verbal puns.'

Puns are mercifully few, now that our former photographer, Marc Atkins, has taken himself off to Paris. But we're overstocked in metaphors. And symbols. The owl is one of them. The Owl pub on Lippitts Hill.

The Leicestershire painter Rigby Graham, doing his Clare walk as part of a documentary film, was much taken by this spot: dripping field, cottage with electricity poles and wires. The film's director, Charles Mapleston, announced that the Essex Man boozer was indeed 'Clare's local'. (Where pubs were concerned, Clare's locals were anywhere he happened to be passing.) Local the Owl undoubtedly is, in terms of proximity to Fairmead; and local in the broader sense of representing the spirit of place. The pub looks out on a booster mast and a secure 'Metropolitan Police Firearms Training' area.

WHEN THE ORANGE FLAG IS FLYING THERE IS A POSSIBILITY OF SUDDEN LOUD NOISE FROM THIS CAMP.

Ill-considered obscenery usurps every hectare of ground within a day's walk of Aldgate Pump. The Owl is an excursionist pub with wooden outdoor tables, kids welcome. It has a nominal garden in which squirrels and pigeons compete for burger traces, hopping from perch to perch. There is a play area for which the management accepts no responsibility. A fire-hydrant-red helicopter with Arab-zapping rocket rays. A stainless-steel sculpture like an autopsy tray. Barbecue spits coagulated with thick black fat. The heady stink of yesterday's good times dissipated by cordite and diesel and fresh horse manure.

The obtuseness of Lippitts Hill is absolute; here is the confusion we solicit. As we descend, we catch glimpses of a distant London through breaks in the thinning forest: a rumour best avoided. We ask a woman for Mott Street and, very obligingly, she points us in completely the wrong direction. Our mistake. We need an owl as guide.

Edward North Buxton ('Verderer'), in his 1905 study of Epping Forest, makes a list of birds he encountered. 'I saw a pair [of Barn owls] close to Fairmead Lodge in the summer of 1884. A chorus of angry jays attracted me to the tree where they were.' Tawny owls and Long-eared owls were also recorded. Short-eared owls were 'shot on several occasions by sportsmen in the turnip fields'.

Rigby Graham chooses the owl as John Clare's totem, a mind in flight. Troublesome avatar. From his perch in the Fleet Street window, Clare watches the traffic of London. He is wrapped in a green coat. Feathers. Claws for hands. Crumpled top hat. Graham's birds are a chorus, tracking the poet as he walks north: owls and herons. Owl for madness. Heron as symbol of place: rivers shadowing roads. The painter catches a heron swooping over the Bishop's Palace at Buckden. The owl that is perched under the telegraph pole in the High Beach cottage is still with Clare at the finish, bloody prey in claws, at Glinton.

Our votive beasts, as we follow Mott Street down to the busy commuter road, are white plaster bulldogs. In matching pairs, fresh painted, they guard wrought-iron gates. The crest of the hill is Nationwide footballer, Russian journeyman, rather than Premier League and Beckhamite. The lethal swimming-pool parties of TV comedians are deeper into the forest, further north. Tall gates soon give way to low gates, temple-sized garages to bungalows and pick-up trucks. Dirtyneck enterprises in the way of roadside horticulture. Plant nurseries: Dotheboys Hall for geraniums, antirrhinums, cineraria. Dusty paddocks, spidery greenhouses. Crystal Palaces of spun sugar, cuckoo-spit. Oxygen tents for premature cucumbers and forced tomatoes.

We're hammered against Sewardstone Road as the rest of London throws itself at the M25. The brownfield acres of Waltham Abbey, suburbs of suburbs, are very brown; horizon-to-horizon mud, smoking machinery. Growling noise. Bright, yellow-brick, non-negotiable, no-through-road dormitory estates. Four-wheel drives bark as you approach, snarl a warning. Civic signs are traduced by the pseudo destinations of developers, locations become locations only when they have been rechristened.

WELCOME TO MERIDIAN PARK.

Barratt Homes, Bellwinch Homes, Fairclough Homes, Twigden Homes, Wimpey Homes. Zero-longitude future somewheres hungry for identity.

A red-and-yellow hoarding – FREE CHOCOLATE – offers: Free Internet Access, Free Web Space, Free Exclusive Email Address. As physical space shrinks, Web space expands to fill the vacuum. Anywhere conquers somewhere. Blink and the 'New 48 Acre Industrial Park' will be old news. Another unsightly blank polyfilled with generic architecture, supercity germ cultures grown in hyperspace. Islamophile minarets cohabit with Islamophobe portraits of chicken-slaughtering Southern crackers with phony Confederate titles. You travel through a projected topography to recover from travelling. Retail therapy consoles you for what you have lost: memory, choice. Mark Kass (in a co-production with Nissan) supplies you with transport. Kass has the edgelands franchise; ranks of gleaming motors cushion Waltham Abbey from motorway slip roads. SMART: the number plate of a black pod. Yours for £7995. Wheels pre-champed.

The bridge over the M25 is a moment worth celebrating, the point where our new walk breaks free from the old one; hanging in space, we bond with the totality of London. Petit strokes his screen. Renchi spatters a chaos of stalled trucks, hurtling repmobiles, blue hoardings, white lines, lighting poles, radio masts, into Kodak-colour vorticism. The next image, in the file he sends me, is a booted foot crunching gravel on the riverside path.

We can't do what Clare did and take the road into Enfield. Cross-river options have been suspended. Put right by an acquaintance coming out of the Labour in Vain pub, Clare is directed to the Great North Road. But roads change: Ermine Street, Old North Road, Great North Road, A1, A1(M). You would have to walk from Waltham Abbey to South Mimms (don't try it) to pick up Clare's route. Golf courses. Unilaterally privatised roads. Boarding kennels for traumatised dogs. Garden 'centres' (symbols of suburbia). Cancelled asylums decanted on to cambered blacktop.

The Great North Road, London to York, was an English myth, serviced by Dick Turpin and the footsore Clare: an escape. The beginnings of the road are complex, two tributaries coming together as they quit the city. Clare, on his visits to and from London, used them both. I feel a shiver of excitement when I read any account confirming the fact that Hackney connects, by lost toll gates, with the fabulous north. Ermine Street made its escape by way of Kingsland Road, Stoke Newington, Tottenham, Edmonton. It slipped its present route to pass through Theobald's Park and on to Cheshunt, Broxbourne.

Posting stations, watering places for horses and passengers, adapt and survive. Milestones, ground down like ancient molars, can still be found in the long grass. Clare, confused after a detour to the Ram public house, beyond Potton, was further discomforted by the dogmatic bluntness of just such a milestone. Information undid him. It was more than he wanted to know.

at length I came to a place where the road branched off into two turnpikes one to the right about & the other straight forward & on going bye my eye glanced on a mile stone standing under the hedge so I heedlessly turned back to read it to see where the other road led too & on doing so I found it led to London I then suddenly forgot which was North or south & though I narrowly examined both ways I could see no tree or bush or stone heap that I could reccolect I had passed so I went on mile after mile almost convinced I was going the same way I came & these thoughts were so strong upon me that doubt & hopelessness made me turn so feeble that I was scarcely able to walk yet I could not sit down or give up but shuffled along till I saw a lamp shining as bright as the moon which on nearing I found was suspended over a Tollgate

Informed walkers fix their position, the distance from London, by examining plants found under hedges, noticing the wildlife that roams free down central reservations. There is more time to experience doubt – and a higher price to pay if you go wrong – when you walk. The Great North Road having so many earlier identities, cattle track, coach route, carriageway, is dangerously plural. Always ready, under extreme weather conditions, clammy mists, flooded rivers, to revert to some previous state. Wandering ghosts are more visible as solid landscape fades.

Anna, smart-suited for a visit to London, met her father at the Great Northern Hotel, near King's Cross. An interview, something of the sort. She would have been – twenty? She thinks I was hanging about, we weren't married. Her father, still living in Lancashire, had business in town. He'd bought a rather grand house in a village, closer to his roots, for retirement. Isaac Newton, so they said, blinded himself challenging the sun in their summer house. They would drive back together, father and daughter, not a common occurrence, to Rutland. The manor house would subsequently be let out, while the family home remained in Poulton-le-Fylde (aka Blackpool).

I know that road, the A1: a memory strip with bloody sprockets. Driving is re-driving, pre-driving, overlaying one journey with another. You are always crawling through extruded suburbia: electronics companies, war simulations, underwater missile-guidance systems, Hatfield estates with shaved playing fields and pavilions. Will Self, in *How the Dead Live*, talks about death as the 'undeveloping' of memory. That condition also applies to English roads. Highway fog is glaucoma, clouding specifics of place, offering pod-people a preview of non-existence. Limbo dreams between life and extinction.

The Great Northern Hotel, when I left the Hadmans, was a wet hulk. Belonging to the river, not the railway. London was grey skin, fouled lungs. Hands slipping on clammy rails. Highgate Village, by the time they found it, looked back on a drowned valley. The A1 was a supposition, a blind guess. Road signs were there to be touched, not read. Geoffrey Hadman was familiar with the routine of late meetings, long drives. Staying awake on whisky and sandwiches. Anna had been his passenger, often, but not on this road, not out of London.

By Norman Cross visibility is, what, six feet? Anna is instructed to let down the window and count the turn-offs: out loud. The car edges towards the presumption of a roundabout. She can barely see the kerb. She counts. Gets it wrong. Not much moving, sensible drivers have stayed at home or booked in for the night at the Bell in Stilton.

Out of nowhere, full beams: blinding.

Honks, shouts. They can't go any slower, they are already at walking pace. They hear the lorry apply its brakes. The driver gets out, comes over to them. He says something. The steam from his mouth, a little whiter than the mist, gives away his position.

They are travelling, so it seems, the wrong way, up one of the fiercest roads in England. They are lodged in the fast lane of the A1; heading north, straight into oncoming traffic. They can congratulate themselves, when they stop shaking, on outperforming Clare: navigating to the outskirts of Peterborough without benefit of mileposts and toll gates.

Through Waltham Abbey and on to the River Lee Navigation, a sanctioned footpath through an area of small lakes and meads, heronries of the secret state, we process in numbed abstraction. Gunpowder mills, bunkers, blast-deflecting ziggurats hold no mystery. We have decided to take the water route, by way of Broxbourne and Ware, to Hertford. Then we'll cross unfamiliar territory to meet John Clare (and the Great North Road) at Stevenage.

We enjoyed a modest breakfast in town, but found the church

closed (quarter to nine in the morning). We therefore missed the recent damage inflicted by a care-in-the-community berserker from Waltham Cross who ran amok with a small axe, striking off the marble nose of Francis Woolaston (of Shenton in Leicestershire). An otherwise obscure youth who died of smallpox, aged sixteen, in 1684. White eye split like an egg. Not one drop of blood.

Our route is dispiriting; too much has been invested by outside parties. Noticeboards offer bubblegum cartoons of local history, ecological advances underwritten by generations of bomb-makers. Twinned narratives press uncomfortably on a path that is squeezed tight between road and railway. A David Starkey presentation about abbeys and kings tries to drown the whispered story of badly paid workers in dirty, dangerous occupations; biographies erased by the Official Secrets Act. 'Best Value' futurology contradicts the sorry shuffle of what is actually happening: grunge, entropy, mismanagement. Tame journalists, columnists rescued from a Trotskyite past, can always be found to cry hurrah, to ridicule moaners and whingers. To be loud, as Thatcher discovered, is to be right.

The River Lee Navigation is not much navigated. Nor the path walked. It is jogged, painfully, by red-faced men and determined women with water-hoops around their necks (like liquid fetishes). There are aggressive cyclists too, avoiding roads and regarding pedestrians as foolish obstacles, less-evolved life forms. Leisure, between Enfield Lock and Cheshunt, is a discipline, a quasi-military regime of self-punishment and frowning excess. Miles are ticked off, goals achieved. One cyclist, male, screams at a female sculler as she fails to meet his stopwatch target. The poignancy of the Olympic bid fiasco, excusing all development scams, infects the Lea. There is no excuse for obscurity, no time for strollers, fluvial excursionists.

Djuna Barnes, profiling James Joyce, zoomed in on his 'spoilt and appropriate' teeth. And that is this stretch of the Lea, precisely: spoilt and appropriate. Hissing trains. Occasional apologetic herons (all spindle and no heft) tipping out of dead trees like faultily assembled kites. Nothing spectacular, nothing to stop your advance on Broxbourne. 'Writers,' Joyce told Barnes, 'should never write about the extraordinary, that is for the journalist.' But, already, she was nodding off. 'He drifts from one subject to the other, making no definite division.'

Petit is unwilling to record so commonplace a scene, the absence of the tragic, suspended melancholia: the Lea is off-duty England. A compulsory holiday with no takers. He recalls that Cheshunt had a factory where old film stock was melted down for recycling, memories boiled in vats. He is thinking about the firm of H. A. Gregory and Co., who supervised the last rites of silent cinema. Two hundred million feet of redundant imagery was liquefied, converted into resin for waterproof paint. London's dreaming turned back into fog. There is a glint in Petit's eye. He likes this idea: that he could paint the next property with smoky Hitchcock flickers.

Riverside Cheshunt manages obscurity and erasure very well. Richard Cromwell, failed son of a powerful father, gave up his position (as Oliver's successor) in 1659. After the restoration of the Stuarts in 1660, he was spared the shame of his regicide father, who was taken from his grave, mutilated and hanged at Tyburn. Richard vanished into exile, before returning to take up residence in Cheshunt. He lived, unknown and uncelebrated, beside the Lea, for another fifty-three years. He took the name of John Clarke. Just a 'k' heavy for our man, John Clare.

In the early days of my expeditions, upstream from Hackney (in the traces of Izaac Walton), I persuaded Anna to burden herself with a rucksack, a sleeping bag: we would walk to Ware. It was at just the point where we now found ourselves, advancing on Broxbourne, wooded hills, moored pleasure craft, that we flagged. A summer day dissolving slowly. Cattle in huddles, snorting, tail-twitching. I suggested that we break into a chalet. Anna was horribly shocked (as I was, much later, reading about Werner Herzog's winter march from Munich to Paris, his cavalier disregard for private property). Our expedition was aborted. Those Lea Valley trains can be useful. We were back home, lessons learnt, before any real damage was done.

It is at Broxbourne that Petit makes his excuses: he has an afternoon meeting, a bit of business in Rickmansworth. Property, social or professional, who knows? The station car park is full. A cinema-screen-sized hoarding features, in moody black and white, a polarised sky. Desktop clouds merge with our clouds: high and flighty. The day is getting warmer. We decide, without discussion, to leave the Navigation in favour of the New River. Renchi's chosen T-shirt has the message: GUESS.

The chalets and bungalows of Broxbourne – I'm grateful now I didn't molest them – speak of a different attitude to the city, the liberties of the railway. Neat plots. Individual decoration. Fields behind, river ahead. Narrowboats with pot plants, smoking chimneys, bicycles. On another, more successful Lea Valley walk with Anna, after the Clare excursion was done, we passed a boat with a very pertinent name tag. 'Last Fling But One', it said.

To Stevenage

Ragwort, mallow, foxgloves. Chris peeling away changes the walk. Renchi stoops over common (common to him) wayside flowers. I'll need the Ladybird book, purchased from Woolworths in Dalston Junction (1974); along with a kiddy-friendly account of the torments of Vincent van Gogh. 'Then he had too much sun, quite a lot to drink. He took very long walks. Colours were too loud, crows mobbed yellow fields. He cut off his ear.'

Renchi's ears buttress a scarlet bandanna. Silver halo of cropped hair. Contour-hugging beard. He is alert, benign, but not-quite-here: the Lea is an old story. Coming off this walk, he will adopt a raw-food diet. Weight, never excessive, will melt away. Ashram retreats and a beaker of olive oil will sluice waste from the body; stones, sand, gravel. He hadn't realised, until he witnessed the evacuation, that he was transporting such a diverse geology in his system.

We stride along the nicely tended east bank of the New River: a cool, clear stream shaded by overhanging trees. Sir Hugh Myddelton, realising that drinkable water was a valuable commodity, the Elizabethan oil, engineered a liquid slalom into the city. His New River travelled forty miles to accomplish a direct twenty-mile transit. Hertfordshire springs at Amwell and Chadwell were the source. This manufactured river, less visible than the Lea, is less prone to joyless recreationists and fishing parties. In retirement, free of heritage prompts, it is good company.

DANGER. FISHERY AFFECTED BY OVERHEAD ELEC-TRICAL POWER LINES.

In Broxbourne, nature provides its own security fence. Willows interrupt our view of riverside development: the glint of swimming pools (blue as chemical toilets). Unloved climbing frames. Burglar-alarmed white mansions parasitical on a bayou of rubber alligators and barbecue pits.

Through shallows of weaving underwater greenstuff, schools of small fish, I think I've spotted a dumped safe. Crime adjusts to suit locality: a New River entrepreneur shot in his car, brains smeared over leather upholstery, outside a body-toning Hertfordshire gymnasium. There are Spanish aspirations in these arched and balconied villas; acceptable retreats for upwardly mobile faces from Hackney and Tottenham. Easy to imagine: dead dogs in swimming pools, a dark-vizored motorcyclist at the security gate.

It isn't a safe. It's a Macintosh computer. The Performa 460? The twin of my own beloved veteran. Sleeping with the fishes. A nest of eels and embryo fictions. Hemingway talks about Greeks, having to embark on some hellish voyage into exile, breaking the forelegs of their mules and dumping them in shallow water. 'It was all a pleasant business,' he growls. No mules in Hoddesdon (apart from retired Stanstead drug couriers), just word processors that have run out of words. And the occasional purple bottle trapped on a floating islet of pondweed.

We are far enough out from London to pick up on the energy surge that comes with breaking free from a weakening gravitational field. I feel the high sun on my unprotected neck. And I remember William Cowper's ballad of John Gilpin. Gilpin was a Cheapside linen-draper who decided to celebrate his wedding anniversary by taking his wife to the Bell in Edmonton. The horse bolts. With farcical consequences (rehearsed in excruciating detail over many pages). Lady Austen told Cowper the story to divert him from a depressive fugue. The ruse worked. On the following morning, the poet hacked out his romping, tumpety-tumpety Lea Valley epic.

When John Clare, in the London coach, passed through Huntingdon, Octavius Gilchrist pointed out the homes of Oliver Cromwell and Cowper. There were books by the troubled evangelical poet in Clare's cottage library. Cowper suffered periods of acute melancholia, during which he contemplated suicide. He retired, for months at a time, to Dr Cotton's Collegium Insanorum at St Albans:

another sanctuary placed at a safe distance from London. Disease, so often, seems to be a condition of residence in the edge-lands. At the heart of the city, mad people are not noticed. They enjoy a general amnesty: indifference.

Clare walked, by Northamptonshire streams, with his childhood friend Thomas Porter. Porter, according to Jonathan Bate, had a 'poetic' response to nature. 'He felt,' Clare wrote, about his friend's taste for vulgar chapbooks, 'as happy over these while we wiled away the impatience of a bad fishing day under a green willow or an odd thorn as I did over Thomson and Cowper and Walton.'

Walking, fishing and poeticising are promoted by Walton as compatible activities. Sheltering from summer storms under a suitable tree, dipping into a pocket-edition of Spenser. Before returning, at sunset, to deliver the day's catch to an obliging landlady. Long evenings drinking and yarning by an open fire. Here was the myth of a vanished England spun by Izaac Walton. Clare bought it. We came too late. The fishermen were still around, but much of the Lea lay under a coat of green, post-industrial scum. So thick, birds could wade, bank to bank, without getting their feet wet.

With two companions (Venator and Auceps), encountered on Tottenham Hill, Walton walks towards Hoddesdon and Ware. Ware is the pun: a no-place, bend in the river. The town is a destination on a Lee Valley Park signpost, but nobody goes there by choice; nobody we meet. The classic Waltonian form, three men walking, telling tales, has been denied to us. One of our company (Vidhead) has already detrained for Rickmansworth. With the promise of joining us at Stilton on the evening of the third day.

Walton lived on the north side of Fleet Street. Then Chancery Lane. He was one of the presences Clare sensed from his Fleet Street window. One of the extinguished of London who nudged him in narrow alleys. Walton's idyll of the river bank is not all singing milkmaids and brown trout. It is also a game reserve of interspecies savagery. 'Look, 'tis a bitch otter, and she has lately whelped,' cries Venator. 'Let's go to the place where she was put down, and not far from it you will find all her young ones, I dare warrant you, and kill them all.'

Our first conversation with a New River native concerned fishy matters. Two men, tethered to the scenery, speak of seeing a pike on the far side of the bridge. I remember that taste, gamey ripeness. Ancient sunlight swallowed in a deep pool. The flavour of a creature who has devoured many lesser creatures. It's the brilliance of the morning, after months of rain, that is unfamiliar. I don't bother with a cap, a shirt with a high collar. I don't employ the anti-burn cream Renchi butters lavishly over nose and cheeks. I will pay later for this bravado.

At Rye Meads, New River and old Lea come together, before running on in companionable parallel. We break off to investigate Rye House. Rye House is in the brochure. Rye House has its own brochure: 'This delightful 15th century moated building is one of the finest examples of early English brickwork in the country. It is the only surviving part of a manorial home built for Sir Andrew Ogard.' The fallout from a pair of barley-sugar gateposts, a patch of preserved grass, includes an historic pub and a winter parking site for showfolk, travelling fair personnel.

We're never easy with restoration. You can't restore Rye House without the meads, the river. The people. Restore it for what? The kiosk with a selection of gifts? The display of brick-making? Privileged zones downgrade surrounding territory. They create a class of explainers and apologists, civil servants of heritage. Decay is heritage too; we must learn to appreciate it. Horace Walpole's Gothic fraud, Strawberry Hill: let it collapse. Deal with it as he dealt with Chatterton: brush off, withdrawal of patronage. A plague on edge-land invisibles dragged into the circle of Klieg lights. A plague on tactful interventions. Anywhere 'rescued' by born-again comedians (serial careerists).

We intervene at Rye House. By noticing it, inventing a response. The Gatehouse opens on Sundays. One story is told, others are erased. Henry Teale bought the pub in 1857 and ran it, lusty and loud, for riverside entertainment: a maze, cricket, feasts, boating. Drink, song. London on the razzle. Or: London obliterated as we move, slowly, separately, around the brick-in-grass outline of a demolished building. Twisted chimneys, no fire. The mapping of a phantom: 'Parlour', 'Spiral Staircase'. A fiction of conspiracy, torture, death. An attempt on the king's life. As Charles II and his unpopular Catholic brother return from Newmarket.

Before we reach Ware, the straps of an overloaded rucksack rub my shoulder; I can feel a rough spot cutting through one of my boots. Could Ware rescue me from Hackney? A place which has become (geography aping psychogeography) Will Self's zombie suburb, his outstation for the dead. Self's Dulston (in *How the Dead Live*) is the precise contrary of Clare's Helpston: multicultural, multicuisined, busy with voices. Old Jewish. Old Black. New Russian (with Greek-Cypriot minicab drivers). Dulston has no horizon. Helpston is all horizon. And no strangers, no incomers. Stagnant gene pool. The Helpston villagers are inarticulate, by choice; by the standards of London. Clare had broken a taboo. Despite all his creeping around field margins, hiding in bushes, scribbling in hollow trees, he made himself visible. He published. He couldn't disappear into the mess of the city, Fleet Street, Chancery Lane; he saw too many of the restless dead. He was stuck on a never-ending road, between two incompatible destinations: in pain.

Ware is a river town, houses overlook slow water; it is also a convenient stopover, equidistant between A1(M) and M11. It is close to Stanstead. That's how they can successfully operate a leather-couch wine bar like the Vine. We don't eat there. I don't raid the charity shops. We take our lunch, despite some reservations ('Smart Dress, Over 21'), in the Saracen's Head. On the riverfront. The standing stones around here are not standing stones. They are interventions. Pallid art works quoting William Blake.

On the long curve, between Ware and Hertford, there are humans, quite friendly: Australians visiting antique shops, fast men on crutches, slow women (in football shirts) lopsided with carrier bags. Local walkers. They are unimpressed by: locks, weirs, the birth of the New River. By the A10, as it snakes on pillars across indifferent fields, under a tired cloudscape. An elevated highway going nowhere and attracting few motorists.

Hertford is the county town (of a county that has no current brand image). It's on the way to other places, you pass through (as do several rivers: Lea, Rib, Beane). Hertford is the end of the line for railway commuters and excursionists. There are plenty of historical traces lying about, if you insist on finding them: castle, Corn Exchange, house of Sir Henry Chauncy, who conducted one of England's last witchcraft trials (Jane Wenham). The East India Company founded Haileybury College, two miles out of town, to keep the colonies supplied with willing young men.

We ignore all this. Renchi exorcises the black statue of some Puritan in a hat: bible in hand, outstretched finger. 'Get out of town.' We asked a bright-eyed couple for directions. And discovered that they had just arrived from Melbourne. In search of their roots. We lent them our map.

It's time to abandon this Dutch landscape of canal and sky, distant town; to go off-map, beyond the ken of my faithful Nicholson, the battered *Greater London Street Atlas*. Hertford is stolidly mercantile, Cromwellian, ready to barbecue heretics. We've had enough of rivers. Clare's was a road trip and the road – now we're getting to it – lies across ten miles of blank country. Let's ditch history and start marching.

There is an undiscovered island between the A602 (east), A414 (south) and A1 (west). The apex of the triangle is Stevenage. Clare's first resting point.

I reached Stevenage where being Night I got over a gate crossed over the corner I forced to stay off a respectable distance to keep from falling into it for my legs were knocked up and began to stagger

We set off towards Bull's Green and Datchworth, expecting woods, busy suburbs. Unlike Clare we were pre-booked at the

Abbington Hotel (no prior knowledge). Our legs were moving nicely, nagging backs eased by the morning's stately progress.

On the outskirts of Hertford we notice catalogue buildings that might be drug companies, animal research, or foundation hospitals. Renchi thinks he visited his father in one of these. The late Peter Bicknell (like Anna's faceless relatives) decides to accompany us on the journey north. The further we pull from London, the more the old ones have to say. Or perhaps it's quieter and we have time to listen. Renchi is prompted by the places we pass – Oundle (father's school), Barnack (expeditions to quarries) – to offer anecdotes that bring Peter Bicknell back to life. (There is a lovely painting of his father and his namesake uncle, aged sixty, doing a sixty-mile walk of their own.) Renchi remembers: Peter, as a young man, ice-skating from Cambridge to Ely. Remembers drives across the Fens to look at buildings the senior Bicknell had designed. Remembers childhood: trying to get the attention of an arthritic parent in a Cambridge garden.

Now the pinkish roads of afternoon are quiet and shadow-pooled, heavy branches meeting overhead. Fields of ripe corn seem to require no visible farmworkers. Insects dance around the drooping heads of marigolds.

In the sudden darkness of a wood, Renchi takes out his compass for the first time: to confirm the fact that we've gone wrong (in terms of heading directly for Stevenage). The track is muddy and little used. Hours are lost. With no comforting sound of distant motorway, we're in the warp. Back roads, when we hit them, are lush anachronisms: hedgeless fields, steepled churches, road signs for places that never made it into maps and guides. We lay out what we've got, Renchi's charts and crystals, on the lids of village tombs, forgotten worthies.

We notice: a white horse, the strong curve of his back, in a cropped paddock. A hare split open, belly-jam, busy flies, on a hot section of road. Small stones coming loose from glistening tar. At a house, decorated with pink and white balloons, Renchi asks for water and our bottles are filled.

In the early evening, we emerge from woodland into a haze of cereals, blue horizon; no hint of a town, any town. A solitary terracotta roof rises above wavering golden fields. We're not the same people who left High Beach this morning. Dusty light has no interest in our approval. This view disproves James Thomson's notion of 'View' (capitalised). Look at it and it dissolves: into thorn bush, sandy track, pillow of cloud. A landscape without structure and form. Call it: off-road Hertfordshire. Unless we achieve Stevenage in the next hour, we'll invade the real Clare story: roofless, hungry, aching in every limb. Grey-haired (no-haired) men on the wrong side of mid-life aiming at mid-lands, Middle England. And finding nobody at home.

As we come on it, the ridge that offers the promise of Stevenage, our terracotta Travelodge confesses to another identity: a crematorium. The inverted oast-house funnel is architectural flimflam disguising two metal chimneys that, on another day, will puff dark smoke over the Constable view. The Stevenage crem is a drive-in corpse-disposal facility: with bonus features. It's right on the road. Edge of town and country. Red tiles. White gables. Non-denominational chapel extension. Multifunctional. Easy on the eye. A missing piece of Milton Keynes: flatpacked, assembled in the time it has taken us to walk from Hertford.

Stevenage is no easy conquest: a laboured entry by way of a non-league football ground and the Roebuck Gate. A New Town laid over the remnant of John Clare's staging-post. Oliver Cromwell heritage country: portraits on pub signs. The killjoy English ayatollah (of myth), stabling horses in parish churches, firing Papist heads out of cannons, finds himself strung up outside a chain of roadhouses and boozers. The Cromwell Hotel, red brick, white woodwork, doubles as a 'Business Centre'. Unfortunately, we're not booked in. (They'd never take us, our business is inexplicable. Our clothes are preoccupied, virtually free-standing. We have no vehicle and no appointments. Before the Glinton rendezvous with Anna Sinclair.)

The outskirts of Stevenage are voluminous; clients do come

off-road and stay here. A virtual landscape of grassy knolls, business businesses and Glaxo colonies. (Renchi's sister is involved with a lawsuit over dyes injected into her spine with unfortunate consequences.) Spur roads, boulevards, overpasses, mirror-glass towers: but no trace of our guest house. We can't tell if we're in town, or through it, suburb to suburb, without locating an obvious centre.

The Abbington Hotel, we discover, is at the northern limits. Stevenage is a cycle city, lacking cyclists. It's dull to walk, even though every effort has been made to allow for such frivolities. So long as you have a certified destination. So long as you smile for the cameras.

It is seven-thirty in the evening. We've been walking for thirteen hours and have achieved a Clare-like state of hallucinatory exhaustion. We have also achieved, at long last, the ivy-smothered, gravel-accessed Abbington Hotel. A signboard, blocked out with credit cards like the flags of all nations, confirms the fact. Renchi ducks into the privet to drop his shorts and assume respectably crumpled jeans. I pull a clean shirt over a sweaty torso. And we present ourselves at the door.

VACANCIES. VACANCIES. VACANCIES.

'Sorry,' says the woman. 'No trace of your booking. Completely full.' Bona-fide reps check in by sundown. And don't clutter up vestibules with ugly rucksacks.

I think she reads the dangerous madness in our eyes. I made this reservation, by phone, handing over credit card details. There *must* be a record. Nothing. Well, fine. One day's walk and my London life is a fiction. She sees that we're going to do a Clare and spread out sleeping-bags in her driveway (remembering to set tired heads to the north).

She's sorry. Truly. So much so that she gets on the phone and makes an alternative booking at the hotel ibis. The ibis is back in town, we passed it thirty minutes ago, on the main boulevard: when we still had skin on the soles of our feet. To be rid of us, before the reps notice how their refuge has plunged downmarket, the Abbington woman offers to drive us to the ibis. At once.

Welcome, Bienvenue. 'Early-Bird Breakfast' available from four in the morning. The ibis is the travelling person's oasis of choice. Forty-four hotels in places you'd rather not be (Birmingham New Street Station, Coventry Ringway, London East Barking, Luton Airport). Places where you are comfortably not-at-home, pampered by indifference, courteous apathy. The ibis (same hotel in forty-four different locations) is serviced by unseen automatons.

'No problem,' says the ibis desk-robot in a computer-generated voice simulation. Welcome, bienvenue. To construction workers in claggy boots, to truckers. To long-distance walkers. Everything is plain and easy. The lights don't work in the bathroom, it doesn't matter. Soap squirts from a wall-dispenser. There is a big firm bed. And you can open the windows.

We sit in the restaurant, the canteen, with other bemused transients. And feel good about microwaved fish, a carafe of sour yellow wine. We are satisfied with the conclusion of the first day's walk. Clare tossed and turned on trusses of clover, pressing against the phantom body of his 'first wife'. She lay on his left arm, waking him.

I didn't sleep. I put my head on an unyielding foam pillow, shut my eyes, and opened them a nanosecond later to a lion-sun climbing over a palm-fringed desert. Stevenage: Cairo of the Great North Road. The sacred ibis, a water bird, lends its head to Thoth, god of Hermopolis; scribe of the gods, inventor of writing.

I make illegible notes on a complimentary pad; head off to the canteen, where hissing machines spit out cornflake-dust. Ibis croissants are scimitars of delight (small but perfectly formed).

At the end of the month, when my credit card scroll arrives with the demand for a Southend cheque, I discover that the Abbington Hotel has charged me for a night's stay. So perhaps, after all, the ibis was a dream: a shelf of perfect sleep, lulled by traffic, allowing us through the Roebuck Gate and on towards the lesser initiations of the waiting road.

Over our facsimile breakfast, Renchi tells me that when he sorted out his belongings, before climbing into bed, he found that two items had vanished during our ramble through Stevenage: the compass and the crystal.

To St Neots

A blameless morning: 18 July 2000. We are back outside the Abbington, on the edge of town. Renchi, plunging into the privet, recovers his crystal but not his compass. (He has resumed his blue shorts. Today's T-shirt announces: LEARN SWAHILI.) The mural on the underpass, through which we have come, is the product of local schoolchildren. It depicts a funeral possession: hearse with yellow coffin pulled by three-masted schooner. The mourners, sticky silhouettes, wear short cloaks like gendarmes. The procession features several coaches, of the kind that carried John Clare from Stamford to London.

Parked, square across the pavement, near the ibis, is a white police car: Noddy-sized, a notice taped to its perspex window. THIS FACILITY IS TEMPORARILY OUT OF ORDER. When we achieve our first major roundabout, going round a woman in dark glasses (backed a body's length into the privet, reading a thick paperback), we find that the road for London lies straight ahead; we must swing away to the right. A last look at the Abbington, last ever, reveals the book and a pair of white hands sticking out of a hedge.

Traffic into Stevenage stretches back for miles: splintering sunbursts on windscreens, mobiles busy as electric razors. Grooming ceremonies: hair twitching, nose picking, lipstick applying. Mirror auditions. Hungrily abstracted cigarette suckling: smoke breakfasts. Buffers of random music. News without novelty. Child murders, men shot by accident. And on purpose. Exploding vehicles. Stevenage cars are nose-to-rump like cattle. Leaking subtle poisons. An invisible necklace around a fortunate satellite.

Our relief at leaving town, being on the road, is immense. Beneath an avenue of pylons, Stevenage has its own Dome. The hint picked up from Mandelson's Folly on the Greenwich Peninsula: temporary permanence. A money pit with accidental benefits. This Dome is more active than its metropolitan model. It has two major attractions: 'The Way Forward in Tennis' and the 'r3 Clinic' (viz. McTimoney Chiropractic, Aromatherapy, Reflexology).

32 MILES FROM LONDON.

A distressed milestone: lettering renewed with black paint. Yellow lichen on north-facing flank. Did Clare touch this stone with his faltering hand?

The road, before fumes become unbearable, before snarling commuters and hissing air brakes, is a tarmac idyll. Walking is effortless, miles tick past; we don't talk. Maps are not consulted. We'll make for Baldock by the most direct route, up the B197, which runs alongside the A1.

Anna gets her revenge.

Our journey to Glinton is her vision, this cloudless morning, and I am experiencing it (if I'm not hunkered down at the ibis, snoring on a foam pillow). It used to work, for years, that she took care of my dreaming; she earthed nightmares that would, in due course, be dressed as fiction. 'You've started a new book.' 'Haven't.' 'You're thinking about it.' 'Well, yes.'

Horrors of London, she endured them on my behalf. Folding houses with soft floors. Rivers flooding subterranean passages. Skull-faced stalkers. One-legged dogs. Bubbles of skin that closed around her, cutting off breath. And, worst of all, a man hammering on the door, wanting to be let in. A man with my face. While this impostor, her other husband, lies beside her in the bed. I wake, untroubled, after eight hours: she twists and turns, sits bolt upright; tense, waiting for first light. A few hours of shallow sleep before the day's tasks begin. Before I stroll, whistling, to my desk.

The young Anna, when I met her in Dublin, was a poet, schooled and approved by her father (supposed descendant of John Clare). A man who successfully escaped Glinton and the farm. And who ran a model chemical plant: no strikes, excellent safety record, wasteground given over to the cultivation of vegetables for the canteen. (She is a poet still, without the fuss. The writing. She operates by momentary abdications of attention that never have to be explained. We trade in such exchanges. I front the business, stick my name on the spine. And wait to be found out.)

Geoffrey Hadman set his eldest daughter to writing a poem a day, verse forms to be mastered. Sonnets, villanelles. These poems were never made public nor commented on; they were a task, a duty accepted without complaint. So that, when she arrived in Dublin, Anna was primed for the tone set by the university's long-established magazine, *Icarus*. Her work, at first, was acceptable. Mine was awkwardly modernist and full of itself.

I was in touch with the barbarians, Beat and Black Mountain enthusiasts. I published, to local scandal, a three-column piece, airmailed from Tangier by William S. Burroughs. Two of the founding Beats, Allen Ginsberg and Gregory Corso, were at that moment visiting Oxford. Henrietta Moraes trailed along.

Afterwards we went to the nearest pub to warm up. Allen and Gregory had a drink or two and started to undress, screaming passionately, 'You bloody English mother-fuckers. You kill your poets. All the greatest, you murder them. Keats, Shelley, Byron, John Clare.'

In Dublin, poetry blotted up booze. In McDaid's, Toner's, the Pearl Lounge, green-livered poets incubated spite. They manfully ignored one another, until the opening arrived for that rehearsed quip, delivered over the shoulder as they departed: hunched and mildewed phantoms of the anthologies (talking loud enough to be noticed in America). You could watch them pissing it away, under the cool stare of cellophane-collared curates with Spanish Civil War pedigrees, fresh-faced country boys setting down platters of thickcut ham-and-cheese sandwiches.

At Anna's request, I carried a bundle of my poems, faintly typed, to a party in Rathmines. The bundle stayed in my coat. The coat was forgotten. We left in a Dublin taxi, making it up as we went along. Times fresh enough, the softness of the seats, the driver's helmet of Sweet Afton, to be reinvented, reforgotten. Indulged for their radiant obscurity.

I come abruptly out of my reverie as we notice another peripheral 'Golf Centre'. We lean into cushions of displaced air: Stevenage reps on the burn, sleek convoys of armour-plated school-delivery vehicles. Relief columns for Baldock. Anna must be waking, now, in Hackney; carrying her breakfast tray back to bed. When I get home, I'll find the evidence: screws of kitchen roll blotted with cherry stones, sheets sandpapered in toast crumbs. I haven't much to report: a faded sign for the A1(M) and a few blood-tipped feathers, claws and mince in a buzzing heap. An empty forecourt with chalet-style petrol station attached. A blue car with the door of a red car rammed through its windscreen. A shattered driving mirror fragmenting sky, road, walker, into Cubist slivers. A very worried man in a crisp royal-blue shirt (frosted Blairite half-moons beneath moist armpits) jabbering into his mobile.

WELCOME TO BALDOCK: Historic Market Town. Twinned with Eisenberg & Sanvignes-Les-Mines.

Baldock, I'm ashamed to say, has never meant more to me than this, a marker on the road north. The town takes its name from *Baddac*, the Old French term for Baghdad. 'This name was given to Baldock (Herts),' concludes *The Concise Oxford Dictionary of English Place-Names*, 'by the Knights Templar, who held the manor.'

Middle England infected by news from elsewhere: Baldock/Baghdad. Grubby invaders, we advance through shady suburbs and broad pavements (innocent of pedestrians). Renchi is charmed to find himself in conversation with a rusting oldie who has been around since Templar times. No mere canine accompanist, the Baldock dame is a willing collaborator. Clear blue eyes. She advises us on tea-rooms and potential cafés.

The town is cruciform, architecturally promiscuous: complacent Georgian properties, rejigged coaching inns and a neo-Egyptian *Tesco Extra* superstore. It is our intention to track Templar Avenue, to search out the fourteenth-century flint church of St Mary the Virgin.

Baldock's former identity as a market can still be felt, our chosen café (reverse lettering on window, plastic cloths, views of lazy street) respects that tradition. Hours could drift while we fictionalise maps, swill coffee, nibble buns. SAND is projected over the bleached sheet of OS Landranger Map (No. 153). WICHES over nothing very much. Renchi sits, head in hands, trying to get a fix on what lies ahead. What *is* our project? We've lost Clare and discovered a captured Templar enclave. Our route, after we have settled on the point at which we'll snake across the A1 to the east, should carry us towards Biggleswade and Clare's Potton. But what is actually out there? Where are the significant features? Landranger 153 is not forthcoming. Renchi's feet are hurting, after only five or six miles; fresh blisters cropping on loose flaps of skin.

My feeling is that stories are waiting, but we are not a part of them, not yet. Sheltering from the sun, among the monuments in the churchyard of St Mary the Virgin, Renchi doctors his feet, while I pocket a pine cone. Pineal eye. A small, dry, resinous grenade, which I decide to carry with me, to place on another grave. This is the moment to tell Renchi about the drownings, and how the next part of our walk will be dedicated, not so much to the drowned child or her drowned father (unknown to me), but to the person who recounted the story, and how it haunted her life. And how, in recent times, the placing of a new gravestone, names, dates, in a riverside church, near the Great Ouse, the site of the accident, has begun to diffuse a terrible memory.

Clare's account of his 'Journey out of Essex' was transcribed on his return to Northborough; the incidents fresh in his mind, before the blisters had deflated and the bruises healed. The spin of the road, the frenzy, set down without calculation, was a desperate attempt to keep alive a set of imposed meanings. The quest to bring Mary Joyce back to life. To recover his youth, the period before he began to write. Before this compulsion to describe a sweep of ground, horizon to horizon; seasons, moods, shifts, social changes. The autobiographies of slugs and stones. Human creatures who required nothing of the sort and damned him for his arrogance.

My own scribbled notes aren't much help: 'St Mary the Virgin, Mary Joyce . . . pine cone, drowning . . . shadow of church follows us down undistinguished road . . . we're better fed but just as confused as Clare, the journal.'

I got to a village further on & forgot the name the road on the left hand was quite over shaded by some trees & quite dry so I sat down half an hour & made a good many wishes for breakfast but wishes was no hearty meal so I got up as hungry as I sat down – I forget here the names of the villages I passed through

Plodding down Norton Road towards a stone bridge that turns road into river, canted verges, rippling surface, no cars, my standard preoccupations are suspended: home, family, books, bills. Thirty-two years worrying at the fabric of Hackney. 'Baldock Cemetery', says the blue sign (white figure like a striding ghost). Then: NORTON. I'm advancing into abandoned fictions. Andrew Norton is my unreliable twin, alternate world fetch: a stand-in through many books. An awkward creature with a gift for disappearing; then re-emerging, burdened with useless knowledge, more confused than when he started. I'm walking, of my own free will, towards Norton's estate, a cemetery at the edge of a Templar manor.

Elizabeth Clare (as she would have been) died a few weeks after her birth on 13 July 1793. John's sturdier twin, Bessy: a potent absence. A stranger to the world (though better suited to it than the poet: 'a fine lively bonny wench'). She stays with him. Helpston to London. High Beach to Northborough. Northampton to the grave.

My only sibling, an older sister, stays with me. As she stayed with my mother. A lost infant, named but barely present in the world: spoken of, remembered. Her place stolen by a bemused successor. Guilt at survival cannot be undone, unwalked. In suspension, it is managed.

Norton, the road sign, triggered memories of another map; a

chart produced by New Age geographer Chris Street. Street tells us, in *Earthstars: The Visionary Landscape*, that he 'has been researching the patterns, alignments and sacred sites of London's Earthstars network for the last eighteen years . . . The revelations were initiated by a series of dreams, visions and psychic experiences.'

Energy lines produced by men of the suburbs favour the suburbs: Burnt Oak, East Barnet, Croydon. Lines forged by Limehouse labourers highlight Hawksmoor churches, blue-and-yellow murder sites, decommissioned hospitals and synagogues. Geography is personalised. A walk is a floating autobiography. Renchi travels in the footprints of Peter Bicknell, bearing his father's library of alpine journals, flower paintings, handcoloured English excursions. Writers improvise and iterate, roads reiterate: they are democratic, crowded, verge to verge – even when, as now, coming away from Baldock, we are in remission, no cars, no tractors, no funeral processions.

One map in Chris Street's book catches my eye: four lines meeting in a cross. From Prittlewell Priory, Southend: down the A13 to London. And on, by way of Silbury Hill, to Brean on the Bristol Channel. A reprise of Chris Petit's 1979 road movie, *Radio On*. Then: from Rottingdean (in the south), up through London, to the section we are now walking. At which point, Street's alignment becomes the plan of our once and future journeys: Stevenage, Norton Church, Buckden Palace, Alconbury, Glinton. Sacred signifiers: 'Lines of spirit'.

Alconbury is a favourite of mine, a truckers' all-day-breakfast stop: rapid service, modest prices and as much coffee as you can drink. A hill between the A1 and the A14 link. I used to spread research papers on the Formica and plot future books. I bought all my clothes in the Alconbury shop; shirts, jeans, boots. Tapes, maps. True Crime shockers. You could take a shower, have a shave. Get a bed for the night. Alconbury, in its pomp, offered roadside hospitality of the kind once available at Buckden Palace. A Travelodge for Templars following England's psychic highways.

Street makes no direct reference to Clare. His north-flowing ley line peters out a mile or so beyond Glinton: at Patty Clare's Northborough cottage? There is some mention of a conclusion at Robin Hood's Bay, 'not far from Whitby Abbey'. A provocative coda that will have to wait for a future occasion. (Renchi is chasing geologist William Smith's limestone reef in that direction.)

WELCOME TO BEDFORDSHIRE, A PROGRESSIVE COUNTY.

Borders come and go. The sun climbs. Side roads are empty. We march along, stopping to take note of anything that confirms our theoretical progress. Renchi addresses a clump of daisy-like wild flowers on a steep bank at the edge of an extended village. 'Greater Stitchwort,' I pronounce (on the authority of the Ladybird primer). Red berries. Haws, rose-hips. Renchi snaps his shutter on a person who looks very much like my father: same set of jaw, the tilt of a man leaning into the wind. A self I don't recognise: older, stripped of pretension. I never saw my father with a rucksack, but my adult life has been a long wrestling match with burdens out of *Pilgrim's Progress*: lights, cameras, book bags, children. When there is nothing to carry, I feel that I'm cheating.

RAILWAY SLEEPERS £15.95.

A hunchback hooked over a wheelchair. He'd crumple without it. His forward-pitching momentum is just enough, when added to the pull of a tiny dog, to advance the old lady in the chair. She grips the dog's leash. The dog sniffs at the verge. The wheelchair tips, veers, lurches into Stotfold, a helmet-shaped settlement on the banks of the River Ivel. We can hear the acoustic footprints of the A1.

40 MILES FROM LONDON TO STOTFOLD. BURGLARS BEWARE. OUR PROPERTY IS POSTCODED. (Notice designed, in red and yellow, to look like a book of stamps.)

Churches: Norman, Saxon. Monuments. Leaded windows, blackened beams. Memorials to children: 'Daughter and sister, aged 7 years, lent not given.' Fields of barley, fields of rye. Banks of daisies. Water towers. We glug at plastic bottles. Renchi repairs his feet. An unpeopled landscape with broad paths cut through cereal fields for hikers who have business elsewhere.

We cross the A1, before Biggleswade, and feel wave-movements, ripples in the land: hillocks, woods. This is encouraging. We hear sheep but don't see them, perhaps they're lost in the high corn. There are no farmers, farm-labourers or livestock. We notice pig sheds, military detritus, bunkers swallowed in undergrowth. Agriculture is a top-dressing to disguise past and present airfields. Ballardian concrete in haze of summer heat. Abandoned hangars, limp windsocks. Corrugated outbuildings, smelling of vanished cattle. Crickets active in long grass.

After hours of dreamlike walking, Renchi is aroused by the distant prospect of St Neots. But it's not St Neots, it's Sandy. There are still railways to cross, a Roman road to relish. Slavering dogs guarding empty properties. Artworks (tin peacocks) in places where nobody will see them.

Clare inserted a footnote into his account of the walk: 'The last Mile stone 35 Miles from London got through Baldeck and sat under a dry hedge.' At Potton he knocked on a door to ask for a light for his pipe. Renchi requested a fill for our water bottles. Questioning villagers in this district was fruitless: 'They scarcely heard me or gave me no answer.'

Yellow hallucinations of early evening. Acres of Kansas corn. We advance on another mysterious hangar, another perimeter fence: JORDANS ('Real Ingredients, Real Taste'). Breakfast of choice. The workers were at the back of the factory, in clusters, practising their smoking. Bored CCTV cameras watched them, watched us. We waved, they waved. A mesh fence made conversation difficult, but it was a relief, after two days on the road, to contact live humans prepared to acknowledge our presence.

Clare headed for a pub called the Ram ('looking in vain for the country mans straw bed'), while we pondered our choice of the Wrestlers at St Neots (a blind booking). And now, at last, my 1,000-mile-guaranteed-no-blister socks were wearing through their double layer. Invisible skin rubbed and puffed. Visible skin was tightened by the sun, the effect of two days blundering across England.

I describe the approach to St Neots, in notes transcribed that night, as a zone of 'busy leisure'. Shooting ranges. Golf courses. Four-wheel drives with kangaroo bars. Red sports cars taking the bends hard, leaving white trails of disturbed dust. We're hitting the wrong Ouse town: hard-living St Neots with its marina, rather than Bunyan's Bedford with its sects and secrets.

There is plenty of town to get through before we reach the river. English dissent is a residual presence: Cromwell and his associates, soldiers, bible-punchers, republicans. Tip your cap to Hampden Way. (John Hampden, 1594–1643, Parliamentarian. One of the five members accused by Charles I of inviting the Scots to invade England. Took part in the Battle of Edgehill. Mortally wounded at Chalgrove Heath. Died at Thame.) 'The King chastised us with whips, but Cromwell chastiseth us with scorpions,' wrote the radical John Spittlehouse. His words are inscribed on a stone in Huntingdon. Renchi scrapes dog shit from his boots on a sign for Levellers Lane.

St Neots conforms to nonconformity, liberties of the Ouse. Neot was a saint without portfolio. 'He has baffled all researches,' says Donald Attwater's dictionary. Possible association with Glastonbury? After death, it is thought, Neot's corpse was removed to a monastery at Eynesbury (we are plodding through there now, an official suburb). Neot had his apostrophe painfully amputated. Leaving: an imposing stone bridge. The usual squabble of coaching-inns. An ivy-choked Victorian vicarage. Monastery ruins. Boat yards. Generic restaurants.

Feet gone, sunburnt, overdosed on Roman roads, cracked airfields, we need a haven. A bed. People. We need: the Wrestlers. Drug notices plastered around the entrance. Prohibition or advert? Early drinkers, the detritus of rubber afternoons, are varnished into place. They surface, from a voluntary catalepsy, just far enough to notice shapes at the periphery of vision. The drama of two men struggling across a darkened room towards the only vertical element.

'You want to stay? *Here*?'

Jaw hits puddled bar. No garlic available, so he makes a defensive gesture with a bunch of heavy keys. Then issues us with complicated instructions.

'Red door. Alley. Mind the bins. Another door, right? Stairs. Go up 'em. Careful like.'

One of the ladies, perched on a leatherette stool, unsticks her skirt and volunteers to act as guide; she needs the exercise. It looks like a long evening. Smirnoff (by the bottle). Garishly coloured mobile phones laid out along the bar like surgical implements. Cigarette bricks in cellophane wrappers. Plastic lighters: auxiliary thumbs. Flick flick flick. Black-and-white posters of Paris bohemia.

Female drinker, slipping off stool, to landlord: 'It's my birthday. What shall I do?'

'Get pissed. Then shagged up the arse. Like every other Wednesday.'

One of the phones goes off. The woman taps the rim of her glass with a chipped red nail. Chews ice. The landlord fires her cigarette. It wouldn't be fair to call them binge drinkers. To be a binge drinker you have to stop at some point. In the gloom of the Wrestlers, it is slow and steady. Like the slap and pull of the river. These are professionals, in the zone. Dedicated to soft focus.

Our rooms aren't too bad. They have beds, nicotine-muslin drapes across the window. A pink tablet of soap: in which is embedded a black question mark of pubic hair. A bath would be good (available, on request, at the end of the corridor). Rinse out the evidence of a recent dog-washing ceremony, sink into sodden carpet, as into the peat of Whittlesey Mere. Feet squelch, up to the ankle. It's quite soothing. I may be able to limp into town, the pub doesn't do food (not even breakfasts). There is something decadent in the idea. Food takes the edge off serious drinking.

Feverish, we stagger downstairs, out of the red door. (Behind which, as we hear, the Wrestlers is livening up.) Our evening is resolved at a Beefeater. Anywhere would do, in fearful anticipation of the next day's haul. Old grey stone: another bridge on which to lean, oily light on water. I gnaw on meat and imagine that it's fish; it might be, it might be. Renchi tries the vegetarian vegetables: peas and chips. And decides that, if he makes it back to Glastonbury, it will be raw food and a blender for the next few years.

Ouse

Emma Matthews is a painter, by instinct, training (Wimbledon Art School), and projected intention. She has arrived at a period in her life, early forties, when such practices can again be considered, attempted: studio time, space in which to work. And subject: the interrogation of memory. Frames of film, faded photographs: they will be challenged, stroked with paint. Vitalised. Friends, looking at the small panels in their pale wood frames, talk of Gerhard Richter. But it's not that. Not Germanic gravitas. Serialism. Newsprint retrievals: Baader-Meinhof, Red Army Faction. Objectivity. Richter told Jan Thorn Prikker that he kept photographs, potential art works, for years. Waiting. In limbo. He kept them 'under the heading of unfinished business'.

In painting from photographs Richter felt that he was 'relieved of the need to choose or construct a subject'. He uses the word 'appropriation'. He is alert to material that will enable him to exercise a particular technique, a way of distancing himself from the product of his labours. This would not be my understanding of Emma Matthews's recent work. Her heart is in a very different place. She rescues a landscape, a group of figures, part of a building, from the prejudice of oblivion. She puts a light source behind a blink of forgotten time, blurring boundaries, dignifying mess.

I met Emma through her day job as an editor. She trained on film and adapted, very successfully, to the new technologies of tape (in its primitive form), laptop wizardry. Fast fingers, supple intelligence. She became Chris Petit's editor of choice, an important collaborator on television essays and experimental projects for gallery pieces and performances. My image of Petit on the road would always include Matthews as aesthetic or moral conscience; influencing material he will bring back, even when she is not physically present. Later, in the edit suite, shoes off, legs swinging, she will run his images, backwards and forwards, until they satisfy her rigorous standards. Petit lounges on the sofa with the crossword, sits up to approve the latest revision. Or creaks away to make a pot of tea, massaging the small of his back, taking requests for chocolate biscuits. In their north London bunker, daylight is excluded; they live behind metal shutters. Phone ringing constantly, change of property in the wind. Solicitors, agents. Chris paces, missing his small cigars, deferring to Emma's familiarity with the raw footage he has provided.

Of course they both suffer with their backs. Ten hours at the machine. And another pass after the evening meal (which he prepares). Undoing the day's tentative rough cut. Back to zero. Voices are never raised, though silences are. The final version, never definitive, comes at a cost. Migraines. Repetitive strain injuries. Snatched meals. Too much strong coffee. Patchy sleep: recutting phantom memories of sequences that were never shot.

The American film poet Stan Brakhage, so it is said, developed cancer from the dye in film; from painting directly on to emulsion, years of intimate handling: scratching, smearing, licking. Brakhage wanted to re-enchant industrial material, with its flaws and foibles, in order to recover that primitive, taboo-breaking excitement of early cinema.

At the finish, Brakhage came back to drawing. His wife, Marilyn, called it 'a process of self-searching and elucidation: elucidation of the nature of his illness, of his experiencing of it, of how it affected his perceptions, of the very essence of his being – and of his impending death'. With the guidance of a hypnotherapist, Barbara Julian, Brakhage 'entered a state of deep relaxation and moderate-to-deep hypnotic trance . . . a borderline area between sleep and waking consciousness'.

The tumour was darkness, everything else was light. 'You can't touch me,' Brakhage said, 'I'm memory.' The first drawing, derived from the sessions with Julian, placed the artist in an arid landscape. He was walking. He sat under a bridge, the river had dried up. 'It's peace, but it's boredom.' Before Brakhage entered the hospice, he saw his present body 'as not matter but the energy within matter – as streaming with sparkling golden and silver light'.

One cold, bright New Year's Eve, in a beach house on the South Coast, Emma let it be known that she had three immediate wishes: to be married, to have a child, and to show her paintings. One out of three isn't bad, I thought, I'd settle for that. There shouldn't be a problem, with her contacts, plenty of good will, in fixing an exhibition. The venue, when it happened, was a post-production facility, not far from Tottenham Court Road. The invitation said: 'Lost Memories'. Emma attended the opening with her husband, Chris Petit, and her young son, Louis.

Photography has been called a form of bereavement. Private openings in tight, packed galleries are wakes. Emma's exhibition was at cineContact; friends and associates spilled on to the pavement, one of those close Fitzrovia evenings. Tactfully hung, the paintings glow like warning lights on a dashboard, seen through layers of surgical gauze. Grafts of fresh colour on slivers of scenery that would otherwise fade into the fog of elective amnesia. Emma is fonder of luminescence than structure; a burn of hot reds through recessive blues and blacks. There is a residual dissatisfaction with the headlong momentum of film or tape; the requirement to fix a narrative, tell a story, when all too often narrative is redundant. Emma's panels are closer to poetry than reportage.

Her early work, after art school, was 'icon-like'. So she tells me. Flat, hieratic portraits built up with washes of glaze, floating skins of varnish. Before that, in the Islington school, down by the canal, she remembers constructing an idealised family group: father, mother, three children and a dog. 'I was in love with the dog.' Talking about it brings back the smell, the texture of stiff, grey, sugar paper. A smiling family of confectionary ghosts.

She explains her technique. A moving sequence is slowed, stopped. A frame is chosen, captured. She picks out the detail on which she wants to concentrate. She grades colour, makes her print. The raw image is bathed in oil. There is a PVA (polyvinyl acetate) primer, paint, and then a Brakhage-like process of scratching, erasing. Richter's formal analysis with Brakhage's emotion. 'During SB's final two months,' wrote Marilyn Brakhage, 'the sessions took the form of visualizing the body as an infinite collection of energy fields, in constant flux, pulsing and flowing. SB retreated from the transitory doings of his cells and metabolism into a sense of his secret self, the self behind the self, the self (or deep consciousness) unyoked to time and space.'

There are images in the cineContact exhibition from an era before memory. A hospital. A drive across flat landscape towards a hill town with a cathedral: Lincoln. Her father the doctor. A young man, a dedicated professional. The hospital paintings are not derived from tape, but from a collection of old photographs found, by Emma, in a frozen-turkey box at the bottom of a wardrobe. 'Memory,' said the poet Michael Hamburger, talking about W. G. Sebald, 'is a darkroom for the development of fiction.'

A family group posed in front of a provincial isolation hospital. Conventional pieties of the period: white shirt, fiercely ironed tie, pipe. The woman's summer dress is fashionable again, the kind Emma might wear. Such serenity, family arranged on the grass in front of institutional buildings, tickles my paranoia; notions of animal experimentation, government-approved research, something nasty behind metal-framed windows sticky with new paint.

When she discovered the cache of hidden snapshots, Emma was the age (or close to it) of her mother, back then. The woman on the hospital lawn. Unborn, Emma was part of the scene. Now she paints her adult self into this fragment of the past: a face in a dark window, caught like a penitent behind pink cross-struts. She is looking down at her father, her brother, her pregnant mother. She has returned from the future to eavesdrop on an episode beyond revision. An unrecorded stranger, a memory man, clicks the shutter.

I told Renchi some of this story, about Emma, her paintings, the box of photographs, and how she paid for a gravestone for the church at Great Paxton. We leant for a moment on the bridge at St Neots, watching cruise boats and growling with hunger. Clare, in his poem 'Recollections of a Ramble', writes of sitting on the bank of a river and thinking: 'if I tumbled in/I should fall direct to heaven'.

The Wrestlers offering nothing more than a handwritten bill, daggered to the bar, we provision ourselves with Scotch eggs and plastic water. On the minimart monitor, we see fugitives, blanket-over-head runaways living rough. First light on an open road is something else, so English that it is not English at all. There are no hedges, mist hangs low over innocent fields. You have to walk on tarmac, the road's edge is rutted and treacherous. Long shadows fall towards the river. The sky is cloudless. We move towards a distant clump of trees.

Then the cars begin, not many, but travelling at speed, in clusters. It's not yet seven-thirty. Amateur make-up artists experiment with lipstick. Smokers nuzzle comfort phones. Open windows deliver dead news with faked urgency. Unscathed, we climb through poplar avenues and designer-stubble paddocks. The view from the crest, so the book says, is the most glorious in England. River Ouse on one side, woods on the other. Parodically compact villages.

The church of Holy Trinity at Great Paxton is down a shaded lane. Tower. Perpendicular arch. Three clipped yew bushes mark the path: broad-skirted, emblematic. We search out the relevant graves. It's not difficult in such a quiet, well-tended place. A granite block, the one planted at the time of the drowning. And the recent addition, Emma's gift to her sister.

I leave the Baldock pine cone, in long grass, against the block. The grain of the stone is yellowed, lettering clear: 'Drowned in/ the Ouse/ trying to rescue/ his daughter/ who lies nearby.'

Renchi digs a feather into the soil, near the grave of Emma's sister: Ruth Constance Matthews, 1963–1970. There was a Wordsworth quotation, chosen by Ruth's mother: 'What hast thou to do with sorrow,/ Or the injuries of tomorrow?'

*

At the time when Emma held her exhibition in Newman Street, I'd started to retrace certain sections of the Clare walk. I decided to go south along the Ouse, between Buckden and St Neots; Emma said she would come with me, bringing Louis, her young son. We would avoid the road and stick with the river bank.

I dipped into William Cobbett, a writer admired by Clare. One of Cobbett's rural rides took him through this country, downriver from Huntingdon.

Above and below the bridge, under which the Ouse passes, are the most beautiful, and by far the most beautiful meadows that I ever saw in my life. Here are no reeds, here is no sedge, no unevenness of any sort. Here are *bowling-greens* of hundreds of acres in extent, with a river windling through them, full to the brink.

Emma has been looking at Anselm Kiefer's pictures of the Rhine (from 1981). Woodcuts on paper. A giant book on a steel lectern in the Tate Modern power station. 'Even clean hands leave marks and damage surfaces,' warns a notice, safeguarding this monumental item.

Out of such Stygian gloom, Emma recognises the solution to her dilemma: how she can make paintings from the Ouse walk that will respect, without being overwhelmed by, dark memories. For many years, childhood and adolescence, the river tragedy was not discussed; the box of photographs remained at the bottom of the wardrobe. Returning to the river, her eight-year-old self, the drama of that autumn day, will be a difficult thing: Emma carrying her son past the place where it happened.

A fine, Indian summer morning; we meet at the old posting-house, the Lion at Buckden. They can't offer breakfast, not without prior warning: e-mail, fax, credit card details. We detour to Alconbury, around the American air base; then back to the marina at Offord Cluny, the basin where Emma's father picked up the cruiser. A new riverside development is touting for custom, a bar/bistro provides sustenance for weekend sailors.

The Ouse Valley Way has gathered its complement of small kids with massive rucksacks, award-seeking juvenile hikers, dog attendants and suspiciously cheery fisherfolk. Progress is slow. Louis Petit, seven months old, sturdy, active, has not previously been confronted with a carrysack. He regards it as a gross invasion of his dignity. He grizzles, mopes, works up to an impressive howl. So he is carried in his mother's arms. Set down beside the river for a liquid lunch, he relents. Bestows a winning smile on his exhausted porters.

Our signposted path in no way resembles Cobbett's 'bowling-green' meadows. Going is soft, faces are lashed by drooping willows. Muddy reeds are woven into treacherous islands. The Ouse is broad, oily, thick skinned. A smear of sunlight shows off the dance of midges and gnats. Currents are powerful, contradictory. Pleasure boats pass with upraised gin glasses, rattle of ice cubes. A yawn from the stretching teenage daughter who is like a cat in the wrong place. A scowl from the son at the wheel. The pattern of wavelets, the wash, stays long after the boats have disappeared. My photographs are gloomier than my memories.

The tower of Holy Trinity Church at Great Paxton can be seen across the river, coming out of the trees. A landing stage on the far bank provokes Emma and brings out the story. It was her duty, in 1970, two families sharing a small boat, a camping expedition, heading towards St Neots, to remember the heavy key that would operate the lock gate, let the water flood through. She failed. She was preoccupied. She forgot it.

The second adult, a friend of her father, went ashore, into town, to fetch provisions. The boat turned back towards the marina, the starting point of our walk. Emma and her father were in the small cabin. The children of the other family were on deck. Ruth Matthews, in the prow, watching reflections in the water, slipped over the side. Her father, a strong swimmer, dived in. He caught the child, secured her in the rescue position, and then – as the others, alarmed by these sounds, watched – they disappeared below the surface. To be trapped in the weave of reeds? Held under by strong currents? It is not known. Perhaps Dr Matthews suffered a heart attack, the shock of the dive into cold water. The cruiser was brought to the bank, the landing stage. Emma and her brother were taken into a strange house, comforted. Returned to London, their mother. Years later, travelling north, the church at Great Paxton would be pointed out through the train window.

The story has been told in the place where it happened. We hear the trains. We hear the traffic on the road. We move on. Carrying arrangements for Louis never quite work, buckles snap. The infant is self-absorbed to an heroic degree. His wriggling actuality over-rides any attempt on my part to clarify an episode buried in thirty years of memory.

RIVER VIEWPOINT: DANGER OF DROWNING. NO SWIMMING. NO SKATING. NO UNAUTHORISED BOATING.

Our outing dissolves into the usual English preoccupations: finding a pub for lunch, crossing a river, a railway line, visiting a Saxon church. Reading memorials. Taking photographs. Worrying about accidents and delays on the road home.

The pub is one for the book: food-substitutes fizz like sherbet on the tongue. 'Chicken' and 'Fish' are courtesy discriminations. Microwaved stuff, ice-pink in the middle, is burnt on the outside. A handsome couple, minimally dressed on this cooling October afternoon, chew one another's faces, between swigs from a shared bottle. She exhales his smoke. His love bites depend into rising tattoo bruises. They have a feral, backwater beauty; eyes unclouded by memory of anything that took place before they walked into that bar.

The narrow metal trough of the Gents has been filled to its brim with copper coins. They glint beneath steaming, bubbling scum: a treasure only the most desperate soul will be tempted to raid.

As he advanced on Stilton, too tired to recall how long he had been on the road, Clare's memories became dreams, his dreams memories. Edward Storey, in *A Right to Song*, described the syndrome:

'Sometimes the dreams do not even come out of memories of the past but appear to project themselves into events that are yet to come.'

Influenced by De Quincey's *Confessions of an English Opium-Eater*, which he had been following through extracts published in the *London Magazine*, Clare recorded dreams that might inspire future poems. He saw himself and his fellow villagers processing into Helpston churchyard to witness the Day of Judgement:

when we got into the church a light streamed in one corner of the chancel & from that light appeared to come the final decisions of mans actions in life I felt awfully afraid tho not terrified & in a moment my name was called from the north-west corner of the chancel & when my conductress smiled in exstacy & uttered something as prophetic of happiness I knew all was right & she led me again into the open air

Place sustains light. Walking discovers it. Emma Matthews helps memory to achieve the condition of dream. A necklace of particulars. Illuminated tower blocks on the edge of a city. Wet drives, at dawn, through a dusty Texas town. Nightfishing in the English Channel. Accidents of perception substitute doctored images for an unreliable past, whose only claim on our attention is the fact that it has been captured on film. The paintings, less sharply focused, touched by human warmth, imminent not actual, cannot be forgotten. Or lost.

To Stilton

As, on the morning of our third day, the countryside becomes more serene, so my expression, captured in Renchi's photographs, is more agonised: screwed up, creased. Eyes narrow, blooded, under the long brim of a sweat-streaked cap. The walk is getting serious. We'll make it but it's going to hurt. Our task is to resupply the pain hidden by the Cambridgeshire landscape. It really is very pleased with itself, pristine roads and unbroken sunshine (when we have lumbered ourselves with bundles of rainwear). Lilies float on harmless water. A signboard, in painted relief, for Offord Cluny. Like the wooden cover ripped from a new edition of Izaac Walton.

We pass the marina, cross the mainline railway, wink at a gravel chute; achieve Buckden. With every expectation of a mid-morning break at a timbered hostelry: 'The Old Lion & Lamb. One of the Oldest Posting Houses.' More significantly, we rejoin the Great North Road and the spirit of Clare (at his most weary, so much done, so far to go).

I felt so weak here that I forced to sit down on the ground to rest myself & while I sat here a Coach that seemed to be heavy laden came rattling up & stopt in the hollow below me & I cannot reccolect its ever passing by me I then got up & pushed onward seeing little to notice for the road very often looked as stupid as myself & I was very often half asleep as I went on the third day I satisfied my hunger by eating the grass by the road which seemed to taste something like bread

Settled into a window seat, coffee and biscuits, we plot the rest of the day's march. As I had carried with me Emma's story of the Ouse drownings, so Renchi felt the need to witness Grafham Water and the submerged villages. He had tales of his own to bring to mind. One of which involved a Native American Sundance ceremony, attended by friends or relatives. A tree tumbled on to a participant, smashing his skull. A dancer, who couldn't deal with this unexpected intervention, took off at high speed in his car. The others, after due consideration, came together to pick up the tree, to carry it away: appeasing hurt by a revised and extended ritual.

As we left Great Paxton, a figure out of Trollope, very much like the previous Archbishop of Canterbury, leant over his trim hedge to let us know that we were looking at 'the oldest Saxon church in Cambridgeshire'. Buckden has an alternative ecclesiastical attraction, a redbrick bishop's palace. Rigby Graham's lithograph, from his Clare expedition, pushes a rather pudgy poet (in battered Sam Peckinpah top hat) against the palace wall; while a heron, swooping overhead, points out the road. Head north, young man.

Studying that hat, I wondered how Clare would work in a western, on horseback. This short, sturdy man crumpled under the weight of transporting memories of the Helpston horizon. He wouldn't register in widescreen. Except as a holy fool: Clint Eastwood's dwarfish sidekick in *High Plains Drifter*. A half-breed deputed to looking after the animals for *The Wild Bunch* (credited below L. Q. Jones and Bo Hopkins). A person who is never more than an extension of landscape, attractive but disposable. (Chris Petit's acquaintance, Bo Hopkins, mad as a raft of monkeys, is shot to pieces before the end of the credit sequence.)

Distressed, road-ragged, we behaved like English gentlemen, not cowboys: coffee and Nice biscuits, a brief tour of the bishop's palace. My photographs play along with the romantic fallacy: Jacobean garden, stone cleric with model of church resting on his hand, a priapic swan nuzzling his privates. The eleventh-century palace housed the Bishops of Lincoln. It was here that Catherine of Aragon, Henry VIII's set-aside queen, was kept. The Lion & Lamb, it seems, was a guest house for the bishop. They still boast of it. Of surviving. And remembering.

Blisters tended, socks changed, Renchi is a new man; so much so that he heads rapidly out of town and straight back towards

London: wrong choice at roundabout, delirious reconnection with the A1. The crenellations of the high wall of Buckden Palace may have had something to do with it. They throw out a ladder of light, down which Renchi, tipped forward by his massive burden, dances. Today's bandanna is pale blue, matching the watery oval on his T-shirt, which is otherwise as green as smoke.

Grafham Water is not so much Grafham Water as Grafham under-water: 1,500 acres of drowned farms, hamlets and good agricultural land. Recreation instead of seasonal toil. Water sports, nature trails, instead of nature in its unredeemed state. The Exhibition Centre offers a video presentation (official history) and the shop is stocked with souvenirs of a non-place you are never going to know, mementoes of absence. The Anglian Water brochure ('Something for Everyone') puffs walking, cycling, eating, avian voyeurism, reduced rates for senior citizen fishermen, but says absolutely nothing about land piracy, decanted villagers. Another nice example of erased or selective memory.

When you arrive, as pedestrians, bruised and thirsty for images of water, you sense immediately that something is wrong. Retro-futurist buildings, on the rim of a low grass bank, loom like UFOs: Grafham Water is an airstrip for aliens. Our boys fly out to combat virtual terrorism and rogue regimes in never-ending oil wars, while grape-skinned intelligences from distant galaxies drop in for their summer break, the Grafham Water package. 'For those wishing to have a different location for a special occasion, we can offer private bookings of the facilities.'

As we approach Grafham Water, destination of choice on all road signs, we notice an ominous glint, red and silver: meridian sun flashing on a mound of lobsters or shelled prawns? Which later reveals itself as: the largest collection of bicycles outside Cambridge (or East London's Cheshire Street market). All of them scarlet with silver mudguards. It's tempting, very tempting. The roads are empty, straight, hedgeless. We should make Stilton in time for an afternoon nap, a drink before dinner.

We settle instead for a rest on the beach. It's not a real beach, a token scatter of shells. Like the bottom of a parrot's cage. No tides. Clear water over imported gravel, with bands of yellow in the style of urban swimming pools after the incontinent kiddies' session. Fishermen pose, floppy hats, multipocketed vests, floppy lines, on jetties constructed from broken boulders. Blue lake. Lazy clouds. What could be more delightful? Sucking on plastic water, munching peppermints. Cooling swollen feet in liquid that will soon be gushing through the hosepipes and shower units and kitchen taps of Anglia's customers. This water is fine in photographs, but it smells bad. Dead. Or kept alive on a respirator.

The Duke of Edinburgh choppered down to Grafham in 1966 to cut the ribbon. The Doddington Brook was dammed and water pumped in from the River Ouse at Offord. Farms disappeared. Farmworkers were dispersed. They were used to it, wartime restrictions had never been repealed. Airfields at Little Staughton, Kimbolton, Brampton Grange, Molesworth. The American base at Alconbury. An epic geometry of crisscrossing runways, now disused, near the village of Thurleigh. Renchi is on the trail of a vanished family, a story he wants to uncover. Memories of commandeered barns, compulsory labour. Official secrets. He thinks that Grafham Church might offer a clue, more names on deleted tombstones.

We exit the pleasure zone by way of a raised metal arm, an obliging security barrier. Nothing obvious to protect; water behind us, dazzling cornfields ahead. When white lines appear, we know that we're closing on civilisation, cottages, pubs. The lines are fresh and they are in duplicate. The new painter missed the original mark, went back for a second attempt, and left a drunken road to make its own way to the Montagu Arms. MONDAY: STEAK NITE. 2 × 8 SIRLOIN DINNERS. ONLY £10.

A water tower. Shadows of overhanging trees. Sections of the road, repaired, floating free between black fissures of melted tar.

Grafham. Ellington. (We skirt Brampton, where the young Samuel Pepys spent so much of his time with upwardly mobile relatives. A cousin of his mother worked as a bailiff for the local landowner, Montagu. Hence: the Montagu Arms. Edward Montagu, Earl of Sandwich, was Pepys's patron. The sponsor of his career as a naval bureaucrat.)

Renchi leads me into yet another church, another shaded oasis. He photographs the grave of the Baker family: 'Frank, Twin Brother of Ernest.' He talks to a woman who has parked her car at the church door. He makes notes. He pieces together the story of a family scattered when the drowning happened, when land under cultivation was lost to Grafham Water.

A man of the village was sent to the Thames Estuary, the Isle of Grain, where he became a shepherd. A shepherd working with London delinquents. The legends are as vague as our register of the loss suffered by people who lived and worked this patch for generations. Fading names on weathered stone. The thing that excites Renchi is the accident of meeting the woman with the car, the confirmation of facts he had previously suspected.

Inside the church, he examines a section in the great black Bible, left open on a lectern: 'Love never fails. But where there are prophecies, they will cease; where there are tongues, they will be stilled; where there is knowledge, it will pass away.'

When we walk outside, into bright sunlight, the time on the church clock is twelve thirty-three.

The relief barman is about to call it a day in the village of Alconbury. His wife's family come from another place entirely, my home country, Port Talbot in South Wales. The only relief barmen need there, in the red smoke of the steel mills, is from the humours of the drinkers; the same faces, day after day, looped patter, residual gloom. The game's up in Alconbury, in Middle England, no field-labourers, no dedicated alcoholics left. Small pubs, once run as a sideline by the wives of ambitious farmers, have to peddle pizzas and welcome kids to roadside play areas. (Proud Montagu's heraldic crest is a pub sign. He gave his name to the sandwich, but none are available here.) John Clare's escape from pressure, family, into the boisterous company of the Blue Bell Inn, the Billings brothers and their associates, poachers and fiddlers in the fellowship of drink, has been discontinued.

Frederick Martin:

It was proposed by the brothers Billing, tenants of the Hall, and adopted by a majority of votes, that a stick should be put firmly in the ground, in the middle of the room, and that they should dance around it in a ring till it fell from its erect position. The way in which it fell was to indicate in which direction the two emigrants were to go.

Swaying inebriates stamp a pattern on the dirt floor, a vortex of footprints. Fate will take the decision for them. Such rituals were denied us in Alconbury. Orange moustaches: two pints of sweet cordial fizzed with lemonade from a hose. It's come to that. Rehydrated, we take our leave of the barman and his wife, grateful for their conversation. They'll be back on the road soon, a new gig in Sheffield. Now we have nothing except a long haul, shoulder to shoulder with Clare, out ahead of us; up Ermine Street, the Great North Road, to Stilton.

A decorated stone block beside the Great North Road. Hand pointing south: TO LONDON 64 MILES (through Huntingdon, Royston & Ware). To LONDON 72 MILES (through Cambridge). Here is an object we treat with reverence (the better for being unreadable by motorists). It is faded, masonic; a lost piece in a game of psychogeographical chess. Through his magnifying glass, Renchi watches a snail crawl up one of the grooves, following the vertical stroke of the T in 'To London'.

Pawns advance one square at a time. As we do, hobbled, reconnected to Clare's exhaustion; he understands, pain has taught him, the quest is futile. There is no wife, no Mary Joyce. No cottage. Nothing behind him and no way back to London. Promised distances are lies. TO STILTON 7 MILES. Seven miles on a road that will exist for a single day.

Stilton was a border marker for Clare; finding the Peterborough road, he would be on familiar ground. Spirits lifted after the collapse of the previous night, the disorientation; feeling stupid, out of his knowledge. After Stilton, he had one task left: to learn to forget.

The promised seven miles were the hardest that we walked; one of my feet was shot, blistered. Shoulders were raw from the chafing of unsecured straps. But it was good to have a road again; a ghost highway little used by motorists, Eddie Stobart's fleet or the refrigerated monsters that service superstores.

Vetch, thistle, tares: the unconsidered bounty of disregarded verges. A diminishing white line, dividing vegetable and mineral zones, hauls us forward on a blindman's rope. The edge is innocent of animal corpses, squashed and splattered vermin.

Ghost roads belong to the vanished. They remind me of Chris Petit: who should, by now, be waiting for us at Stilton. With Petit, I've explored many roads that have abdicated their original identity: the A13, out of Rainham. And others. Traffic stolen by a flashier replacement. Leaving a microclimate of entropy and nostalgia. Off-highway enterprises that have run out of puff.

The B1043 is of that family. Pressed against a busy section of the A1(M), it retains a vagrant charm. You have to walk it to know it. Motorway travellers, heading south, visible over tall grass, don't notice you. You might as well be dead. I think of Petit's first feature, *Radio On*, made before he was thirty. It was when I heard that scoreline – 'Norwich, two. Chelsea, nil.' – as the Rover comes down the ramp into Bristol, that I understood. Another fantasy. A posthumous dream. The traveller, trapped on the road west, is dead from the start. Suicide in the bath. Subjected to morbid monologues (roadkill rockers, Belfast), Petit's driver can never come off the road – until it is time to rebury himself in a quarry. *Radio On*, shot in classic Ilford monochrome, is impossible to date, outside time. With every viewing, it seems more contemporary, and comes from a place that is further away.

Ermine Street, in late afternoon, is a catalogue of extinguished enterprises. Prefabricated cafés, overtaken by tumbleweed, have chipped paint, cracked windows. Poppies, saxifrage, daisies burst through blackened pots and pans. Filling stations have drained tanks. Gates open into wilderness estates. Stone furniture: acanthus overwhelmed by green creepers. A Petit movie that was never commissioned. His stubborn cameraman, Martin Schäfer, brought back from the grave.

We don't talk, we listen. We see bridges over the A1, direction indicators, speed warnings, as a march of invaders, *War of the Worlds* tripods, heading for London. We sample ice-cream from the one surviving garage. We walk, in shared reverie, as distance stretches. The motorway is a temporary nuisance, choked into immobility; a conduit for the 'M11 corridor'. A preordained future of estate housing, retail parks and out-of-town shopping cities.

To our right is a country we barely notice: encroaching Fens, rivers, the old island town of Ramsey. Fields and woods where Whittlesey Mere, with its armadas of pleasure boats, once gloried in scale, impregnability, nationwide reputation. The Mere was drained on a whim in 1851: in the perverse way that the area around Grafham was flooded a hundred years later. Holme Fen, which we passed, all unknowing, at the end of the third day's walk, was somewhere to which I would return. By car. With Anna.

The woods of Holme Lode Covert are the strangest in Britain. Draining an expanse of water like Whittlesey Mere throws time into reverse. A notice beside two metal posts boasts that you are standing at the 'lowest place in England'. So low that you breathe through your gills; you breathe earth, dark fathoms of the vanished lake. Water is a magician's medium, a substance with its own memory: you cannot simply pour it away and ignore the outcome. The post crowned with a small pyramid is a marker, set in 1852, to measure peat shrinkage. A second pillar was erected in 1957. The cast-iron column was apparently taken from the original Crystal Palace (built for the Great Exhibition of 1851), before it was removed to Sydenham. So here, in this obscure wood, favoured by dog walkers, antiquarians, adulterous lovers (two cars kept apart), is a piece of Victorian London, a high rib of Empire. The post is not sinking; it is rising, inch by inch, out of the soft black ground.

We abandon the car. Nothing, nobody. The feeling persists: we are watched. I persuade Anna into the woods, over a gate; our path is soft, springy. Pools of friable earth around the roots of fallen trees: run it through your fingers. Sniff them. Damp sawdust, stagnant water. An eros of decay to overwhelm invaders. Better not to come too close, touch or embrace, the consequences would be irreversible. Whittlesey Mere takes no prisoners.

Peter Ashley, the Oundle-based photographer and writer who alerted me to the Crystal Palace post, also suggested that I investigate Engine Farm. A sinister location protected by a steep metal ramp, locked gates, a sluggish irrigation channel: Holme Lode. The map offers no inducement to carry on. A car out of nowhere pulls up alongside, the driver is mystified by my search. 'Engine Farm? Nothing there but stones.'

Stones? Stones are good. You cross a bridge, make yourself known to the farmer: 'Don't want to take no bugger by stealth, boy, not out in the Fens.' You dodge potato lorries: to discover a group of limestone blocks, thirteenth century, intended for Ramsey Abbey. Moving in, you register masons' marks (arrowheads). Embedded fossils. The blocks, lost in transit, had been shipped down the Nene, in flat-bottomed boats, from the Barnack quarries. They had sunk in Whittlesey Mere, deep sediment, for five hundred years. Then, Mere drained by Victorian engineers, they floated to the surface. Peat levels fell away. In brackish hibernation, the Engine Farm stones outlasted the dissolution of the monasteries, the execution of Charles I. Epochs of revolution and restoration. The sanctified blocks, so ley line enthusiasts assert, emerged from the Mere in perfect alignment with Barnack and Ramsey Abbey.

'When we first moved up here in 1996,' Peter Ashley told me in a letter,

we went to a local pub that sits on the banks of the River Nene. It was a crowded Sunday lunchtime and we all sat round a table where a man with wild staring eyes (we've got used to that round here now) quietly supped his beer. I got into conversation with him and he started to recite yards of Clare, the syllables dribbling out with drops of ale into his grey beard. As he got up to go he told me he had been a patient in the same Northamptonshire asylum as Clare, and I watched him slowly cycling away up the street in the rain.

Under a quilt of cloud, we crossed the A1, by way of a splendid bridge. Evening light picked a thread of gold from fading fields. We walked the length of the village, south, to the Bell Inn. Where Chris Petit was already established, bathed and fresh, ready for the final day's stroll to Glinton.

In the courtyard for the evening meal, we suffer nothing worse than a troop of compulsory Morris Dancers (the sort that turn up in the Rigby Graham film). This side of Ermine Street, away from the Fens, dancers are inoffensive hobbyists working up a thirst. Not like the revenant mob, the drunks and madmen of my Welsh youth; the Mari Llwyd rhymers who pranced, house to house, on New Year's Eve. Excavated horse's head, scarlet-lipped, draped in a white sheet. Bells. Footsteps in the snow. The dead try to gain entrance. To fire, warmth, cakes and ale. Improvised poetry, verse for verse, is the only way of keeping them out. The Stilton bell-jinglers, stick-bangers, are not the Shitwitches or Molly Gangs of the Fens. Wild, black-faced, travestied. Unemployed ploughboys taught to beg, midwinter, brick in the hand, by near starvation. Such creatures, displaced from the drained Whittlesey Mere, roam the backroads. Waiting their time. At Stilton, spectral riot disturbed the broken Clare: 'I heard the voices but never looked back to see where they came from.'

DROWNING

I will not remember. I will not remember anything. She is all memory – she remembers so much, she remembers the memories that are not her own.

Iris Murdoch, *The Italian Girl*

Salt Green Death

After a period during which Anna suffered from troubled dreams, and I felt myself torn between the attractions of Hackney present (slo-mo apocalypse) and Hackney past (i.e., Hastings), we settled to our double life. Familiar routines of work in the old house, occupied since 1969, and snatched excursions to a flat in a Thirties cruise liner, seafront building in St Leonards. A crumbling white monster that should never have been built, carving as it did through a substantial portion of James Burton's Regency development. The guilt was piquant. Such easy-paced pleasures, morning swim, hours on a balcony, no phone calls, leisurely walks, shouldn't be allowed.

At home, I tinkered with a novel; on the coast, sliding doors open to the light, the English Channel, I let it all drift. After a dip, a wallow, a tumble in the waves, I did my bit to support local trade (Hungarian minimart) – NO CASH KEPT ON PREMISES OVERNIGHT – by carrying home an obese Saturday newspaper. 'The habit of newsprint,' Charles Olson called it. He's right. Worse than cigarettes. Fouling the fingers, muddying the mind. Passive browsing, addiction. The degrading of our ability to concentrate, evaluate, make independent judgements. I used gloomy noise, growling and screeching on a cheap sound system, as an antidote to cultural grazing: the sorry parade of puffers, fudgers, backscratchers. With the occasional gem chucked in to justify the experience.

And Anna's dreams, what were they? Anticipations of another life: London houses flooding, floating away. Previsions of the novel I was about to write: husband split into separate entities, both with my face. Husband carrying her, in miraculous flight, star-high above a black sea.

Saturday, 21 January 2004, was one of the good days. The *Guardian* offered a W. S. Graham poem: 'Put on your lovely yellow /

Oilskin to meet the weather . . . Hold on to me and stop/ The world's thorns.' (A walk with his wife, Ness, on Penwith moor.) And a lead piece by the biographer Richard Holmes on the drowning of Shelley.

Drowning and flying were themes to be resolved in the Clare book that I was plotting, preparing to write. Drowned villages, flights across England. The painting by Renchi, from his walk to Land's End, undertaken between 1990 and 1997, hung on my Hastings wall. A memory he summarises as: 'Pilgrim setting out on journey beneath guardian tree with Greensand Goddess towering above.' An overpainted word (in loud red): 'Drownings'. Drownings in earth. In chalk. In Wealden clay. Flying, dreaming, walking, drowning: that would be my underlying structure.

Then there were lines I marked, for possible Clare insertion, from Chris Petit's novel, *Robinson*: 'Sometimes the road disappeared under water, and the surrounding fields became lakes.' A sentence from a *Guardian* review of a Bram Stoker biography: 'The worst he did was wave his stick and shout at the sea.'

That's one of the things I liked about St Leonards. I lay on the sofa, picking out volumes at random, books I hadn't seen in years, and noted down paragraphs, prompts, phrases that might become titles of unwritten poems. I cultivated a notebook. I watched fishing boats, small yachts. And plotted voyages.

Holmes tested material from his 1974 book, *Shelley: The Pursuit*, against a sharper sense of what the act of biography now meant. The interplay of one life on another, the risks. He polished a myth, teased out connections. He fingered mementoes of the drownings, 8 July 1822, in the Bay of Spezia. Holmes loves thanatology: 'An astonishing array of pictures, poems, inscriptions, memoirs and Victorian monuments.' A death cult. 'Shelley could always fly, but he could never swim.'

Flight is a shamanic fugue (when practised without aeroplane or wings), an involuntary or induced lifting of the imagination into another register: vision. Hallucination. The lip of the world. Swimming is abdication, universal memory; weightlessness, supported struggle. Learning to let go. Passengers in Shelley's homemade skiff, stitched canvas and reeds, were frantic to escape; they leapt over the side at the first glimpse of sand beneath clear water. The poet struck out for the open bay with the cry of 'Now let us together solve the great mystery.' Feeling himself a 'glowworm' beside Lord Byron's dazzling sun, Shelley swore that he would abandon verse (while heaping up mounds of unfinished translations, historical dramas, projected epics). He wrote to Trelawny asking if he knew anyone 'capable of preparing the Prussic Acid'. Suicide: my mail-order bride.

He was a river sailor, Thames excursionist, book in one hand, tiller under the elbow, not a deepwater man. Byron commissioned the *Bolivar*, a decked, seaworthy yacht; while Shelley, with help from his friend Williams, designed a cranky and unstable twenty-four-footer. A wooden craft with too much sail and not enough hull. She had to carry two tonnes of pig iron as ballast. Along with a name Shelley didn't want: Byron arranged for Captain Roberts to paint *his* choice on the sail. So *Don Juan* it was. The closest Shelley came to his preferred *Ariel* was the quote from *The Tempest* that Trelawny put on his grave (in the Protestant Cemetery in Rome). 'Nothing of him that doth fade / But doth suffer a sea change / Into something rich and strange.'

The Casa Magni, a former 'Jesuit convent', looked, as Holmes says, like a bleached skull. This house, near San Terenzo, taken for the summer, was rife with premonitions. Or so posthumous Shelley cultists would have us believe. Shelley suffered from nightmares, driving his wife from the bed with terrible screams. He said that he had not been asleep but had seen a vision.

Edward Dowden (in his 1886 biography):

He dreamt that lying as he did in bed, Edward and Jane [Williams] came in to him; they were in the most horrible condition – their bodies lacerated, their bones starting through their skin, the faces pale yet stained with blood . . . Edward said, 'Get up Shelley; the sea is flooding the house, and it is all coming down.' Shelley got up, he thought, and went to the window that looked on the terrace and the sea, and thought he saw the sea rushing in.

Worse was to follow: Shelley met himself out on the terrace, a double who said, 'How long do you mean to be content?' The fetch established an identity quite independent of the poet, the dreamer. But located firmly in place, the broad terrace of the former convent. The position from which Mary Shelley would watch the sea, when her husband did not return from his voyage to Leghorn.

The last emotional attachment of Shelley's life was for Jane, the (courtesy) wife of his friend Edward Williams. He presented Jane with a guitar which was to become one of the most notable relics of the Shelley cult. This dark, calm woman seems to have had the gift of suggesting much by saying little, keeping clear of literary squabbles, the posturings of poets and pretenders. Mary liked her, as a companion for afternoon walks. 'Jane and I are off together,' she wrote to Mrs Leigh Hunt (Marianne Kent), 'and talk morality and pluck violets by the way . . . She has a very pretty voice, and a taste and ear for music which is almost miraculous.'

Living communally with this troop of world-class neurotics, anarchist rentiers and bluestocking totty, Jane Williams was taken for a person of sensibility, but no great imagination. They liked to make a picture of her, a plaintive soundtrack for their experiments in auto-destruction: sweet Jane floating on the bay by moonlight, strumming her guitar.

Anna Sinclair, in her youth, knew the syndrome all too well. She weathered maelstroms of performance angst, expelling kitchen-squatters, poets and camp followers, into the street (after three or four days of herbal monologues and ill-tuned guitars). She beat off dazed admirers who turned up at our Hackney house claiming a lifelong fascination with ley lines or multiple-superimposition 8mm film. It dawned on me, very early in the game, that most of the men, husbands, pre-famous sculptors, who arrived late with invitations to very private views, or expressed their eagerness to chauffeur us to a cinema club or Charlotte Street meal, were not acknowledging my remarkable talent, my brilliant conversation. They wanted the chance to feed, however circumspectly, on Anna's aura: that impenetrable look called unconcern.

Even as a child, an adolescent, she had been the still point, as outsiders saw it, in an outrageous family. Letters of acid denunciation from co-drivers on trips through France – ruined picnics, tragic treats, stinking cheese – would single Anna out as 'calm, serene and beautiful'. It's an unbeatable act, absence. Detachment. Going deep into your own thoughts. Letting furies exhaust themselves: before you erupt, to everyone's amazement, with a kitchen-pot projectile, a brick aimed at your brother's head. It was always Anna who was sent for, to be with her father when he was in one of his darker moods.

The terrace of Casa Magni, a house in which every occupant dreamt competitively, becomes a platform of psychic manifestations. Jane on the water with her guitar. Jane anticipating Shelley's split self, the flying soul and the drowned soul. Dowden describes the episode:

She was standing one day . . . at a window that looked on the terrace . . . she saw, as she thought, Shelley pass by the window, as he often was then, without a coat or jacket; he passed again. Now, as he passed both times the same way, and as from the side towards which he went each time there was no way to get back except past the window again . . . she was struck at seeing him pass twice thus, and looked out and seeing him no more she cried, 'Good God! can Shelley have leapt from the wall? Where can he be gone?' 'Shelley?' said Trelawny; 'no Shelley has past. What do you mean?' Trelawny says that she trembled exceedingly when she heard this; and it proved indeed, that Shelley had never been on the terrace, and was far off at the time she saw him.

Children abandoned in nunneries. Miscarriages. Barbarous natives singing and shouting on the beach. Family bankruptcy back in England (Mary's father, William Godwin). Bills to be settled. Fantasies of living quietly on some Greek island. Visions arrived more frequently than the post. The Shelley circle were disturbed by the news that Claire Clairmont's young daughter, left by her father (Lord Byron) in a convent in the Romagna, had died of typhus fever. The poet, walking on the terrace at Casa Magni, 'observing the effect of moonshine on the water' (as Edward Williams reports), felt uneasy; gripping his friend by the arm, he 'stared steadfastly on the white surf that broke upon the beach'.

He recovered after some time, and declared that he saw, as plainly as he then saw me, a naked child (Allegra) rise from the sea, and clap its hands in joy, smiling at him. This was a trance that it required some reasoning and philosophy entirely to awaken him from, so forcibly had the vision operated on his mind. Our conversation, which had been at first rather melancholy, led to this; and my confirming his sensations by confessing that I had felt the same, gave greater activity to his wandering and ever-lively fancy.

In so many texts of the Romantic era, there is a collective delusion: poets exploit images of drowning, naked Blakean babes crying for joy. Time is an unstable medium, devalued by prophetic dreams. Shelley, so Trelawny and other witnesses insist, is childlike, a boy. Hair flopping across his eyes, he is mired in voices; torrents of verse from which he must extract two or three serviceable lines.

'I often saw him in a state of nudity,' wrote Trelawny, 'and he always reminded me of a young Indian, strong-limbed and vigorous, and there were few men who would walk on broken ground at the pace he kept up; he beat us all in walking, and, barring drugs and accidents, he might have lived as long as his father – to ninety.'

As the excesses of Shelley's life began to unravel, the hours of his days ceased to be atomic and became oceanic: he developed a theory of time. None was available to him, his store was used up. He had lived so intensely, spent so recklessly, that he was now an older man than his father, his grandfather. 'I am ninety years old.' Poetry plea-bargains with an uncertain future. Always a weak bet: the poem as a machine for achieving immortality. Shelley bought it. Subtle mnemonics. Secret music that burrows through our defence systems like an intelligent virus. Original clichés laying their syrup over dull tongues. 'He hath awakened from the dream of life.'

Romantic poets, dying in clusters, killed the poetry franchise: and just at the point when John Clare was launching a public career. Keats, coughing his last in Rome, set the pattern. All his contemporaries were obliged to pen a tribute. (Mick Jagger, in gauzy drag, tried a cover version of Shelley, at the Hyde Park 'Free' concert: his immediate response to the face-down swim of Brian Jones. And the launching of a nest of conspiracy theories that would rival those generated by the wreckage of the *Don Juan*. Shelley's first wife, Harriet, carrying his child, also died in the park. By drowning herself in the Serpentine.)

'Here lieth One whose name was writ on water.' Shelley, in his 'Fragment on Keats', quotes the consumptive poet's chosen epitaph. Keats dies in 1821 and is buried in Rome's Protestant Cemetery. Clare writes a sonnet in his memory and sends it to their shared publisher, Taylor: 'Just a few beats of the heart – the head has nothing to do with them.' Shelley composes *Adonais*, while staying at Pisa, in June 1821. He is drowned on a voyage between Leghorn and Lerici on 8 July 1822. Trelawny adds a tag from *The Tempest* to Shelley's memorial stone. He burns his hand, pulling the poet's heart from the improvised funeral pyre on the beach. Byron swims out to his yacht, the *Bolivar*.

Williams was grilled on an iron furnace, slowly, splashed with wine, oil and spices. The author of *Don Juan* decided to 'try the strength' of the waters that had robbed him of his friends. He swam until he became sick, a mile out. On his return, there was nothing left of Williams but 'a quantity of blackish-looking ashes, mingled with white and broken fragments of bone'. Two years later, Byron died of a fever at Missolonghi. His funeral procession in London was witnessed by John Clare.

Coming back to England, after the European tour that gave him the material for *Childe Harold*, Byron learnt that his Cambridge

friend Charles Skinner Matthews ('Citoyen') was dead. This 'brilliant and witty' young man had drowned in a river, having become
tangled in weeds.

Personal tragedies are mythologised, reported by such unreliable
witnesses as Trelawny and Shelley's cousin Thomas Medwin. Mary
Shelley's memoirs of her husband, her edition of the poems, have
to be tempered by the requirement of not offending Sir Timothy
Shelley; and thereby forfeiting her small allowance. Continental
Europe, in the wake of the Napoleonic Wars, was sticky with
officers on half-pay. Disgraced society figures faffing about Florence
under assumed names. Minor aristocrats and younger sons
borrowing on their expectations. Most, it seems, had pretensions
to write. They hunted extant wildlife with guns and dogs. But
above all they hunted literary lions.

In summer months, the English exiles liked to play at being
sailors. Shelley with his skiff on the river, his paper boats. Marine
doodles in the margins of manuscripts. Lord Byron commissioned
the *Bolivar* to complement his exotic servants, Italian mistresses,
catamites, horses, hounds, apes and cockatoos. Tales of the club-
footed poet reached the young Clare in Helpston, at the time when
he was considering an apprenticeship with the cobbler Will Farrow.
Farrow's brother Tom had been a sailor. A sailor who kept a
journal.

Jonathan Bate:

Only one passage stuck in Clare's memory: an account of a traveller who
once sailed on a ship on which Farrow served, 'an odd young man lame of
one foot on which he wore a cloth shoe – who was of a resolute temper,
fond of bathing in the sea and going ashore to see ruins in a rough sea
when it required six hands to manage the boat.' He was so demanding
that 'his name became a bye word in the ship for unnecessary trouble.'
The name – and this was the first time that Clare heard it – was Byron.

By the time he is taken to High Beach, the asylum in Epping
Forest, Clare is possessed by the spirit of Byron. He is recomposing

'Don Juan' and 'Child Harold' as parallel texts. Romanticism is dead, but the energies it sponsored are still active. The first two cantos of Byron's *Don Juan*, published in 1819, three years before Shelley's fatal voyage, can be interpreted as rehearsing the coming tragedy in the Bay of Spezia.

> Juan embark'd – the ship got under way,
>> The wind was fair, the water passing rough;
> A devil of a sea rolls in that bay,
>> As I, who've crossed it, oft, know well enough;
> And standing upon the deck, the dashing spray
>> Flies in one's face, and makes it weather-tough.

Juan is in flight: 'steering duly for the port of Leghorn'.

> At sunset they began to take in sail,
> For the sky show'd it would come on to blow,
> And carry away, perhaps, a mast or so.

Poetry, like the neurasthenic dreams of the Casa Magni, precedes human drama. A spectacular death will underwrite a legendary life, sell future volumes. It establishes a necrophile industry, a taste for epitaphs. As Richard Holmes concludes, in his *Guardian* essay, Shelley will have to be 'undrowned'; recovered, reassembled. His biography, up to this point, has been forged from sanctified relics, provided by dutiful descendants, pious benefactors. A Catholic cult grows up around an avowed atheist. Museums and colleges manufacture shrines.

Lady Shelley, wife of Percy Florence (Shelley's son), made a votive chapel of Boscombe Manor, the family home. She burnt letters, clipped out offensive passages, harried potential biographers. She designed an inner sanctum with domed turquoise ceiling, set with gold stars. Female visitors were advised to remove their hats. A memorial was shaped like a pietà. The boneless poet: a sacrificed corpse in Mary Shelley's arms. Letters, books, fragments of bone, locks of hair. The barbecued heart was wrapped in a copy of *Adonais* and laid in a silk-lined box.

A pilgrimage to Italy was arranged for Lady Shelley and her son. She slept in the poet's room at Casa Magni, willing the visions that wouldn't come. Elderly fisherfolk were interrogated for their memories of the fatal voyage. Cultists wanted to prove that the *Don Juan* had been rammed by a Leghorn felucca, pirates after Lord Byron's gold. Spars and shattered oars: relics of the true cross. A ninety-three-year-old woman claimed to have witnessed the burning of the bodies on the beach. It was said that the ashes of the two gentlemen had been taken to England so that they could, by witchcraft, be brought back to life.

Old Trelawny, irascible as ever, made a fiction of Shelley, a distorted mirror image. 'He wrote his poems in the open air; on the sea shore; the pine woods; and like a shepherd, he could tell the time of day exactly by the light. He never had a watch.'

Richard Holmes has whetted my taste for relics. I want to view, in Northampton, the gathered volumes from John Clare's library, the notebook with 'Journey out of Essex'. I want to gawp at his snuffboxes and his watch (he did have one). I'm fascinated by objects associated with the *Don Juan* legend: the spy-glass recovered from the wreck, the 'mostly rotten' books preserved in blue mud. It would be especially unnerving to handle these. The copy of Keats, borrowed from Leigh Hunt, spine split by being crammed into Shelley's pocket, was gone. Burnt. A 'drowned' notebook, salvaged by Captain Roberts, survives: 'A quickening life from the Earths heart has (burst).' The notebook was presented to the Bodleian Library at Oxford in 1946. The original is fading fast. It is harder to read than the photographic reproductions made in 1992.

The *Guardian* essay wraps up with a meditation on time. 'What is the "time of death"?' Holmes asks. He mentions the fact that Shelley's gold watch, like so many of his manuscripts and memorials, is now kept at the Bodleian. I knew that I would have to break away from Clare, come at him from another direction: I made plans to visit Oxford. Anything to delay the writing of my book.

Oxford

'Can you fix it for me to see Shelley's watch?'

I had one contact in Oxford, in academia, and I exploited it shamelessly. My man enjoyed a challenge, the opportunity to demonstrate his status, the ability to open doors that would otherwise require painful negotiation, explanatory letters, covering notes from publishers. Brian Catling, Head of Sculpture at the Ruskin School of Fine Art, was a prophecy come to fruition. Years ago, when I'd known him as a fellow labourer in breweries and dog patches, Limehouse graveyards, Ratcliffe kennels, I'd promoted him to professorial status in a novel called *Downriver*. I mythologised Catling as a committee man, enthusiastic diner; a social being who would never compromise the thing that mattered most, his work. Which was frequently out of sight, elsewhere (Norway, Iceland, Israel, Japan); or published in limited-edition chapbooks, abandoned (show over) in the nearest skip.

Catling was an old soul. In an old town. He was happy to facilitate my request. We would meet for lunch at a restaurant in a converted bank, a few doors up the High Street from the Ruskin School of Art. Then we'd amble over to the Bodleian for our appointment with the wondrously named Mr B. C. Barker-Benfield. Who would produce the drowned watch. Catling worked hard, doing the bureaucratic stuff, dealing with those pests, the students, but left time for gun clubs, haunting the Pitt Rivers collection, taking his boat on the river. That had always been his obsession, water; if he didn't drink much of it, he enjoyed nothing more than cruising the Thames, canoeing through Oxford's labyrinthine and overgrown backstreams, heading out into the North Sea with a paralytic skipper and a phantom crew.

Oxford is Fleet Street with a hangover: slower, longer in the tooth. Nothing much happens in the tolerated gap between Uxbridge and Headington. (Somewhere to plant microwaved celebrities.) The road west is Thames Valley phenobarbitone, play country. You leave the metropolis with red contact lenses, a thick tongue, too much blood washing against the lid of your skull, and Oxford confirms it. The distance is just enough. Close your eyes, suck one of Catling's superstrength cough sweets, and you're there: among refused-entry colleges, a centre given over to war memorials, martyrs' crosses, bus stops and deep-trace cultural busking. Gargoyles leer. Gothic architecture preens. Heritage shops have run low on stock, lost their Americans. Professor Catling travels backwards and forwards, Oxford to London, family obligations, art business, on the coach: nursing a bottled Scottish nightcap. In town, he patronises taxis. 'I gave up public transport years ago,' he says. 'Don't have the time for it.'

If I can't walk to Oxford, I'll drive. I like to feel the umbilical cord stretching. This is safe, this is still London. Cowley Road has the feral, dangerous charm of Clapton. You can buy the *Evening Standard*. Eat ethnic. Get tattooed, fixed up, mugged. Cross Magdalen Bridge and you'll be trampled by a conga of overexcited dons rushing towards the station, on their way to TV studios, bookshop events; the media hassle that proves their continued viability.

With this new hotel, the Old Bank, Oxford comes into line with Clerkenwell. Invisible cash converted into visible design. And back again. You no longer have to rely on the dreadful Randolph, with its embargo on courtesy, its complicated parking and time-warp dining room (bus queues of Bosch-monsters pressed against the windows). The Old Bank displays an original sketch by Stanley Spencer in every bedroom, corridors of Wyndham Lewis, Patrick Hughes, Sandra Blow. A catalogue is available at the front desk. You have to speak advanced Sewell before they'll let you near the Quod Restaurant, with its devastatingly slick service and novel food (you can eat it).

A cold, moist day: 20 February 2004. I spot Catling, ahead of me, weaving effortlessly through released office workers, newly risen students. He might be a banker or one of the hotel's featured artists. I notice his doppelgänger in the City, Brighton, Cologne. It's my age, everybody looks like somebody else. The man with the thick silver hair, long black coat, moves with stately intent. A type. Touch his shoulder and prove your mistake. But, for once, I call the right name; we are nodded straight through to our table. An actor-manager of the old school, Catling throws off his coat, orders a pair of chilled vodka martinis and settles back to scan the menu.

Food taken, wine swilled, I produce a small collection of photographs from a recent tour, with Anna, through Clare country. There are things I want to show Catling. I have the prints arranged in a particular order. I click them down, one after the other, on the cleared table. An inscription on a Northborough grave. A child's toy in an unexpected location. A young girl riding a shaggy horse through the outskirts of an ugly town. Tall chimneys on the rim of a quarry. An unidentified skull (with snout) impaled on a stick. A canal seen through the smeared windscreen of a car. Ramsey Abbey in the rain.

A loose narrative carries us back to another expedition, undertaken thirty years ago. A strange period: auditory hallucinations, too much cider mixed with Russian stout, books beginning to be published. Much wandering, late and early, across London. Somewhere, it might have been the deserted Whitechapel Gallery or the Roebuck in Durward Street, I heard a voice say: 'Ramsey holds the key.' Which I took, for no good reason, to be a reference to Ramsey Abbey. That ancient island in the Fens.

We drove up the A1. Found the town and the church. But no key. Too rushed, I thought. We should have walked, allowed time for the right questions to form. Londoners in an amphibian environment, we paddled around unwelcoming streets: bakers of monumental loaves, funeral parlours, decayed warehouses servicing a dead river.

The rest of the afternoon, under lowering skies, we toured the Fens; Catling was not then much of a map-reader. Long, wet roads on raised banks above canals. Lone bungalows. Clumps of trees

standing forlorn in hedgeless fields, reclaimed from the water. We circled this unknown and unknowable territory, until we arrived at Ely. The spire had been a marker of sorts. Defeat.

Nothing was settled. That phrase, 'Ramsey holds the key', nagged. Stayed with me. Did it refer to a Scottish occultist or the poet (who had his place in Clare's library)? Should I visit one of the other Ramseys? I tried a few without revelation. Then let it go, until now.

We discuss bears (remembering them from the window of the Ramsey undertakers, child memorials). And why people in such a flat landscape, with no experience of mountain and forest creatures, except as fairground freaks, should adopt the bear as totem. I quote

Clare's phrase about being dragged into Stamford like a bear to a wake. Why would that be? Dancing bears, I supposed, were exhibited at village fairs. But funerals? I recall the skinned and headless bears found floating in the River Lea. Catling says that his wife, Sarah Simblet, has an interesting notion about the potency of such animals in the Fen country. It's verticality in a horizontal world, the looming power. Like iron posts rising out of drained Whittlesey Mere. Like chimneys at the quarry's edge.

When I walked over to pick up my coat, the vertical Catling, smoothly ursine, had vanished. I found him at the bar, taking a quick shot, before we braved the Bodleian. There were a few minutes in hand. He suggested a look at the Shelley memorial in University College. A delightful notion. I am now an approved visitor, the treasures of the colleges are available. It is all slightly unreal, the arcana of Oxford, under the glaze of drink.

At the north-west corner of the Front Quad, Staircase Three, exposed in its chill nakedness, is the Shelley autopsy by Edward Onslow Ford. The effigy was carved in 1894, intended for the Protestant Cemetery in Rome (they declined the suggestion). The human Shelley was removed from Oxford University (after a few months of shooting, walking, pyrotechnic experiments and accosting women with babies), for publishing a pamphlet advocating *The Necessity of Atheism*. Shedloads of relics bring him back: letters, manuscripts (genuine and forged), locks of hair, snuffboxes, touched-up portraits. The Victorian necrophile apparatus. This was a second matriculation, initiated by Lady Shelley (his son's formidable widow); a matriculation in doctored memory, improved and improving biography. Atheist as secular saint: overseeing a sorority of drowned wives, suicided camp-followers, disappointed mistresses and sorry infants who gave up the ghost.

Shelley was painted less frequently than Clare: who lived long enough to be photographed. The Northampton peasant is recorded in his youthful pomp (the Hilton in the National Portrait Gallery), in maturity, in madness. The sole portrait of Shelley, by Amelia Curran, has to be adapted, fudged: for use as a future frontispiece, a locket miniature for the lovesick. Shelley's likeness, vague as Shakespeare's, is as liable to misattribution. (He was lucky to avoid being turned into a novel by Anthony Burgess.)

What we want is a way of hiding the poetry, that difficulty, so we trade in the fiction of biography; selective quotation dresses a dramatic life. Dead as mutton, the veggie republican Percy Shelley is neutralised in satin-finish marble: a premature trust fund hippie. The accident of the boat wreck is rebranded as martyrdom. A chaos of wives, debts, bad karma, justifies the neurosis of composition.

The first boat that Williams and Shelley kitted out was intended to save them from the tedious walk between Pisa and Livorno. They sailed up the canal by moonlight. The boat capsized, foundered. The non-swimming Shelley was rescued.

Our ducking last night has added fire instead of quenching the nautical ardour which produced it: and I consider it as a good omen in any enterprise that it begins in evil: as more probable that it will end in good . . .

But fire, like the bright moon, was unquenched, it was waiting on the beach. Those leisurely cruises up the Thames – Marlow, Oxford, Lechlade – were no preparation for the Bay of Spezia. The sickly poet, advised by his medical man William Lawrence, had to choose between relocation to the English South Coast or another Mediterranean tour.

The Ford sculpture in University College offers a version of Trelawny's naked boy: Shelley, drained of blood, a hairless albino. Sprawled on a bed of salt. Rescued from quicklime. He is like one of those modelled wax exhibits in medical museums that Catling loves, a romantic conceit symbolising the death of poetry. Or the shift of poetry, from a medium that could factor complex scientific experiments, political theory, refractions of Goethe, to vapid song. Mourning crêpe and yellow waistcoats. Ford's Shelley is a radiant fish on a baroque mount (bare-breasted, drooping muse): better suited to cathedral aisle or catacomb. Horribly exposed and shameless in this Oxford cage.

The autopsy aspect seems quite modern; the way that the sprawling, flaccid Shelley is a minor detail in a grander composition. The space in which the monument is contained is part of the argument: a drained pool (out of Leighton), a drowning chamber, an operating theatre for a poet whose heart has been ripped out. Dry leaves have blown through iron gates (which are intended to exclude students and pranksters). They dress the base of the monument, scattered rose petals. Acanthus leaves are gilded. English Romanticism atrophies into Hammer Films Gothic: part theatre, part ritual (botched). The scale is wrong. A diminutive corpse lying on its side, ready to donate a kidney. A plump, unemployed muse contemplating her navel.

Professor Catling, the sculptor who doesn't sculpt, recognises the ensemble (stiff, slab, plinth, pool) as a potential location for performance. For voice. Recently, he has been afflicted by an entity he calls 'Large Ghost'. A being who 'signs its presence in tricks, enigmas and predictions, small visions, jangling keys, blood spots hours before the accident; haiku of mortality'. Energy escapes from mute stone, from slow meat. And Catling is preternaturally alert to its passage. His poetry is abrupt, spare, briskly purposeful. Shocking. It snatches at breath and never wastes a word. No padding, no fat. No apologies.

> Sad and foreign: a shaved panda,
> a twin of violence coying
> in its buff squint.

Two gentlemen in very tight suits, one with spectacles, one without, lurking in a doorway: Mr Barker-Benfield and a colleague. The quadrangle of the Bodleian. An enclosure in which I once watched John Thaw do his walk; a hobbled equine kick that struggled to disguise a malfunctioning leg, as he investigated yet another Oxford massacre (an assassination during the encaenia procession). You never know when one of these ceremonies will erupt out of the cobbles and courtyards; even the likes of Professor Catling are expected to perform, dragged up in robes, ratty trimmings. They march, stern or stoic, through a mob of dull watchers, lazy cameras.

Scooting up stairways with Barker-Benfield is rather like being in an episode of *Morse*: finger the guilty man. For failing to appreciate real ale and choral song. Chippy remarks are hedged by inverted commas. This is a viva for which I'm horribly underprepared. If I was expecting a cobwebby attic, creaking muniment chest, I was rapidly disabused. A small hot office. A locked stationery cupboard. The kind of storage boxes in which VAT returns are kept. Then, before I caught my breath, two pocket watches of immaculate provenance are set on the desk. My challenge – fail and we'll see nothing more – is to decide which watch belonged to Edward Williams and which to Percy Bysshe Shelley, poet and gent.

Catling steps back. The archivists smirk. It falls to me, the outsider who made the nuisance request, to do the business. And in that instant I realise how stupid I've been. The Richard Holmes essay, 'Death and Destiny', seemed to suggest that Shelley's watch had been recovered from the body of the drowned man. How so? The watches gleam like golden eggs. They haven't been dug from quicklime, preserved in mud. The frisson I solicited, death rattle, loss of heat, was not available. Laid out for inspection were two sober relics, left behind at the Casa Magni when the voyage to Leghorn was undertaken.

Visiting an exhibition of literary manuscripts in Ferrara, November 1818, Shelley said: 'You know I always seek in what I see the manifestations of something beyond the present and tangible object.'

I studied marks on the surface of the desk; vinegar-grey leather pitted with deep scratches. What other relics had been examined, fondled, lovingly evaluated by B. C. Barker-Benfield?

One watch had a case and a heavy, serrated ring (by which to attach it to a chain); the other was plainer – more elegant? I didn't hesitate. I stepped forward, twitched a sleeve, made a mysterious pass over the meticulously positioned objects. I felt the heat on my open palm. The riddle was simple. A low murmur: 'Ah yes.' A grunt. 'This one,' I said. 'No question. Shelley.'

The library men were impressed. Now all the treasures of the Bodleian were available to us. They scuttle about, sliding open drawers, unwrapping packages, smoothing tissue. It was like a divvy-up between consenting antique-dealers in Camden Passage: expensive clutter smothers the neutrality of the stilled watches. Rather nasty stuff. A bloodstone. A seal with Shelley's coat of arms. An oval onyx *Judgement of Paris*. An amethyst engraved: 'Mary Shelley'. The date-letter on the watch-case is 1814. This instrument, Barker-Benfield surmises, replaced the one Shelley sold in Paris. The desk is littered with potent scrap: gold chains to tangle around the legs of a drowning man. The watch is a mechanical heart to balance in the palm of your hand.

How had I worked my magic? A trick, of course. The watches gave out at different times, death being susceptible to the laws of relativity. I remembered the Holmes article, his inaccurate assertion that Shelley's watch had 'stopped at precisely sixteen minutes past five'. The plainer watch said: eighteen minutes past two. Shelley's fat gold job, from which heat could still be dowsed, was fixed at eighteen minutes past five. Perhaps it had gained a couple of minutes since Holmes carried out his research? Time leaked very slowly in this hot room. My photographs of the watches are fuzzy, Dali-soft. The witnesses have aureoles of flame emerging from the necks of their close-buttoned suits.

We touched sheets of manuscript corroded with brown ink. But, once the connection with the drowning, the beach barbecue, the visions and presentiments of the Casa Magni, was lost, my involvement with the relics was polite. A draft of *Frankenstein* was produced as the curator's final flourish. Mary's holograph with Shelley's revisions and editorial suggestions: 'A pale student of unhallowed arts kneeling beside the thing he had put together.'

We take it in turns to view the pages. Mary's phrase about 'the dreams of forgotten alchymists', Barker-Benfield reckons, could be 'a specific echo of the Oxford visit of 1815'.

Frankenstein (or, The Modern Prometheus) was another workable Clare metaphor. 'I continued walking in this manner for some time, endeavouring by bodily exercise to ease the load that weighed upon my mind . . . My heart palpitated in the sickness of fear, and I hurried on with irregular steps, not daring to look about me.' Dr Frankenstein and his creature walk. Compulsively. The monster, assembled from spare parts, ex-human quotations, is another Clare. He speaks, moves, suffers. Patrons and medical men revise him to suit their picture of what a peasant poet should be. Grateful. Innocent. Sober.

The *Frankenstein* manuscript had been part of a successful bicentennial Shelley exhibition: first editions, relics. Barker-Benfield wrote the catalogue. Now something on the Godwins is proposed. Budget: three and a half million. Small change. Three is already in place. Can Catling help to make up the shortfall? Favour for favour. The professor pats his pockets, coughs. Time to be moving on. Lectures, engagements. See what he can do.

Where next? The cigar shop on the High, obviously. Another privileged space. Private cabinets. Humidifiers. Rituals of subservience and discretion. Even the wall displays are occulted: scarlet triangles and swords on a Montecristo lid, the Masonic symbolism of enlarged dollar bills. Catling rummages, fondling the goods, sticks of dynamite. He's not smoking these days, not really, a modest Cohiba will suffice. Gold band like undersized wedding ring: *Habana, Cuba*.

We're back in the flat above the sculpture studios, last night's feast on the table; whisky bottle for the prof, wine for me. We plot a boat trip, down the Nene from Peterborough, reprising Clare's adolescent voyage to Wisbech. Catling thinks he can get his cruiser, by easy stages, to Northampton. Then, through almost fifty locks, to Peterborough. It will take most of the summer.

We watch the video version of a film by Philip Trevelyan, *The Moon and the Sledgehammer*. Which shifts, very neatly, as Catling knows it will, between my pursuit of John Clare and my fondness for the work of the playful documentarist, Andrew Kötting. (Who has recently relocated to St Leonards. Given his preoccupations, an inevitable exile.)

The film witnesses a submerged family in a Sussex forest. English eccentrics, who tend traction engines, are languaged in ways the rest of us, chewed over by urban life, have put aside. My cigar is a soggy stub. Certain passages of this epic are, no doubt, replayed. We are spared interventions by the director, gibbering by presenters. Faces. Voices. Black kettles. Shotguns. Stubbled cheeks. Rollups grafted to rubber lips. A woman, illuminated by real and imagined sleights, speaks of the harshness of her hidden life. Mad monologues achieve the condition of poetry. A floating moon. A bloody hare. Solitaries, cohabiting in an extended family, wait for a chance to escape. Or kill. Or make their song.

The only way to get anywhere near this profligate blend of inbreeding and seclusion is on water. Water slows time to a walking pace. Catling's proposed Fenland boat trip will resolve our confusions, float us free of duty, the necessary mundane of everyday life. John Clare travelled by water, as an initiation, and was refused. He marched to the sea with a sack of his own books. Many hours of his life were spent beside rivers. Northampton was a river town, served by the Nene. Northampton kept the notebook with the journal of Clare's walk. I would go there next.

Northampton

John Clare returned to Northborough, to the home that was not a home, the wife who was not a wife, children (actual and imagined): the existential pointlessness of freedom. 'Poet's Cottage' was a future teddy bear reservation, a twenty-first-century toy shop waiting to happen. It didn't belong to him and it never would. Northborough was a dark place on the edge of a greater darkness, it was not Helpston. He was out of his knowledge and out of work. He had betrayed his heritage by celebrating it. He was condemned by the journal he kept. The walk from Epping Forest divided him from his former self, left him playing out time: an unscripted performance. Three and a half days on the road cancelled the four London visits, the memories accepted and authenticated by family and friends. Clare's walk confirmed his non-existence, a fugue of forgetting.

Mary Joyce, dead Mary, was the only constant in this mental landscape: a muse to be reclaimed. She was the force of the last poems written by Clare as Clare, before other selves, Byron and the rest, absorbed him; before the no-self of Northampton. 'The vast shipwreck of my lifes esteems.'

Patty tried him and found him wanting, a stranger, a man of unpredictable moods and uncertain temper. His melancholy was a potent infection. He would walk out with one of his sons; it was a leave-taking between generations, the living and the dead. He might prowl the confines of the garden: as a rehearsal for the grander spaces of Northampton, woodland overlooking a river. The despair clutching his heart might be a matter of sluggish blood, diet, thyroid deficiency; treatable dysfunctions of body chemistry and inheritance. Poisoned dreams. There is fear here, the inability to walk further into the fields. Watchers. Doctors' men. Clare's intelligence struggled with crushing circumstance and composed an apologia, a settling of accounts.

A letter to Matthew Allen:

I should [like] to be to myself a few years & lead the life of a hermit – but even there I should wish from one whom I am always thinking of & almost every Song I write has some sighs & wishes in Ink for Mary.

A meditation on 'Self Identity':

I shall never be in three places at once nor ever change to a woman & that ought to be some comfort.

'Autumn': an elegy for a known and loved horizon, after which he could be disposed of, locked away, trained in oblivion. A mental flight before banishment.

The plot of meadows now dont look bigger then a large homestead & the ponds that used to seem so large are now no bigger then puddles & as for fish I scarcely have interest enough to walk round them to see if there is any . . . Now the man is putting off his boat to ferry over the water where an odd passenger may now & then call to be ferried over the lake to the other bank or high road.

The ferrymen came, came for him. Parson Mossop reported on Clare's 'want of restraint'. Patty applied to Earl Fitzwilliam of Milton Hall. The Northamptonshire peasant poet, certified by two doctors, Fenwick Skrimshire of Peterborough and William Page of Market Deeping, was removed to the recently built Northampton General Lunatic Asylum. Where he would be kept for twenty-two years, the rest of his life.

If he journeyed along the axis of the Great North Road, he was allowed to return. The road was his spine. Sideways, crab fashion, to the east? By river? This too was permitted. Sent home from Wisbech as: 'unfinished'. But the lurch, south-west, to Northampton, could never be rescinded: meat thickened on the bone, before melting in dissolution. No more to be said. Fate accepted: a necessary dole.

The one thing I knew about Northampton, walking up the hill from the railway station (where I'd failed to meet Renchi), was that I'd got it wrong. My previous visit, fifteen years earlier, left me with a grievously warped impression; twitched by reading Alan Moore's serial novel, *Voice of the Fire*. It was Moore who invited me in the first place: a signing at a local bookshop, followed by a poetry reading in a Templar church, the Holy Sepulchre. With Brian Catling. Another Northampton virgin. (According to Moore, bears were kept at 'the top end of a lane', near the church.)

The bookshop event was salutary; it disabused me of the notion that I might, one day, sell a book outside London. Until you've been there, somewhere like Northampton, you don't understand the system. I used to imagine that published novelists made livings comparable to bus conductors (remember them?) or postmen (another anachronism); new titles, pre-computerisation, would be distributed throughout England, after having been reviewed and promoted.

This was a proper do, the kind now reserved for non-writing writers, faces with hovering PR accompanists: refreshments, a heap of books ('returns' on day release from the warehouse), folk milling around the display (lifting a title, reading the blurb, returning it to the pyre). We kept up the weather talk, motorway talk, until it became obvious that they were all employees. It was a duty, to play the crowd, drink the drink, nibble ostentatiously. A rep breezed in, to witness the debacle. I had the courtesy title then of 'poetry editor' for one of Rupert Murdoch's satellites, which meant that I approved hardbacks that would appear as paperbacks. And I initiated mini-anthologies, career retrospectives soon to be pulped. I couldn't find any of these on the shelves. Making conversation, I asked the rep why this was. 'Do we publish poetry?' he said.

Not one book sold. All the non-shows at the shop were already camped out in the round church, a nice cross-section of longhairs, bright eyes (no pupils) and red eyes (deltas of blood). Benevolent occultists. Cashiered Hell's Angels. Dopers, anoraks. The pre and post sectioned. Scorch marks at the temples. 'Carve here' tattoos around the throat.

I read first at the Holy Sepulchre. I preached my profane sermon, quietly, making no real impression on the space. Then, as Catling delivered his coded-language formulae, sticky with nerve and edge, a man groaned. Climbed to his feet. And was rapidly expelled. To return with a revolver.

It was, Alan explained, an ordinary Northampton night. The intervention by this 'homicidal medicine-head of local notoriety' was a felt response to Catling's challenge: words nudge the world. The overexcited literary critic was beguiled into a pub, offered a drink. He smashed the glass, lunged at his minder's throat. Teeth were spat on to the floor.

Moore describes the outcome: 'Thrown from the barroom in the wake of his attacker, to the street outside, Fred (the minder) found himself staring into the quivering muzzle of a gun and hoping that he wouldn't die between the Labour Exchange and the Inland Revenue, a victim of that local speciality, the stroll-by shooting . . . Slept downstairs with a sword that night, unconsciously sucked into the crusader aura of the church and the event.'

Warned of the psycho sniper, we dodged through the graveyard into a muted celebration; and, later, the Labour Club. Alan was a member in good standing. Old boys nursed their drinks in a narrow, sepia room. The bearded Northampton magus, recognised and saluted in London, was integrated into this dim and smoky scene; a figure no more or less extraordinary than any of the recreational pint-swallowers. Northampton was Moore's family. He eavesdropped on conversations and conspiracies, waiting, as we all do, for something to exploit.

Place expresses itself through the person you choose as guide: Northampton, in effect, had become a monologue or graphic script by Alan Moore. I hadn't been paying close enough attention. On

Tuesday, 12 August 2003, I returned. To meet Renchi. To stay at the hotel ibis. To inspect the Clare collection in the Central Library. To walk the bounds, the poet's last traces. What struck me about St Andrew's, the revamped Northampton General Lunatic Asylum, was the status of the hospital as a retreat, a green Arcadia, walled off from the seething, boiling dementia of the town. Lovingly-tended grounds were a respite from an excess of normalcy: Carlsberg Brewery, credit card towers, Church's shoe factory. Without knowing it, Northampton had sponsored Alan Moore as laureate. *Voice of the Fire*, a collection of twelve linked tales, was a grimoire of occulted imagination: myths, crimes, witch-burnings. Human legends of the Railway Club, the stolen crates of beer, eccentric uncles with amputated legs, played alongside particulars of geography, geology and gossip. John Clare's shoes might be kept in a glass case at the Central Museum, but you won't find a single copy of Moore's book.

What other notables, in the years after Clare, lodged in the Priory-style hospital? Sheiks, arms brokers, inconvenient royals? Rumours abounded: Dusty Springfield (drying out), Michael Jackson (hiding from the press). Lucia Anna Joyce, daughter of the other James (not the Glinton farmer). J. K. Stephen, Ripper suspect and Cambridge poet, was committed to St Andrew's in 1891. He died there, never having recovered from a blow to the head, received during a visit to Felixstowe. Stephen was a cousin of Virginia Woolf.

Emerging from the station, climbing Black Lion Hill, you appreciate St Peter's, a Norman church (key available from pub): beds of lavender, stone-flagged paths. The house where Cromwell lodged on the night before the Battle of Naseby. The railway station built on the site of the castle where Thomas à Becket was tried. The postern gate has migrated. Or so the plaques, the brochures, inform us.

The railway usurped the power of the river, but the Nene remains a presence, snaking around a hill town. The Northampton template is still visible, a loop of development emphasised on present maps: the noose formed by St Peter's Way, Victoria Promenade, Cheyne Walk, York Road, Broad Street, Horse Market. A town fixed by its cardinal points: gallows at North Gate to Eleanor Cross on the London Road. A market square as generously proportioned, commercially sound, as a Flemish town. Such solidity of purpose demands its Bosch, its painter of demons: its Alan Moore. Along with a supporting cast from the bestiary: bin-bag Goths, discharged squaddies, minicab maniacs cruising for victims (somebody who will listen). A town of random violence. Of parks and pathways: scorched-foot walkers passing unscathed through floods of urgent traffic. Close streets. Old pubs with new signs. Libraries. Nightclub conversions. The county cricket ground. Northampton, above all, is a model of contrary opinions; a displaced capital, seat of alternative scholarship.

'In the thirteenth century,' writes Henry Bett (in *English Legends*), 'as a result of quarrels at Oxford, a large body of students migrated to Northampton, and Henry the Third ordered the authorities of the town to receive them.' Royal licence revoked, numbers of students migrated to Stamford: 'where the lectures of the Augustinian and Carmelite friars were in high repute'. A tradition of hermetic knowledge was established: Stamford and Northampton. A curious door-knocker, which gave title to Brasenose College, survived for years in St Paul's Street, Stamford. The knocker, Bett claims, was identified 'with the brazen head Roger Bacon made for himself by magical arts, which answered every question put to it'. When the head disappeared, the town became the oracle. Mad voices behind leather masks.

Northampton, unlike Peterborough and Oxford, has not been ruined by traffic, by planners. It can support Alan Moore in his terraced house. His cave of books and heretical impedimenta. 'Seaview', he calls it.

I lost Renchi. I met the right train, he was on it; we didn't recognise one another in this context. Our reunion was accomplished at the ibis. An hotel ibis is singular and universal, somewhere and everywhere; customised oddity, generic virtue. Breakfast is available, always, without attendants; fill a bowl, plot your day.

Northampton and Bedford, Renchi reckoned, should be treated as twins, river towns: darkness and light. Each with its own voyager: John Clare and John Bunyan. A tinker imprisoned on a bridge, a farm labourer kept in a park. Northampton sits on a limestone reef, the Jurassic Way from Bath to Lincoln; Bedford floats in water meadows. Alan Moore nominated Bunyan as the 'first to chart the land of spirit and imagination lying under Middle England, mapping actual journeys undertaken in the solid realm on to his allegorical terrain'. I recognised the syndrome, but in reverse: towns were allegorical, peopled by ghosts. The fictions and parables, of Bunyan and Moore, were the only solid ground. Trust what you read, not what you see. My eyes, like Clare's, had skinned over: an inward gaze of virtual navigation. Suitable to towns with too much literature.

We had relics to inspect: Clare's shoes, his books. The death mask. If there was any narrative left, it would be delivered as a catalogue of solid objects, hidden in provincial libraries. I rang Alan Moore and arranged a meeting, later that day, at the portico of All Saints' Church: his suggestion.

As soon as we're moving, on foot, Northampton reveals itself: an illusion. Gold Street. The Guildhall. A display commemorating the day (8 June 1989) when 'HRH the Princess of Wales received the freedom of the Borough'. Painted chart like a board-game: fame and death. The Guildhall, extravagant Gothic revival, does history as theatre: tableaux in alcoves, murals, starry ceiling. A single, tiled and flagged cell beneath the pavement, in which they kept Alfie Rouse – philanderer, accidental murderer, torcher of cars – before he was taken to Bedford and hanged.

There is a statue of a British prime minister, Spencer Perceval, remembered, if at all, for being assassinated; shot, at close range, in the lobby of the House of Commons, by John Bellingham (described as 'a lunatic'). Perceval was once recognised, no minor distinction, as the most reactionary of nineteenth-century premiers. A cobweb spreads, unbrushed, from flared nostril to left shoulder. Dead flies trapped in sagging gossamer. The little finger of Perceval's left hand has been snapped off, restored. Pink drips down white stone: a recurring wound. A motif nobody can be bothered to record, or celebrate.

Northampton librarians are used to Clare fanatics, bursting in without letters of authorisation, research permits; off-road relictrufflers hoping to be pointed in the right direction, let loose among the stacks. We're not trusted with the original 'Journey out of Essex' manuscript, but we are allowed to crank through the microfilm version.

A cabinet of curios, at the head of the stairs, doesn't delay us. Postcard portraits. A bust by Henry Burlowe (plaster toshed to look like bronze). Numerous representations of beings who were never John Clare. A death mask like a wet sheet drawn over a sleeping man: closed lids (eyes without pupils), thin smile. The sharp chin of Mr Punch. A confirmation of absence. The municipal shrine is a secondary imprisonment, keeping the poet in Northampton, along with his papers, his much-prized library. Patty cleared the shelves. The books travelled, as he did, into a definitive exile.

The librarian's counter is high, heaped with papers and forms. She listens to my garbled request, permission to view Clare's books is immediately granted. I wait while the paperwork is completed. Above the desk are two oil portraits, titular Northampton worthies. Thomas Grimshaw's rather wild 1844 vision of Clare parodies the Spencer Perceval pose; left hand clutching lapel, head twisted to observe an approaching figure. The poet stands at the edge of a dark wood, a studio wood. His elevated brow is a kind of pregnant dome. The prominent overhanging eyebrows have been bleached. The beaked nose has butterfly shadows in place of Perceval's cobwebs.

The complementary portrait is of Charles Bradlaugh, atheist, radical, member of parliament. Another of Alan Moore's local heroes. Bradlaugh's statue, islanded in the traffic flow of Abington Square, black finger raised aloft, is a marker in Northampton's psychogeography. Drunks, Moore asserts, try to mount the patriarch from the rear: simulated statuary rape. Students paint footsteps

Edge of the Orison

from plinth to Gents' urinal. Alan depicts the raised digit as: 'pointing resolutely west towards the fields beyond the urban sprawl, assisting Sunday shoppers who've forgotten how to get to Toys 'Я' Us'.

Looking at Clare's books, such a modest bequest, so neatly fitted to a corner of the local history room, I thought again of Joseph Merrick, the Elephant Man. Those who visited the rescued fair-ground freak, in his London Hospital apartment, brought books: to prove their liberality, his redemption. Clare's cottage library is contained in two, free-standing units. A dark wood cupboard and a set of glass-fronted shelves. There is some confusion about the provenance. The lady at the desk tells me that the cupboard belonged to John Taylor, Clare's London publisher. But this is not the case. It was another John Taylor, another publisher, a Northampton man. He bought Clare's books from the widow, Patty. They were transported, with papers and cupboard, to Helpston railway station. In two donkey carts. (As Clare's coffin travelled the other way.)

I scan the shelves, conscious of limited time: the meeting with Alan Moore. The first name to catch my eye is 'Ramsay'. (Shelves have been arranged in alphabetical order, restored after Patty's face-down, book-on-book, Northborough stacking.) Could this be the Ramsay who holds the theoretical key? The clue I missed on my expedition with Brian Catling?

(1) Allan Ramsay: *Poems on Several Occasions*. In two volumes. Berwick, 1793. With ownership stamp: J* CLARE.

I carry the book to the readers' table, scour it, flick through the pages: nothing. A memorial to Clare's sympathy for light verse, the period when he became an elective Scot. No revelation. A sniff at the cloth. Phrase noted: 'How vain are our attempts to know.'

I must proceed in a more methodical fashion, begin with the cupboard. It is too close: the presence of the dead man, the heat of the room. To learn anything of value, I would have to dedicate two years to the business: records of the asylum, critical essays.

Manuscripts examined under Renchi's magnifying glass. Try another approach. Go for the books with fingerprints, personal markings: Clare's confident signature. Name, place, date: 'John Clare, Helpstone, 1820'. The optimism of that moment when his career was launched, his destiny revealed.

Fragments of letters tipped in. Presentation inscriptions from minor and forgotten poets. A coherent collection assembled in a Helpston cottage: poetry, natural history, science, rudiments of grammar. Treasures of an autodidact, a self-improver. In my time as a bookdealer I saw many attics, packed with scavengings of stalls and charity pits, brought together by men of modest means. (They were men, all of them.) Clare's library was no accidental heap. Volumes represented his tribute to contemporary poets (those from whom he could steal with advantage). Theology. Trigonometry (uncut pages). Biographies. Sermons. Base material from which a practical philosophy might be assembled. A working library, not a reliquary protected by initiates. Clare's forlorn bits and pieces, gathered from local sale rooms, haggled carts, left him exposed: peasant poet. A hanged man given for dissection to future anatomists.

(2) Thomas Eastoe Abbot: *The Triumph of Christianity*. 1818. 'The Author of these Poems having received a copy of Mr Clare's poems through his Friend Mr Sergeant begs leave respectfully to present . . .'

(3) John Bunyan: *Holy War*. 1810. With Clare's signature. The name of the previous owner, John Hunt, has been struck through, cancelled.

(4) Lord Byron: *Don Juan in 5 Cantos (A New Edition with Notes)*. n.d. (1818). With three engravings after Corbould. A drowning scene: storm-tossed beach, two women, sprawled man. A prevision of Shelley, mourned by Mary and Jane Williams?

> And, like a wither'd lily, on the land
> His slender frame and pallid aspect lay
> As fair a thing as e'er was form'd of clay.

(5) William Cowper: *Poems*. Clare's signature: 'Helpstone 1819'. And the additional signature of Sophia Clare, his sister. Shared ownership, shared purchase?

(6) Daniel Defoe: *Robinson Crusoe*. 1831. With the inscription: 'Frederick Clare. The gift of Mr. Taylor. Feb 15th 1834.'

(7) Thomas Rowley: *Poems, Supposed to have been written at Bristol by Thomas Rowley, & others. In the Fifteenth Century*. 1757. Published by T. Payne. Clare followed up on his mother's gift from Deeping Market, the Chatterton handkerchief. Pastiches, forgeries. He learnt the art of passing off Elizabethan imitations on unsuspecting (or indifferent) editors of almanacs.

(8) Izaak Walton: *The Compleat Angler*. A handsome beast. Decorative boards.

(9) James Thomson: *The Seasons*. 1818. A new edition of the fatal volume, Clare's introduction to poetry. Carried into Burghley Park.

Volume after volume reveal the history, slanting ownership signature, of a man who refused to soil books with annotations, marginalia, challenges to false authority. Clare was no Graham Greene, 'improving' dull texts with inventive scribbles, in order to boost future sale prices.

The librarian summoned us. The 'Journey out of Essex' microfilm was ready. Winding it through a lightbox, we saw a spread of words: different inks, different spacings, boxed footnotes. Nothing wasted. Clare's narrative strides: it ploughs the field, knitting with barbed wire. The act of composition is physical, you feel the nib gouge at the paper. The escape from High Beach is re-enacted in blocks of vivid prose: 'Reccolections of the Journey from Essex'. Script slants against the breeze. As the days pass, so lines draw closer together; breath comes harder, final flourishes are less flourishing. Clare limps but his story pushes remorselessly towards its conclusion.

Viewing the screen feels like a betrayal: of author and quest. We have been presented with Clare's secret before our own walk is concluded. The key for Ramsey remains obscure. No connection has been discovered between Anna's family and that of John Clare.

The meeting with Alan Moore, the circuit of the asylum he offers, is our farewell to a project that defies resolution. And which may, very soon, be consigned to the storage boxes and dead files of Northampton Library. Marked: 'incomplete'. Abandoned.

The Sun Looks Pale upon the Wall

All Saints' Church in Clare's day was an island, raised above a dirt road by the height of a coach. The present railings, an annoyance, are replicas of the originals; church and business (the caves of Gold Street) were kept apart. Northampton, with its taste for scouring fire, has a long tradition of meaningless feuds, human barbecues. Dislike of successful incomers. On Good Friday, 1277, a number of Jews were drawn 'at the horse-tail' to a chosen place outside the city walls, and there hanged. The following year, the Jewish community was again attacked; property forfeited, men executed on suspicion of clipping and forging: stoned to death.

Twin alcoves, I'm not sure which of them Clare favoured, are worn smooth. They are popular with loungers, tourists wanting to sit where Clare sat: in the local version of Wilhelm Reich's orgone accumulator. A device for concentrating energy, sexual potency. The slots are tall and arched, bald as the peasant poet's skull, his double-decker dome. Stone is warm, shaped by human weight like an outdoor privy: buttock indentations in the polished seat.

We're early. We go inside to inspect another Clare trophy, another severed head: gilded, beaked like a parrot, dumbly prophetic. Friar Bacon's automaton willed to silence. A penny-swallowing toy in memory of Clare's days as a public beggar. Allowed his liberty, a walk from the hospital, the poet filled his alcove, behaving, pen in hand, like a flesh statue. For a plug of tobacco, the price of a pint, he would write to order: a fortune-telling machine. Stout Farmer Clare, strolling down Billing Road (remembering Bachelor's Hall?), takes his place, benevolent gargoyle, in the otherwise incomplete church.

Charles II, high above the portico, is crowned with a garland of oak leaves in memory of his escape after the Battle of Worcester.

His flight from England. Now he can fly again, a second Bladud, a stone Icarus. Alan Moore has written about a Second World War bomber crashing on this street: 'a great tin angel with a sucking chest wound fallen from the Final Judgement'. It skidded into the Market Square, an object of interest to the gathering populace; only one of whom, a cyclist, was slightly injured.

George Maine drew Clare – leggings, waistcoat – perched in his alcove; quill in one hand, notebook in the other. Top hat on the ground: available for alms, a dropped coin. Renchi, as we wait for Alan Moore, duplicates the pose: writing and sketching. I sneak a glance at the page. 'Northampton ANNA,' it says. Anna Sinclair, so far as I know, has never been to Northampton. Nor stayed in an ibis. The cultural deprivation in her life is shocking.

Alan manifests: curtain of hair tossed back, snakehead stick brandished. A wand. His black vest is rimmed with body salts. A sticky day. He's walked from his home, out to the north, above Abington Park. Alan's property faces a mini-anthology of poetic terraces: Milton, Byron, Shelley, Moore, Chaucer. An eccentric gathering: Tom Moore being the odd man out. Alan says that, in years to come, guide books will have Moore Street named after him: creator of *From Hell* and *Swamp Thing*, convener of *The League of Extraordinary Gentlemen*. After all, he got his start at Northampton Arts Lab with poetry gigs. He remembers Anne Tibble, the Clare scholar, receiving a round of applause for a reading laced with gracefully handled obscenities. Her gesture to the times, the Non-Swinging Seventies.

They shake hands, the artists; Renchi's sheet-washing, bed-making, paint-smeared digits and Moore's silver claws. Alan's a post-ironic scissorhand, tin man, jumped from the pages of Marvel comics. John Dee's roadie made good. Scryer, tapper of tables, voice-catcher: mythologist. Fingers flash in dazzling thimbles; a heavy-metal scrap of rings pulls him, effortlessly, through the hill town's sluggish magnetic field.

We shamble down St Giles Street, a tour of the Guildhall (decorations by a Moore ancestor, amateur artist, professional drinker):

before our assault on St Andrew's Hospital. But first Alan sidetracks us into the Wig & Pen, a wannabe lawyers' pub, formerly known as the Black Lion. Before this *Rumpole of the Bailey* makeover, there was a ceiling painting, spirits of place: John Clare acknowledging Alan Moore. An art student's unknowing variant on Rippingille's conversation piece, *The Stage Coach*. A lick of paint obscures Northampton's culture heroes; they've vanished. And, in vanishing, have acquired the dignity of legend; something forged in tipsy memory.

Revamped pub signs are the tarot pack of county topography. Moore rescues the Labour in Vain, the hostelry Clare passed on Enfield Highway; where 'a person coming out' set him on the right track for the Great North Road. In *Voice of the Fire*, Alan places this refuge, which has never been found, outside time; an anomaly located by solitary travellers in states of crisis or extreme anxiety. A false oracle of the English road.

The car-burner Alfie Rouse, heading out of London towards the Northampton field where he will smash the skull of a man picked up in transit, visits a roadhouse called the Labour in Vain – in which he encounters an 'old tinker with a funny stand-up hat': the misplaced Clare. Eric Robinson and David Powell, editors of *John Clare by Himself*, admit that they have 'no knowledge of a public house at Enfield Highway called the Labour in Vain'. *Robson's Directory* (1839) lists nine pubs. The mysterious 'Labour in Vain' is not one of them.

In less confident towns, we might offend the eyes of sober citizens; crowds would part, squad cars slow. Not here, not now. We've erred on the side of discretion, anonymity. Picture it. The black-vested Moore with his swinging stick, silver fingerstalls. He claws back a damp curtain of thick hair, reddish-brown hemp of Jesus length. Salt-and-pepper beard teased out like a Robert Newton pirate: Blackbeard without the burning tapers. Advancing through broken suburbs, he's the dead spit of one of the 'Vessels of Wrath'; the fire demons depicted in Francis Barrett's *The Magus (or Celestial Intelligencer)* as 'Powers of Evil'. *The Magus* is the magical primer

Moore searched out in a Princelet Street attic, years before; a Whitechapel fantasy, a film. In performance, he became that thing: 'The worst sort of devils are those who lie in wait, and overthrow passengers in their journeys.'

We struggle up the steady incline, away from the town centre: a carnival of mountebanks fleeing the plague. Expelled jugglers, confidence tricksters. Renchi: blue bandanna, long shorts, lightly bearded. Moore: striding out with upraised staff. And your reporter: sun-bleached cap from fisherman's hotel, desert jacket. A spook embedded in the madness. Traitor. Manipulator of fictions.

Moore announces that on his fiftieth birthday he will retire from mainstream comics, the grind. Give himself over to the twin disciplines of magic and the writing of prose, a sequel to *Voice of the Fire*. He has already signed away future income from Hollywood; the films of *From Hell* and *The League of Extraordinary Gentlemen* were nothing but aggravation. Court cases loom, million-dollar plagiarism suits brought by disgruntled careerists who failed to understand that invention has no copyright. The Faustian contract between graphic novels and movies is based on mutual cannibalism, brain-sucking rip-offs, canny lifts from the dead or the powerless.

Ghostly legions of the reforgotten know that remakes are the only true originals.

'There is a magical virtue,' writes Barrett,

being as it were abstracted from the body, which is wrought by the stirring up of the power of the soul, from whence there are made most potent procreations, and most famous impressions, and strong effects, so that nature is on every side . . . and by how much the more spiritual her phantasy is, so much the more powerful it is, therefore the denomination of magic is truly proportionable or concordant.

As we walk, Alan unfolds, in a way that only a lifelong victim and lover, bridegroom of the town, could do, his account of certain buildings, certain people. Anecdotes. Family reminiscences. He grants Clare a chapter in *Voice of the Fire*: an exercise in ventriloquism pastiching the journals. But nothing carries you further, or deeper, than the poet's own prose; the slanted script we experienced in the library. The hospital was always the conclusion of the walk from London; a purgatory in which to shake free of identity, the compulsion to scribble. Spoil paper. Northampton was a good place for the eyes to lose their inward fire.

There was never to be a second escape. Mary was gone. Madness was the loss of her, the missing portion of Clare's soul. In a grubby asylum notebook, he inscribed the names of one hundred and fifty women. Mary Joyce was omitted. He sat at a window, for hours at a time, attempting to recall those faces, the lost harem of beauties; admired, forgotten.

William Knight, one of the asylum staff, a good friend, helped to preserve the Northampton poems, troubled fragments. The music of the Nene infiltrates the verse; rhythms of water, water memories.

> Love's memories haunt my footsteps still,
>   Like ceaseless flowings of the river.
> Its mystic depths, say, what can fill?
>   Sad disappointment waits for ever.

A second walk was impossible, flight pointless. There was nowhere to go. In two days, Clare could have been back in Northborough, having travelled across soft country, tracking the river. But he refused to consider escape, even when other inmates discussed their plans. That book was written. A new journey would undo it. Northampton was an occulted principality: the asylum its seminary, Dr Prichard its magus. Prichard could draw invisible wires from men's heads. He knew their thoughts because he planted them. Composing delusions, he was benevolent but absolute. Two runaways got as far as Hertfordshire before they were captured and brought back. 'I told you how it would be, you fools,' said Clare. He could wander freely through town, fields and woods, to Delapre Abbey: because he was psychically tagged. Branded. Watched.

St Andrew's was not the gothic prison of my imagination. A grim redoubt in which Clare was held, until he was leached from the memories of family and friends; put away for the crime of being addicted to 'poetical prosing'. The asylum years were a sponsored exile, underwritten by Earl Fitzwilliam. The peasant poet was housed, fed, clothed, encouraged to write. That was the problem: kindly Mr Knight standing at Clare's shoulder, eager to carry off defaced paper; ready to mend broken sentences, repair rhymes. Prompts leading nowhere. 'Clare,' he reported, 'will seldom turn his attention to pieces he has been interrupted in while writing: and in no instance has he rewritten a single line.'

The stout verse-farmer, Mr John Clare of Helpston, sat in his alcove; silent until approached, questioned about the sources of his inspiration. Rivers of deep image in which to drown. The natural world imitated by an invented language. Poetry came to him, was his strategic reply, as he walked in the fields. As he kicked his ignorance against clods of sodden earth. The fools nodded in sympathy, made notes, published the lie.

We could be invading a public school in Cheltenham: a hint of the military, honeyed limestone flushed in afternoon light. Neoclassical pediment. Pillared porch. Symmetrical blocks with regimented windows. A country house for a battalion of the moderately insane. Alan Moore poses for the snap, puffing out his chest, gripping his cane like an RSM's swagger stick.

Croquet lawns shaved in alternate bands. Crowded flower beds. Avenues of proper English trees: oak, elm, beech. The chapel in which they held, in 1982, the funeral service for Lucia Anna Joyce. She had been here much longer than Clare; a gaunt presence whose writings (including a novel) were destroyed by the Joyce Estate. Annulled. Denied. Clare, in the end, returned to source, the burial plot in Helpston. Lucia remains in Northampton, a cemetery on the edge of town; you notice the sign as you drive towards Corby and the A1.

The grounds are landscaped, leafy walks, broad paths. Golf, tennis. White figures stooped over croquet mallets. Why would you leave? St Andrew's is the best kind of hotel, every facility and no visible surveillance. Nobody to challenge our lack of credentials.

Alan Moore is nudged back towards adolescence, when his school was just over the fence. Avoiding compulsory sport, Alan and his mates bombed around the perimeter of the hospital grounds on motorbikes. They swam in the pool. John Clare, between biographies, was in limbo. Lucia Joyce, in body if not spirit, was present. A remote witness to acts of trespass, mild testosterone hooliganism.

The bright boy, future graphic novelist, was expelled from the grammar school for selling LSD. False move. (Hallucinogenics, given the behaviour of most of the townsfolk, proved an unnecessary refinement. On one side of the hospital fence, pharmaceutical trade was punished; on the other, disciples of Dr Laing dished out superstrength doses.) Alan declined the standard career curve: crime as profession (with Thatcherite enterprise allowances). He prepared for a lifetime operating at the limits of the system, certified free-lancer. Cards marked: disbarred troublemaker. Alan remembers the headmaster very well. After the school (founded 1541) lost its status, in one of those ill-considered policy shifts, the poor man hanged himself. A successor was nicked for fiddling coins from a slot-machine.

I ask Alan about 'Beckett's Park', which I noticed on the map; down by the Nene, between bus depot and Cattle Market Road. I was thinking about the second great love of Lucia Joyce's life (after her father): eagle-nosed Sam. I hoped the name of the park might commemorate his cricketing feats at the county ground; two first-class games for Trinity College, Dublin. But, no; Moore reckons it's a characteristically misspelt reference to Thomas the Martyr. Becket has a holy well in that part of town. My own instinct, after poking around All Saints' Church, is that there might be another explanation.

On the west wall, I found a memorial tablet to Mrs Dorothy Beckett (relict of Mr Thomas Beckett, late of Congleton in the County of Cheshire). Mrs Beckett, together with Mrs Anne Sergeant, provided funds for 'cloathing and teaching 30 Poor Girls of this Parish'. Surely Mrs Beckett would be thanked, even when forgotten, by having her name attached to an obscure patch of grass?

I was approaching overload. Too many blank faces in asylum windows. Discussing Clare with Bill Drummond (writer, art activist, sampler of pop songs), he told me that he'd worked in St Andrew's as a male nurse. On the back of his enthusiasm for Ken Kesey's *One Flew over the Cuckoo's Nest*, he arrived from Corby and got himself a job. He'd been in the hospital while Lucia Joyce was incarcerated. There were tales to tell. He would take care of them in his own time.

We pause outside the Beckett-sanctified county cricket ground. 'Eight tight, economical overs for only seventeen runs,' while playing for an outclassed student side: useful. Scores, batting down the order at number eight, of eighteen and twelve. Above average for an English test player against Australia. Sam bowled at medium pace, reckons biographer James Knowlson. 'Off-breaks,' retorts Deirdre Bair. Call it: Derek Underwood on a sticky wicket. Beckett, the near-blind, left-hand bat. Slow to start, difficult to dislodge. Two appearances at Northampton got him into *Wisden*. The only Nobel prizewinner with this distinction.

Moore's contacts at St Andrew's report that Beckett made an annual pilgrimage, to visit Lucia – and also to return, for sentimental reasons, to the cricket ground. Certainly, in the last years, they corresponded. Beckett, prompted by Lucia, made a generous contribution to the nurses' fund. But it was a ghost play, this relationship in which human warmth and pain were so remote they belonged to textual exegetists, playwrights rewiring literary history. The principal actors, safely buried, were redundant: pale flames guttering in an antechamber. Reported sighs. Death rattles. A discontinued monologue.

'Seaview', Moore's house, is a self-curated museum, customised, by the author's continuing and growing success, into something like that terraced street in the Beatles' film *Help*. An attachment to class roots, memories of his grandmother in the now-demolished warren of Green Street (behind St Peter's Church), is reasserted by the employment of local craftsmen: carving figurines of Pan, intertwined serpents for the door, painting blue walls with glittering stars. Brickwork was pointed by Big John Weston, 'former junky, former biped'; while the attic conversion was left to Fiery Fred (veteran of the assault at the poetry reading in the round church). Through this patronage, Alan has created a modest version of the Guildhall.

We sink gratefully into sofas and chairs, while mugs of tea are brewed. The set has been tidied by Moore's visiting daughters: otherwise it reminds me of a student house, a student of peculiar means and taste. A student of magical practice. Mounds of books and tapes. Hinged Tibetan skull. Nudes by Austin Spare. Enochian tables. Crowleyite wand. Clocks, tins, bottles. Family photos in frames. Hand-crafted Egyptian ritual mask with beak and feathers. Tiled fireplace with fake coals. I note, with envy, a lovely first edition of William Hope Hodgson's *The House on the Borderland*, bound in green leather.

Alan discourses on the migrating coffin of Princess Di. The tale is confirmed by two witnesses. One of the craftsmen improving his house had been working at Althorp when the cavalcade arrived.

(Moore's relatives travelled out to the motorway to witness the most significant returnee since Lord Byron.) A second account was furnished by a member of Ayrton Senna's pit crew. They had been celebrating, all day, in a pub on the back road between Althorp and Great Brington. (A track success, apparently. Not Diana's funeral.)

Dead queens were always part of the climate, Moore reckoned. Di's black limo covered with petals. Queen Eleanor transported to London, her journey marked by funerary monuments. Mary, Queen of Scots, at Fotheringhay. Catherine of Aragon in Peterborough. Unhappy women laid to rest in unhappy places.

Here's the story. The island business was a feint to divert trippers, necrophile tourists. The Althorp island was the burial ground of family pets: dogs, cats, monkeys. Dig deep enough for a human-size coffin and the hole will flood. A contingent of marines was supposed to have built a bridge, carried the coffin to the island, demolished the bridge, moved out. Neither of Moore's witnesses, on the day in question, saw any such activity. They reported a large black van heading down the back road to the church at Great Brington, the Spencer vault. Church closed, visible police presence. Diana laid, without fuss, alongside her ancestors.

Such unconfirmed rumours suit the town and our situation in it: trying to figure out how we can process all this stuff. At which point, happily, Alan's girlfriend (and sometime collaborator), Melinda Gebbie, drops in. Melinda, dark-haired, in loose, flowered dress, has a camera of her own: which she turns on us. Moore describes her as an 'underground cartoonist late of Sausalito, California: former bondage model recently turned quarkweight boxer'. Now, alert to currents already stirred, the woman who has been 'sucked in by this urban black hole', helps shift the conversation away from conspiracies, mad walkers, to human enquiry. What happened to Lucia Joyce in Northampton? Can her silence be set against Clare's painful and garrulous exile? Visitors came to the hospital to pay their respects, to report on the poet's health. Biographies of Lucia cut out, abruptly, after she steps into the car at Ruislip and drives north, never to return.

Cousin Sam

And cousins, there never was a man with so many cousins.

Samuel Beckett

In the Northampton ibis, I dreamt; re-remembered. The drowning. Weaving back, no licence required, on my motor scooter: to Sandy-cove, the flat beside Joyce's Martello tower. Wet night. A tinker woman had been pulled from the canal. Drunk. The smell of her. My first and only attempt at artificial resuscitation, meddling with fate. Met with: green mouth-weed, slime, bile, vomit. Incoherent pain. Language returns, curses. Better left in water was the consensus of other night-wanderers: 'Leave her be.' World of its own. Woodfire on wasteground within sight of a busy yellow road. Bring someone back from death and you're landed with them.

Blame Alan Moore for this plunge into darkness. According to the journalist Jeremy Duns, Alan 'converted to Gnosticism in the mid-1990s' and was now a worshipper of 'the Roman snake-god Glycon'. His terraced house was frequented by jewelled toads, black dogs bearing information: 'The world will end between 2012 and 2017.'

Lucia Joyce was drowning. Or recovering slowly, fighting for breath; fighting to remain in the shadows. James Joyce (always) and Beckett (at the beginning) constructed their works by a process of grafting, editing: quotations, submerged whispers. Correspondences. Joyce read other men's books only to discover material useful to his current project. Libraries were oracles accessed by long hours of labour: at the cost of sight. The half-blind Beckett, aged twenty-two, reading to a man in dark glasses (waiting for the next operation). A theatrical image reprised in Beckett's play *Endgame*. Which would be revived in London, 2004, to run alongside

Michael Hastings's *Calico*. A drama about Lucia Joyce: the high-bourgeois family, her relationship with the callow Beckett.

Lucia, entering Beckett's room-cell at the École Normale, surprises him stepping from the shower. She dries him with a dirty towel. 'I can smell sea water in your hair. You're half the swimmer you think you are. I know a great deal about drowning oneself.'

Echoes of Clare (writing to Taylor): 'Yet I know if I could reach London I should be better, or else get to salt water.'

One of Lucia's cabal of expensive doctors, Henri Vignes, prescribed injections of sea water. To no evident effect. Beckett was a vigorous swimmer, in rough seas off Donegal. In the biographies, you'll find a photograph of him, with his brother, Frank, in the dunes; both smoking. Beckett dressed in heavy black boots, loose white shorts. Smiling sardonically: as if resting, between tank battles, on the road to Tobruk.

Michael Hastings proposes incest, real or metaphorical, fathers and daughters, brothers and sisters: the shamed daughter hidden away. White purdah. Beckett, adopted son, takes Lucia's place in Joyce's workroom. Nora Barnacle, her mother, says that she has 'never seen two more drunken men'.

Joyce: 'Not a drop has passed our lips.'

Nora: 'Then it is your eyes again.'

Magnifying glass over etymological dictionary: blood-globe, headache. More wrappings around Joyce's head than a mummy. Bandages under grey Homburg, smoked glasses. Stub of period moustache, just like my father.

'Did you ever see my eyes?'

'No.'

'Did you never have the curiosity, while I was sleeping, to take off my glasses and look at my eyes?'

'Pulling back the lids? No.'

'One of these days I'll show them to you. It seems they've gone all white.'

I refilmed, on outdated 8mm stock, garden footage my father shot of his father, shortly before he died. Wartime in Wales. My grandfather slipped away, forgotten face over the rim of the cot, while I was a baby. He is trapped in a home movie: convalescent, dapper but unwell. Bones push against flesh as he holds up seedcake for his dog, a Scottie, to jump. Tilted hat, good tailoring; thin legs crossed. The dog jumps and jumps. My mother is there, by his side, in a summer dress. This man, a doctor, is very tired. He performs a reflex ritual, perhaps for the last time: remembering how to lift an arm. A moment that parallels Gisele Freund's 1938 photograph of Joyce in a deckchair. More dead than alive. Moving image slowing to a still: bleaching to nothing.

When this clip, recycled as a memory induced by motorway travel, was logged for the script of the film of *London Orbital*, the young woman doing the job wrote: 'James Joyce in garden.' Thereby confirming my fantasy of a physical resemblance between two dandified grandfathers: Henry Sinclair and James Joyce.

Joyce died in Zurich, 13 January 1941, of peritonitis from a duodenal ulcer; leaving Lucia, dependent on distracted relatives, in occupied France. A clinic in Pornichet. Lucia saw her father's obituary in a newspaper, an accidental reference that preceded the letter from her brother, Giorgio. She wanted to get away from hospitals: to Paris, Zurich, Galway. Harriet Weaver, her father's patron, agreed to try her in London.

When she was in Weaver's care, before the war, Joyce sent a camera. Something to replace the stress of drawing: the *lettrines* supposed to decorate private editions of his work. Photographs reveal Lucia's strabismus, the turn in her eye that failed to evade the Kodak's inquisition. The flaw that emphasises her dark-browed beauty: the height, the dancer's athleticism. Dead photographs speak of the aborted beginnings of things: careers, night walks, lovers, cities.

'When Lucia forwarded snapshots to him in mid-October,' wrote Carol Loeb Shloss (in her biography of this troubled daughter), 'Joyce saw a sullen, immobile young woman lying in a hammock with a book.' A lost girl swinging in a net, enjoying the warmth, the pointless eros of an English garden. Practice for the asylum years. The nunnery of mental hygiene. Lucia, who would soon be threatened by Nazi eugenicists, culling difference, is captured at Loveland's Cottage, where Miss Weaver brought her, along with Mrs Middlemost, a Scottish nurse chosen for 'her splendid physique'. The snapshot Joyce received was taken as evidence of Lucia's deteriorating condition: an upraised hand, palm open. Her belt tight, a restraint. Long, loose cardigan. Overhanging leaves: coarse and spiky as the girl's hair.

Joyce wrote to Weaver: 'My daughter is in a madhouse where I hear she fell off a tree.' Once more he echoes Clare: the fall associated with epileptic fits. Doctors soothing hot bruises with cold baths, lukewarm mutton.

Dr Macdonald, Lucia's London psychiatrist, was a needle man; an associate of Naum Ischlondsky. They worked on a supposed connection between the endocrine glands and the nervous system: blood affecting mood. Serums were made, as Carol Shloss explains, 'from the tissues of embryonic animals'. Lucia could be injected only after a 'violent struggle'. Macdonald laid out a grim regime: confinement to bed for seven weeks, no visitors, no other medication. Clammy London summer. Lucia 'sang incessantly in four languages'. She threw books from windows.

The story moves towards an inevitable destination. Macdonald arranged for Lucia to be returned to St Andrew's Hospital, which she had visited, briefly, in 1935 and 1936. A three-time loser, lifer. Maria Jolas escorted her from Paris to London. Dr Macdonald was waiting at Ruislip airfield with a car. He drove Lucia to Northampton. In her luggage she had: an identity card, a little money, a pack of Lucky Strike cigarettes bought by Jolas. The cigarettes, prison currency, were used. The other items, after Lucia's death, were gifted to the library of the University of London. More boxes, more forensic bags, more permission slips.

Outlasting Clare, in silence and stamina, Lucia Anna Joyce remained in Northampton from 15 March 1951 until her death on 12 December 1982. She had already been living at St Andrew's for two years when Alan Moore was born.

*

In mid-England, mid-journey, flying and drowning become confused. Drowning and writing. Dreaming and walking. *Finnegans Wake*: Lucia searching out words for her father, the book for which she is the inspiration. The problem. The role of secretary (sub-author) taken away from her by Samuel Beckett. Until he is banished, for the crime – as Nora Barnacle sees it – of trifling with her daughter's affections.

She is drowning. Agenbite. Save her. Agenbite. All against us. She will drown me with her, eyes and hair. Lank coils of seaweed hair around me, my heart, my soul. Salt green death.

Joyce asks Lucia to look at the song 'Dublin Bay', to change it: the young couple must not be drowned. The man will bide his time at the bottom of the sea, then rise to the surface. Joyce, fond father, continued to believe that Lucia, dosed on sea-water, would swim back to him, to health. Hospitals taught her to breathe underwater.

She visited Jung. He couldn't help. There was an unresolved argument with the author of *Ulysses*: a book that dared to trespass on his territory. Beckett, marooned in London (in the Thirties), went with his therapist, W. R. Bion, to hear Jung lecture. He picked up on the notion of patients having their horoscopes cast. He used it in his first published novel, *Murphy*. 'If Joyce was diving into a river,' Jung said, 'Lucia was falling.' Voluntary or involuntary immersion: it depends on who is telling the tale.

Hypnotised sleepwalkers dance, movements choreographed by alienists. Beckett retained the photograph of Lucia in performance; barefoot in a scaly, shimmering, mermaid-skin. Carol Shloss sees Lucia falling like Icarus into the sea: flying and drowning. 'O cripes, I'm drowned!'

Stopped Lucia, kept back from the excitement of theatres and dance halls, was put to making designs for her father. Joyce persuaded his daughter to draw complex initial letters: turning his 1927 collection, *Pomes Penyeach*, into an illuminated gospel (for private subscribers). The experience proved both stressful and unfulfilling:

like the capitalised correspondence of Clare's madness. Those High Beach poems: 'The Rose Of The World Was Dear Mary To Me'. Lucia was permitted to express her pain, one letter at a time. A saline drip. An agony compounded by work on another alphabet project, the *Chaucer ABC*. Brenda Maddox (in her biography of Nora Barnacle) says that 'Joyce tried frantically to breathe life into Lucia's career as a designer of *lettrines*. He pretended that she was, as he saw himself, an unappreciated artist whose brain was on fire.'

In his confinement, John Clare lost language: word by word, syllable by syllable, letter by letter. Too much kindness. Too much interest. Too many helpers eager to take away his agonised fumblings, his failures. 'They have cut off my head and picked out all the letters of the alphabet,' he told Agnes Strickland. 'All the vowels and consonants – and brought them out through my ears; and then they want me to write poetry!'

He leaked blood and pus. Lucia, when she was visited in St Andrew's, had nothing to say. She had been dosed into sexless neutrality. She told Nino Frank, and repeated it several times, that her father was under the earth: 'watching us all the time'. A double surveillance. By nurses and attendants. And by the concerned dead. While we think of them, they watch. Open eyes. All white. Sight recovered, postmortem. Skull emptied of letters.

'Eyes,' as the great European poet Paul Celan wrote, 'talked into blindness . . . Visits of drowned joiners to these submerging words.'

An exile in Paris, Celan died at the age of fifty: suicide in the Seine.

Walking through twilight Northampton, I have to force myself to let go of the back story. Through accidents of literary history, we know something about John Clare and Lucia Joyce, and something about the celebrity aspect of St Andrew's – but the anonymous patients and sufferers have gone: recorded, unremarked. Moving through the darkness, you are at liberty to choose your own relatives, revise your autobiography.

I had been searching – library records, photo albums, birth and wedding certificates – for a direct connection between the Clares and the Hadmans. There wasn't one: if you discount Clare's spirit children, by Mary Joyce, the ones who haunted Helpston and Glinton. The ones who were not buried with Patty Clare, against the church wall in Northborough. The relationship I had missed (or suppressed), until I started on this genealogical truffling, was between myself and Samuel Beckett. Cousin Sam.

The link is as tenuous as Geoffrey Hadman's wished-for association with Clare. I enjoyed finding out about Anna's antecedents, I prefer to leave my own in obscurity. Let them out of the box and they'll have you. A life dedicated to cramming oversize feet into delicate footprints.

Dublin, 1962. I met Anna in Sandymount. A student house on the sea. I saw her at the turn of the stairs, coming up, brown jersey with silver-coin clip; tall, dark, hesitant. Should she wait or climb further? There was a discussion, subdued, about her appearance in a play. And, shortly after that, my parents in town, I went with my father to visit relatives, cousins, aunts, in polite Ballsbridge. I have done my best, of course, to expunge the memory. The last thing I wanted, back then, was a conduit that might filter news

home to Wales: no tea parties, no written reports on academic lethargy.

The Ballsbridge aunt, I recall (or re-invent), was gracious and interesting. She had a connection with Sam Beckett and attended his lectures in Trinity. She kept, and now produced, detailed notes. There was the lecture on the imaginary poet Jean du Chas. There were recollections of Beckett's appearance in a play put on by the Modern Languages staff, cut-up Pierre Corneille. There was talk about the agonised delivery of material to dull-witted and rowdy students. This woman, who was related to Beckett, was also related to my father. Let that suffice: I handled the notes, I wiped the tape.

When Beckett arrived in Paris, he carried a letter of introduction to Joyce, written by Harry Sinclair. His Aunt Cissie (mother's sister) married William 'Boss' Sinclair. Harry and William were twins. They have the standard issue Sinclair names: my father and grandfather were both called Henry, my son is William. The Dublin Sinclairs were Jewish or half-Jewish (and were famously libelled by Oliver St John Gogarty). Beckett's first real affair was with his cousin, Peggy Sinclair, daughter of Cissie and Boss.

The Sinclairs, removed to Germany, were a refuge for Sam; an escape from the cramp of the Beckett villa in Foxrock. From his fearsome mother. From nightsweats and a racing heart. Bohemian, after their fashion, dealers in paintings and antiques, the family were travelling fast towards poverty. They were established in the wrong place, at the worst time.

Peggy died young, of tuberculosis, drowning in air. Boss Sinclair had a house on Howth Head; where I lived in a caravan that threatened to take off during winter storms. In summer, I rowed Anna out to Ireland's Eye (a rock in the bay). We disturbed colonies of roosting birds. Returned to Howth for the first night of our marriage, in 1967, we met a girl I knew, former runaway, involuntary patient, earning a few pounds by escorting an overweight lady in black velvet on an excursion from the asylum. She suffered with radio voices in the head, inconvenient broadcasts. Dublin was full of such marginal figures, hovering somewhere between the status of cancelled artists and inspirers of fiction. One character, who lived for years by positioning himself with forensic precision at the edge of drinking groups, talking Yeats and Joyce, William Faulkner and Douglas Sirk, followed us from Dublin to London. You never knew when you'd wake in the night to find him sitting on your bed, shaking coins from your pocket. Visiting the mother, a widow, he dropped into a Baggot Street bar and saw, on a newly installed television, the image that had him hospitalised (or sheltered) for the rest of his life. James Joyce stepping out of a plane at Dublin Airport. Peace made with the Pope. Come home to kiss the tarmac. Nobody could tell him that it was Giorgio, the son, looking after family business. Taking care of a valuable and litigious estate.

If there is common blood with Beckett, however diluted, so much the better. I won't investigate it. I salute him as a great walker, out alone in all weathers, or with his father, tramping the Wicklow Hills. (William Beckett, a quantity surveyor, kept an office in town, which Sam frequently visited. It was in Clare Street.)

Elective affinities: I acknowledge Beckett, from the period of *Murphy*, as a notable London psychogeographer. James Knowlson tells us how the frustrated novelist trudged for hours through streets and parks, making a narrative of the city. 'The regularity of his movement acted as a kind of anaesthetic, easing his troubles.' Beckett noted, for future use, street names, pub signs, bread companies, manufacturers of bath mats. 'He could cover as much as twenty miles in a day.'

Reading the Beckett biography, I came to understand how relationships are based on shared topography, not mere accidents of blood. Beckett had preceded us to the asylums of London's orbital fringe. Through his friendship with Geoffrey Thompson, he arranged to visit the Bethlem Royal Hospital at Beckenham (where Thompson worked as a Senior House Physician). This was old Bedlam, twice removed; first from Bishopsgate, then from Lambeth. He penetrated secure wards, viewed 'melancholics, motionless and brooding, holding their heads or bellies according to type'. Years later, I walked through those gates with Renchi. The expedition was part of our tour around the M25; a direct line from the Millennium Dome to Clacket Lane Services. Samuel Beckett was ahead of us, every step of the way: his silence, his eagle stare (the poster portrait, in the alcove outside the bathroom, that terrified my children).

Before we left town, we made an attempt on St Peter's Church. Once again, Beckett beat us to it. James Knowlson reports that, after the cricket match against Northampton, Sam took to the streets. 'Instead of going off whoring or drinking in the local pubs with the others, he went on his own around local churches.'

A key is obtained, without difficulty, through the window of the pub. It's that kind of morning: bright sun, beds of lavender scenting soft air. Malfate in remission. The church, under threat of restoration, is balanced between shafts of light, shadowy recesses: past worshippers, present silence. Romanesque arches. Celtic beasts. This is somewhere in which to sit, while the mind is cleared of its froth and babble.

A memorial bust, all knobble and lump, takes me by surprise. Renchi, in his epic walks across England, gathers up chips of chalk, slate, flint. They are incorporated into his paintings as part of the meaning, the weight of the journey. The presiding spirit, on these jaunts, is visionary engineer and duff poet William Smith. Who was responsible, as Simon Winchester would have it, for the 'map that changed the world'. The colours of this 1815 chart are those of a living body, after the skin has been stripped to expose rivers of pulsing nerves and fibres.

TO HONOUR THE NAME OF
WILLIAM SMITH, L.L.D.
THIS MONUMENT IS ERECTED BY HIS FRIENDS
AND FELLOW LABOURERS IN THE FIELD OF
BRITISH GEOLOGY

William Smith, stalker of the limestone causeway, Bath to Lincoln, died in Northampton. And was memorialised in a locked church, across the road from the hotel ibis. An obituary is carved, in capitals, on a marble tablet. Born: 23 March 1769 (at Churchill in Oxfordshire). Works on collieries, canals. In 1815, he publishes his geological map. The artfully delineated strata come at the period of enclosures. Pinks, greys, greens: England divided like the villages of Helpston and Glinton.

The Jurassic Highway drew Smith, as we had been drawn to investigate the mysteries of the M25. His nephew reported: 'In the winter of 1819 Mr Smith, having perhaps more than usual leisure, undertook the walk from Lincolnshire into Oxfordshire.' He intended 'to pass along a particular line through the counties of Rutland, Northampton, Bedford and Oxford'. He listened to 'odd stories of supernatural beings and incredible frights which were narrated by the villagers'. And as he walked, like Renchi, he picked up stones at the roadside; even the 'dull red sandstone found in unexceptional middle-English cities like Northampton'. Pedestrian excursions of 'fifty miles or so' were 'a casual stroll' for this driven man.

It was the Scottish poet Allan Ramsay who provided a verse tribute at the geologist's anniversary dinner in 1854. 'To Father Smith we owe our thanks / For the history of a few stones.'

Travelling home from Oxfordshire, Smith's coach stopped in Northampton – where he chose to lodge for a few days with his old friend George Baker. A cold 'settled on his lungs'. He died, 28 August 1839, and was buried, with due ceremony, in St Peter's Church.

We packed up to move out: a last Clare walk, before Renchi returned to Somerset. We would make a circuit, Glinton to Crowland Abbey, to Market Deeping, to Northborough, back to Glinton. Alan Moore, reflecting on the evening's talk, rang the ibis, telling us to go to the crossroads of Marefair, Gold Street and Horse Market, and to look downhill. We would see the place where St Gregory located the centre of England. Gregory, it seems, made a pilgrimage to the Holy Land. The *Northampton Chronicle* fleshes out the story: 'Visiting the supposed spot where Christ was crucified he noticed an unusual shaped stone projecting from the ground. Scraping it out he discovered an ancient stone cross just 10 inches long.' An angel ordered him to plant the cross in Northampton: on the spot where he was subsequently buried. The notion of 'centre' is a spiritual conceit, significant for local mystics. The 'true' centre of the English landmass, according to geographers, is a little closer to the territory from which Anna's ancestors emerged.

We drive to Barnack, to explore the ancient quarries, the 'Hills and Holes': a favourite walk of the orchid-hunting Clare. And of Renchi's father, Peter. Memories flood back. As we walk, Renchi recalls those conversations. Butterflies. Thorn bushes. Healed declivities from which stone for Peterborough Cathedral was excavated. Rafts on the Nene. Cambridge colleges lying in wait, already formed, beneath a thin carpet of soil. Miniature hills on which to catch unexpected views.

After paying our respects to Helpston and Glinton, we strike out, down North Fen, towards Clare's bridge; and away, birds rising affronted from bare fields, to Crowland. Renchi worries that he has left his boots in Barnack: in the church with that curious grave, a stone palm tree lying on the ground. I brood on the dissolution of my quest but decide that it doesn't matter. Touring Northampton, church to church, laid down a pattern that activated a series of overlapping narratives. We must walk them out, empty-headed in an empty landscape. Searching for Anna's Hadman relatives, I found Beckett. Listening for Clare, I heard Lucia's silence. Trudging beside water, under unforgiving skies, we hope that our twinned stories will loop back on themselves; bringing us to that unknown place we must learn to recognise.

REFORGETTING

& we often see clouds which we identify by their curling up from
the orison in seperate masses as gass clouds which ascend into the
middle sky & then join the quiet journey other clouds & are lost in the
same colour.

John Clare (Northborough. October/November 1841)

Glinton

Clare: Farewell, dear Mrs Joyce. We shall return with tales to tell.
(Pauses)
One more thing before we depart. You mentioned my travels
earlier and spoke of my home with a certain familiarity. I
was wondering, do you have family in Glinton or Helpston?

John Mackintosh, *A Song of Summer*

Commentators assert that Samuel Beckett, in *Krapp's Last Tape*,
drew on memories of Peggy Sinclair: 'a girl in a shabby green coat,
on a railway-station platform'. The association is presumptuous
and unnecessary. I remember, I have the photograph in my hand,
the three-quarter-length tweed coat, leather collar, Anna wore
when I took her to the 'Hills and Holes' at Barnack: hoping that
she could give me the names of the wild flowers, the bushes. I saw
instead how much returning to this part of the world meant. The
animation that came with the road from Stamford to Helpston.
The pleasure she derived from walking the mounds. Barnack was
a quiet, moneyed village with handsome church and vicarage (traces
of Charles Kingsley).

Coming off the A1, away from London: the lift in the landscape,
before the falling away into flatness, is an exhilaration. We've given
ourselves three days to sort out the business of the Hadmans and
Glinton. We'll start at the family grave, St Benedict's Church, then
work across to the Red House, before making a circuit of the
village. What we understand, from the modest heights of Barnack,
is the way Glinton functioned: cattle brought down from the hills
to feed on rich summer pastures, ground recovered from water.
Beds of mint. Hemp from which shoes were made. Dampness and
flooded fields the perpetual winter condition. How the young Clare

moaned about his sodden feet when he tried working as a gardener at Woodcroft Castle.

Guided by Glinton historian Val Hetzel – who produced enclosure maps, copies of parish registers – we learnt that the Red House stood alongside a pen for strayed cattle. There were two cottages in Rectory Lane: a policeman occupied one of them, the other was a reading room. The Hadmans owned no fields at the time of the enclosures, neither were they landowners in 1886. Websters were active. They intermarried with Vergettes. James Joyce put together a nice parcel of land, a strip here, a patch there. He lived at the Fen edge, beside the path where Mary Joyce is supposed to have kept company with Clare.

The village spreads like a stain, out from the church, on its green island. Tenant farmers, satirised by Clare, were the coming men: active, energetic, socially ambitious. There was no sentiment for cottage life, nor any aspect of heritage standing in the way of immediate profit. One of the Webster properties was a Custom House, occupied by the military; decent quarters for officers, dormitory for other ranks. They patrolled the rivers and dykes, to prevent the movement of contraband by water (there were no serviceable roads).

The Titmans, the most recent of the farming families, so Mrs Hetzel told us, were parish and county councillors. They were sufficiently well informed about Peterborough's coming status as a 'New Town', about legislation forbidding the replacement of thatched roofs with Collyweston slate, to buy up and rapidly tear down examples of the picturesque (the Glinton equivalent of Clare's cottage). Bungalow developments and convenience stores prepared the way for Glinton to be absorbed into Peterborough: a desirable satellite accessed by dual carriageway. Farmers become developers. Or they vanish, disperse, lose their nerve.

We couldn't turn right into Glinton: flooded road. The journey from Helpston, a reprise of my original walk, was fouled up by a system of roundabouts that try to suck everything into Peterborough's gravitational field. Clare's trudge home from the village school has been overwhelmed by superstores, retail parks, exhaust-replacement centres. I prompt Anna, looking out of the car at naked fields, to remember where the Auster landed. She can't. An area known as the 'Stacks' was part of the Hadman farm, but she can't place it with certainty. Perhaps the field sliced off by the road? Peppery-brown mud, combed flat, fenced by brutally hacked hedges. The hum of the bypass.

Denied access to Glinton, we make the long detour by way of Northborough. An opportunity to look for the Clare graves, Patty and her children, in St Andrew's churchyard. Damp morning, no definition in the sky. Church locked, key available from cottage down the street.

I begin, in the dimmest corner, with slabs that are waiting to be broken up, cut to dress a cottage garden. There are no Clares, but plenty of Catlings. Joseph and Elizabeth. And their children. Brian Catling's biological parents come from Sheerness, the Isle of Sheppey, but his adopted family emerged from these parts, floaters. They kept the stock healthy by getting away; pubs, army, ducking and diving in the Old Kent Road and Rotherhithe. The gene pool in some Northamptonshire villages, according to Alan Moore, is so shallow you're lucky to find partners with eyes on different sides of their noses.

Catlings face the east window, while Clares face them, and look beyond: to the sewage works, the River Welland. Flat fields. Straight roads. Crowland Abbey. Gravestones are readdressed like misdirected mail. Names added until there is no space left on the grey envelope. Northborough was a family reunion to which John Clare was not invited. Martha (Patty) Clare is present; the 'wife' part of her title faded from the inscription, black paint gone. Sons and daughters are lovingly remembered. Children of children. Definitively asleep. Until prodded by biographers, scholars obliged to set the record straight. Patty's association with Helpston is put aside. The family sinks back into the element from which it emerged. John Clare's fret of language is kept at a safe distance, a couple of miles down the road, with his father and mother, in St Botolph's churchyard.

I take down some of the names. 'William P. Clare. July 31st, 1887. Aged 57.' John's third son. He lived with Patty in Northborough. He married Elizabeth Pateman and had three children. The family owned Poet's Cottage until 1920.

We find no Hadman/Clare intermarriage, before or after the poet. Turner, Morris, Sefton, Stimson, Gorge, Garfet, Woodward, Stapely, Ward, Kettle, Crason, Snow, Preston, Bean, Dove, Bowery, Stallebrass, Humber, Baxter, Hornblow, Pryce, Jones, Griffiths: names to stock a dozen Shakespeare comedies, novels by Dickens. It would be easier, if we had the stomach for it, to find a link to my family. Jack Clare, the poet's second son, worked for the railways as a carpenter. He lived in the Welsh borders with his second wife, fathering six children. My mother had connections in Brecon and Monmouthshire. Then there was the rogue schoolteacher, John Donald Parker, itinerant Scot. Who knows where he came from? Or where he went?

William Hadman, Anna's grandfather, died a month after she was born. He was churchwarden of St Benedict's at Glinton, from 1921 to 1943. His wife, Florence (maiden name Rose), followed him within seven months. Unlike the Websters, Vergettes, Titmans, Joyces, there was only one Hadman grave to be found. It was multiply occupied with memorial prompts. And tended by surviving family members. Gravel combed, lettering repainted, the Hadman grave stood apart from the chaotic enclosure map into which the Glinton churchyard had been converted by the other notable farmers. A strip here, a mound there. Grandiose monuments, broken slabs buried in long grass. Avenues of relatives, shoulder to shoulder, in neighbourly proximity. The Hadmans stood alone. All on one raft. They had come from nowhere, vanished into nothing. There were no uncles, aunts, cousins. The singular grave lacked the soil for elaborate planting; skimmia, roses, chrysanthemums (from garden centres or garages) brought a splash of colour. The record was clear, but stark. Anna's paternal grandparents. Her father, Geoffrey. Her mother, Joan. Her aunt, Mary. Recorded and remembered on one stone.

That's as far as we can take it. Gravestone and family album. Two photographs of Florence Hadman with her three children: Florence Mary, Lawrence William ('Lawrie') and Geoffrey. (The workforce at ICI called him 'Skipper'.) Florence Hadman isn't happy about this performance, kids gussied up, hair brushed; in bright sunshine, backed against a bush. In the first photograph,

Geoffrey is a baby, perched on his mother's knee; bemused, bald, affronted by the impertinent camera. A little old man, dignity ruffled. By the second photo – it must have been an annual agony, same cast, same positions – he is about five or six; the only one of the trio who has not yet perfected the Hadman scowl. A tall, solid, beetle-browed gang. With low tolerance for nonsense of any kind. The five-bar gate places them on Rectory Lane, looking at the apple orchards on the far side.

Here, at last, is something to work with. We pass the Blue Bell pub (tricked out with antique farm implements), and start down the lane. Anna notices how the redbrick frontage of the family house has been grafted on to the armature of a much older cottage. A metal fire-insurance badge is visible between the upstairs windows. Anna recalls the rectory, now a private house, as a rather gloomy children's home. The fields beyond may have been where the Auster landed, bumped to ground. Leaving her deaf for the walk to the Red House. Unable to hear her own footfalls.

As we come out of the field, on to the busy road, across from the Community College, Anna realises that she has lost her brooch. A Celtic silver device, zoomorphic, swans (like the Peakirk village sign) entwined – and representing, so the leaflet says, 'shape-shifting abilities, transformation in the physical and spiritual sense'. A small sacrifice to our quest, another Barnack vanishing (to set alongside Renchi's Beckettian boots). Brooches disappear and are replaced like the children of the rural poor. The clip of silver coins I remembered from Sandymount was stolen, the usual toll, shortly after we moved to Hackney, along with most of Anna's inherited jewellery. A replacement brooch went the day Tate Modern opened on Bankside. Now this: no glint in hedge or gutter, as we retrace our steps. I'm sure the brooch dropped off as we clambered around the 'Hills and Holes'; to be found, in years to come, by a metal-detecting enthusiast. A nice wink to the culture: limestone molehills revised as New Grange theme park. A pocket of renegade Celts rafting up the Nene. An attraction to rival Flag Fen.

As tourists offer boots and brooches to unsuspecting fields, so chunks of Barnack stone rise from their long hibernation in Whittlesey mud. Blocks designated for Ramsey and Ely shake free from the peat, to parade their thirteenth-century brands. Peter Ashley, English Heritage researcher, told me that after he'd photographed the Ramsey blocks at Engine Farm he was drawn to search for other Barnack stones, sunk with their rafts or dropped over the side. The Old Plough Inn, between Ely and Prickwillow, so he discovered (from a book by A. K. Astbury, called *The Black Fens*), was 'built partly of Barnack stone which never completed its journey by river to the site of Ely Cathedral'. With this reference for a guide, Ashley jumped in his car. 'I did go out on to the Fens at Prickwillow,' he said. 'And found that pub (now a home), with very obvious blocks of medieval masonry built into it. It now sits right out on the Fen away from all roads except a grassy track that was once the Ely to Norwich road.'

Ashley photographed one more thing: a pond with a little rushy island which contained a great church bell. Another drowned item dragged from the depths: to be rung when a novice entered a convent, bride of Christ. The bell's provenance was surprising. It had escaped from an Iris Murdoch novel (the TV dramatisation). And found its rightful place: a real fake. A relic slowly acquiring mystique by erasing its previous history, sitting mute on a piece of damp ground.

We settled in the pub with papers and documents we'd scrounged or been given by relatives. Val Hetzel, tracking back through local records, came up with a list of the owners of the Red House and its surrounding land.

At enclosure claimed by Mrs Elizabeth Webster.
1825 John Webster of Thorney sold to Walker.
1841 J. Webster willed it to Mrs Frances Walker and died 1850.
1861 Under the will was sold, purchased by Ancell Ball
who built on to the house Eastward.
1889 A. Ball died, sold to R. Vergette.
1899 R. Vergette sold to J. T. Smith – Mr Smith bequeathed it to his cousin, Mrs Fanny Warwick.
1909 Mrs Warwick died, buried at Glinton. Purchased by Mr Hadman for . . .

Amount lost. William Hadman was established, not as a tenant farmer, but as the owner of the property, and the land behind it, running back to the road, and beyond. Our understanding of the

farmers and how they operate is becoming clearer; the social gulf
that yawned between the Joyces and the Clares (who could aspire,
at best, to cottager status). Families with push, Elizabeth Webster
as prime example, went for land at the time of the enclosures. If
the children of farmers spurned Glinton, the power base was lost.

Clare's satire in 'The Parish' shows what he thought of these shifts:

> That good old fame that farmers earned of yore
> That made as equals not as slaves the poor
> That good old fame did in two sparks expire
> A shooting coxcomb and a hunting Squire
> And their old mansions that was dignified
> With things far better than the pomp of pride
>
> . . .
>
> These all have vanished like a dream of good
> And the slim things that rises where they stood
> Are built by those whose clownish taste aspires
> To hate their farms and ape the country squires

So William Hadman owned the Red House. He farmed. His
eldest son, Lawrie, took over the property. His daughter Mary had a
written contract to cook for the men. Talking to Lawrie's daughter,
Judy, who now lived on the west side of the A1, we discovered that
her grandfather had not always been a farmer. He started as a
forester. Judy supplied us with copies of William Hadman's obituaries. 'A Glinton Worthy,' says one of them. Chairman of the
Parish Council, churchwarden, school manager, special constable.
Member in good standing of the Peterborough Unionist Club.
Stalwart of village bowls. Keeper of a herd of Lincoln Red dairy
cattle. A man famed for his hospitality. Nothing he enjoyed more
than feeding friends and neighbours, until they couldn't move from
the table. His pet name for the Red House was 'Starvation Cottage'.

Judy had her grandfather's chair, decorative mirrors from the
Glinton house. And, with that chair, presence. Looking over the
photographs, in her kitchen, fleshed out the family portrait. We

learnt about social ambitions, of the sort John Clare noted, that went with the rise in status. Judy's mother was Madge. That was her name. Geoffrey and Mary Hadman decided it would never do. They rechristened her: Margaret. Aunt Margaret she became. Judy, on the other hand, was born Juliet Mary. Then rebranded to fit with a perceived notion of what she should be. Lawrie, it seems, never wanted to take over the farm. He trained as a butcher.

Identities can be assigned to figures in the group gathered in the Red House garden. The rather elegant woman in the back row, beside Geoffrey, was a London friend. Anna thinks she sponsored the publication of the unique copy of her father's lost poems. Judy, as a young girl, admired this woman so much that she wanted to become her: the style, the clothes, the perfume. She took to hiding a stone in her shoe, so that she could imitate the rather sexy limp. Anna, in her turn, was captivated by Judy's kidney-shaped dressing table, with the pink frills; make-up, lipstick, preparations for a party. Her very own mirror.

Family photographs present a severely edited narrative of the past. As if all life happened against that hedge, in that garden: in sunlight. One by one, the participants disappear. Geoffrey Hadman, blazer, cap crumpled awkwardly in left hand, takes up the pose he has practised from childhood. Shuffle the wilting pack of images in any order, reverse time. Anna, as a baby, with mother and aunt. Cats, dogs, dolls. Open-top cars. The Auster parked in a field. William and Florence Hadman: bespectacled, hatted. Their pipe-smoking son, much taller than his father, rests a hand on the old man's shoulder. Infant Anna, in Churchillian siren suit, braves Rectory Lane with her cousin Judy.

Anna's brother William told us about the only Hadmans he had discovered. One worked for the railway. His name is published on a wall, between Hackford (S) and Hale (E): the memorial to the war dead in King's Cross Station. ('To the immortal memory of the men of the Great Northern Railway who gave their lives in the Great War.') So Hadman (E) escaped from his home country, on at least one occasion, to die in a foreign land.

Alan Moore disputes the fable about Boadicea being buried under a platform at King's Cross. He thinks she's lying beneath a Northampton mound, returned with honour: like the victorious Margaret Thatcher being landfilled at Grantham. Hadman (E) is no fiction. He is visible to anyone walking between ticket hall and train: black lettering on white marble.

The second rescued Hadman, Oscar, was ambitious. Determined to stretch his horizons, he booked passage on a liner headed from Southampton to New York, pride of the White Star Line. A new beginning in a new country: courtesy of the *Titanic*. He is listed among the survivors. (Further research disproved my notion of Oscar as a country boy, escaping Fenland inertia. Probably German, he shipped out from Cherbourg, giving his destination as: 414 West First Street, Sioux Falls, South Dakota. One of a minority of Third Class male passengers to find a place in a lifeboat, Oscar was picked up by the *SS Carpathia* on 18 April 1912. At which point, bowing modestly, he slips from our story.)

In June 1938, William and Florence Hadman sat for passport photographs; a strange moment to be contemplating a European holiday. Anna isn't sure, but she thinks they had never been abroad before, and that her father, with his affection for Germany, might have been taking them there. Signatures on the documents are clear and firm. William has the high cheekbones, grey moustache, of his grandson and namesake. Steady stare: straight through photographic paper. Through meddlers troubling his memory.

The last item we examined, that day in the Glinton pub, was a copy of William Hadman's birth certificate. Born: 28 December 1872. Registered: 17 January 1873 at Peterborough. Father: Robert Hadman. Rank or profession: cottager. Mother: Louisa Maria Hadman, formerly Devonshire. Place of birth: Werrington, Northants.

That's it, I thought. Move out. Move on. Werrington. Anna winced, she was beginning to flag. 'We never did a trip with the kids, heading west, without two earthworks, a cathedral and a germ-warfare facility, before breakfast,' she moaned. The family learnt to gang up on me. 'He's reading the country,' they chorused: as I plunged into a thicket, across a stream, through head-high nettles. They stayed on tarmac. 'Can dad fetch the car *now*?' one of them would ask before we negotiated the first incline.

Werrington was where it would begin to connect, the cottager Hadmans and the peasant Clares. John Clare's mother, Ann Stimson, came from Castor; her father was town shepherd. Castor is separated from Werrington by Milton Park. You could form a triangle between Helpston, Werrington and Castor: improvise the rest of the story from that. Hadmans may well have been in Werrington in July 1841; when John Clare arrived, broken down, at the limits of his endurance:

when I got on the high road I rested on the stone heaps as I passed till I was able to go on afresh & bye & bye I passed Walton & soon reached Werrington & was making for the Beehive as fast as I could when a cart met me with a man & a woman & a boy in it when nearing me the woman jumped out & caught fast hold of my hands & wished me to get into the cart but I refused & thought her either drunk or mad but when I was told it was my second wife Patty I got in & was soon at Northborough but Mary was not there neither could I get any information about her further then the old story of her being dead six years ago which might have been taken from a bran new old Newspaper printed a dozen years ago but I took no notice of the blarney having seen her myself about a twelvemonth ago alive & well & as young as ever – so here I am homeless at home & half gratified to feel that I can be happy anywhere

Werrington

Glinton is free of Peterborough, by a breath, but Werrington has been swallowed, split. There are estates, screened highways on the Milton Keynes model, along with the preserved fossil of the original village: a cluster of pubs, a church, the road that Clare travelled. It generally takes longer to drive to Werrington from Glinton than to walk: make an ill-advised turn and the system is unforgiving. Here is another of England's virtual landscapes, a proposal, a drawing laid down over something drowsy but not quite dead: sculpted earthworks, tactful plantings, traffic-calming measures that induce apoplexy. Movement is method. Trust the road and it will carry you to the next retail park, the next Travelodge. The ever-present but teasingly inaccessible cathedral.

We drive. There is nobody at home; deserted Church Street, deserted village green: nowhere to park on either of them. The populace, if it exists, is indoors, keeping its communal head down. Afternoon television in empty rooms. A Northborough farm cart, deranged walker, a bit of a domestic: that would be a headline event in contemporary Werrington. A cat crossing the road would make the front page.

It's early afternoon, never a good time for Anna, she knows how it will be: locked church, knocking on impervious doors, phone numbers of discontinued agencies. Clare's pub, the Beehive, is not to be found (it was never here). Trade directories from the period list the Cock, the Blue Bell and the Wheat Sheaf. The nearest Beehive, according to Eric Robinson, was at Stamford. The Cock and the Blue Bell have survived; in the course of our Werrington labours we tried them both.

We march on the church, our obvious starting point, Anna on one side of the road, myself on the other. I photograph the pub, the village sign, and a thatched cottage: complete with visible quotation marks. Whenever I notice a whitewashed (mouth-washed, deloused) property, blinking at the twenty-first century, I feel obliged to snap back. Werrington is post-ironic, freeze-dried, brittle with anxiety. Rightly suspicious of intruders, fabricators of false memory. With the disappearance of the Beehive, there is no reason for thesis writers, Clare brokers, to step out of their cars.

The road is the road. It used to go somewhere, now it's a self-referential loop, a circuit that is reluctant to let a potential client (toll-payer) get away. Settlements are unsettling. Rate-payers are busy with this new, electronic hobby: inventing ancestors, shaking the family tree. The great genealogical game show. We suffer from a compulsion to apologise for the present malaise, the mess we've made of things. (Just as they did, our fathers, in their own way.)

I'm ahead of Anna, when I walk through the gate at the west end of the Parish Church of St John the Baptist (with Emmanuel). I see the stone, it had to be there; I wait. Anna should go first. We've crossed an invisible line and made contact with a previously unknown Hadman. Mary Annabel Rose has returned to roots she never knew she had. To Werrington.

On the left, inside the gate, is a large, grey-white stone which has been split in half. The memorial to Anna's great-grandfather, Robert; father of William Hadman of the Red House. The damage to the stone, recent vandalism, runs right through Robert's name. The rubric patches together the family dead, as and when they became available.

SACRED TO THE MEMORY

OF

LOUISA MARIA,

THE BELOVED WIFE OF

ROBERT HADMAN

WHO FELL ASLEEP

OCTR. 19TH 1907

AGED 68 YEARS

+

SO HE GIVETH HIS BELOVED SLEEP

ALSO OF

ROBERT HADMAN

DIED SEPTR 21ST 1924

AGED 87 YEARS

–

AT REST

From nowhere, Anna has acquired a great-grandfather with her junior brother's name. The senior brother, William, acknowledges the Glinton farmer. This vandalised Robert opens a new chapter. He must have visited Glinton? His son had been living there for fifteen years when the old man died. Anna's father was born the year that William bought the Red House, 1909. But Anna says he never mentioned Robert, his Werrington grandfather, or any other Peterborough-fringe relatives. The only Glinton event she remembers him talking about was a row with his father, over his reluctance, as an Oxford undergraduate, to help with the harvest. He was pushing socially, she reckons, moving up (in the fashion Clare decries). Geoffrey was the first member of the family to make it to university, to escape. And in some style. (That was her assumption. The farm life, she knew, was a hard one.)

Keeping Robert and Louisa company are more fading Hadmans. Henry who died in 1893. George. Alice Machin (daughter of Robert). Her sister, May Wright. Then, after I try the church door, another Robert. A favoured position beside the path. Anna's great-great-grandfather? Born 1808. Died 1863. Married to Rebecca. A second churchwarden in the family?

The vicar, I notice, has a house at the far end of the village, a safe distance from importunate brass-rubbers and drive-by genealogists. We'll try him. The signs aren't promising. St John the Baptist at Werrington has opted to go with the spirit of John Prescott's M11 corridor: the off-highway city that will stretch from London to

Stansted, Cambridge to Peterborough. Satellite estates. Service stations selling everything you don't need. Car-boot sales twinned with collectors' fairs. Motels that specialise in American breakfasts for jacketless reps. Churches have to find a marketable pitch or shut up shop: peddle historic properties to downsizing urbanites with a taste for the bizarre.

'The Alpha Course – an opportunity to explore the meaning of life,' whispers a church notice. 'Can you Handle the National Marriage Week 10 minute challenge?'

The burial grounds of St John's are composted with ex-Hadmans; Hadmans and Stimsons, side by side, contiguous in death. The family of Anna's father cohabiting with the relatives of John Clare's mother. Anna is beginning to feel weighed down with names, dates, biographies teased from the ground. Werrington has been made into an island, cut off by Peterborough ring roads; a motorway circuit between Fenland and the softer country where Ann Stimson's father looked after the Castor flocks.

The padre, disturbed at his afternoon leisure, can't understand why anyone would want to see inside a church when no performance is taking place. 'My wife's family,' I mutter. 'They come from here. Generations planted in your graveyard.'

He walks with us, down the village street, past the Blue Bell; a Canadian, slightly poached around the edges. We are let in at the side door. Church and office are indistinguishable: carpeted, rigged for video projection. 'It's a crying shame about these things,' the vicar remarks (of the Norman pillars with their zigzag patterning). 'They sure spoil the throw.' He meant the lightbeam that magnified his preaching self on to an elevated silver screen.

'The church is not buildings but people,' he explains (in the parish magazine). 'Jesus Christ. Here we can come to know him personally.' The vicar's editorial goes on to regret the fact that Our Lord wasn't able to make a personal appearance this season, due to prior commitments; he reassures parishioners (clients) that the next instalment of Hollywood's Tolkien saga, released in time for Christmas, under the title *The Return of the King*, is a portent. To the initiated, movie trailers are subliminal prompts. Other items flagged on the magazine's cover include: 'Coping with Cancer, Energised by the Lord' and 'Recycling a Goat and Saving the World'.

We realise, very quickly, that messing about with old bones is ill-advised and probably perverse. The church of St John has been around since the twelfth century. It is inconvenient for present needs (inadequate parking facilities); it might have to be relocated to a custom-built municipal hall. Werrington, one of five manors in the parish of Paston, dates its settlement to 1013, when the manor was held by, and worked for, the benefit of Peterborough Abbey.

The current operation is slick and persuasive: 'all sermons are recorded and kept in the Parish Office'. But it doesn't come cheap. 'All members of the church have the privilege and responsibility of enabling the financial costs of the church's work to be met through the giving of money.' One tenth of income is suggested as 'a good guide'. By Banker's Order: 'monthly payments'. Or Stewardship Envelopes: 'each week in offering basket'.

Other churches in the Peterborough outwash are sullen, silent, ashamed of their neglect, preoccupied with petty arguments over flower arranging. Energetic course leaders (such as our Werrington friend) organise their parishes like pyramid salesmen: worshippers become 'one of the family', under the umbrella of a great corporation. Actual families of farmers, butchers and bakers are redundant. The village Clare reached, four miles out of Peterborough, was a thin line of cottages, two or three pubs. The present church serves an ever-expanding network of housing estates; it has adapted accordingly.

We have to look elsewhere for news of Anna's relatives: starting with the Parish Office in Twelvetrees Avenue. Here is new Werrington, wide roads branching into generic estates; a civic block with parking bays and security doors. Local history is on file, on-line. The relevant official, Mrs Val Watkinson, gives us the name of a woman who might be able to help. This lady has made it her business to gather up friable newspapers, parish records, census listings: to put flesh on the bones of graveyard names. She lives down the lane from the church. A phone call is made. The amateur genealogist, overwhelmed by many such requests, is prepared to see us. The Werrington Hadmans? They are in the files, certainly. If she can dig them out.

Very soon, in an L-shaped bungalow, across a hospitable table, tea and biscuits, we are looking into the eyes of dead Hadmans. The paterfamilias with his coven of daughters, women you would be foolish to cross. The grand lady who wouldn't ride on a butcher's cart. A church choir. A wedding party. The story comes in fits and starts: a farm here, a property there, a pair of sisters marrying brothers. Prosperity for some, ruin for others.

The local historian, Mrs Judith Bunten, heard of a cache of glass negatives, about to be scrapped. She rescued them, had prints made. The archive of a village photographer became the basis for a book: *Werrington through the Ages*. Numerous Hadmans were on record. The family had been embedded here, Werrington and Paston, for centuries. The Robert Hadman (1808–1863) who married Rebecca was indeed the father of the Robert (1835–1924) of the split memorial stone. The one who married Louisa Maria Devonshire (1839–1907). Father of William Hadman of the Red House.

'I'm hung about with them now,' Anna said. 'They're waiting, waiting – watching.' It was too sudden, this stampede of Werrington ghosts. Lifeless faces pressing against the window. Familiar names worn by unfamiliar people. Great-grandfather Robert's older brother, Henry, what became of him? And Robert's children: Robert Henry, William (who married Florence Rose), Edith Caroline (who married George Tyler)? And: George, May, Alice, Percy, Alfred?

We'd seen a plaque for George and Caroline Tyler in the church: 'In Loving Memory of George Henry Tyler. 12 September 1871–14 March 1946, church warden for many years, and Caroline his wife, Dec 1 1874–July 30 1962. The Lord shall give thee rest.' Anna remembered, as a child, when she was staying in Glinton, talk of this considerable personage, Aunt Car. She'd married well.

The Tylers were prominent butchers. Tyler was in partnership with Twelvetree, the man who became a street in new Werrington.

Photographs are easier than parish records. Photographs are always contemporary, our brazen gaze hazarding a gulf in time and culture. Thinking we can know these lives by noticing stiff poses, arrangements of hair, brave outfits exposed to brass-mounted cameras. We survey lost streets, in the belief that the dead will move again. Here is Tyler's cart; in which Caroline was too ladylike to ride (unlike Patty Clare, who came to Werrington in search of her vagrant husband). Fire engines. Primitive airfields. Those images caught my fancy as I riffled through Mrs Bunten's book. It seems there was a long-established tradition, around Peterborough, in the villages, of flying.

In 1920, Tom Stimson flew from a field near Marholm Wood. Werrington had its own aerodrome, a disused barn. Geoffrey Hadman's exploits in the Auster were true to a custom of freelance flight that ran all the way back to the shamanic schools of Stamford, the gobblers of dream-inducing mushrooms. Old planes looked like agricultural machinery expecting a favourable wind, a gale. Men in caps stood around primitive sheds, waiting for farmland to be converted into parks for premature-retaliation American bombers.

October 1911: an aeroplane, canvas and wire, circled Peterborough for the first time. Early flight is a record of spectacular accidents. Mr Ewen, sportingly avoiding large trees near Werrington, 'failed to land on skids' and ploughed into the earth; the heavy engine burying itself like one of the Ramsey stones. Boys of the village inspected the carnage. As did the photographer. Farmers looked for ways to turn land, heavy and wet, into cash: a slaughterhouse, a bakery, a battery farm, an aerodrome. One of the Hadmans, with a strip of useless ground, 'lying on the side of a good road', attempted (May 1872) to peddle: 'Four acres of TARES, an excellent crop.' Tares are featured in the Old Testament as 'a noxious weed', probably darnel. Grass with flat leaves and terminal spikes. Fodder a starving mule wouldn't touch.

In such a field, 25 June 1920, there was a passenger flight from

Werrington. The pilot, Donald Hastings Sadler (twenty-one), said 'Cheerio' to his mechanics and saluted a small group of onlookers. At 2,000 feet, 'wings dropped away from the fuselage', his machine plummeted. The pilot, who bailed out, smashed into the ground at Cock Inn corner.

Mrs Bunten's archives, her memories, rescue Werrington from its present malaise: sleepwalkers in the trance of motorway England. Robert Hadman and his brother Henry lived in Hall Lane, across the road from the village's grandest property: Werrington Hall, home of the Everards. The brothers were listed on census forms as 'cottagers', a kind of rural middle-class between tenant farmers like the Joyces (Websters, Vergettes) and peasants like the Clares. (Patty Clare's father, William Turner, was a cottager. He employed labourers to help with his land.) Cottagers kept a few animals and worked a strip or two of field, acquired at the time of enclosures. Despite outward appearances, village society never stood still: the energetic adapted and thrived, while steady labourers, waiting for seasonal employment, felt the bite of the times. The smarter children moved on, following the railways or the potentialities of industrial towns.

Henry Hadman, between 1860 and 1870, was empowered to keep a 'sparrow book'. Boys of the village were paid a few pence for every dead sparrow they brought to Henry's door. And he, in neat hand, would enter the details of the kill, the money dispersed, in his ledger.

Further down Hall Lane was a cattle trough and a pond. One night, so Mrs Bunten told us, drawing on a story she'd heard from Albert Plant (who, at a hundred and one, was the oldest man in the village), there had been the sound of a car, a very unusual thing. Albert, a lad in his nightshirt, crept to the window, to witness the sweeping lights of the vehicle. Two passengers: a gentleman and a young woman. Next morning, the woman was found dead, drowned, a supposed suicide, in the cattle trough. Why, Mrs Bunten wanted to know, had this girl, who had been in service and was making her way home, not thrown herself into the pond, which she must have passed?

Another Hadman, John, cousin of Robert, illustrates the darker side of the rural economy: thrive or perish. He married well, so it was thought, the daughter of Edward Pitts the wheelwright; he was set up with a bakery. The shop was in the wrong place. Werrington had two superior establishments. John's bakery foundered: stale loaves, dead sparrows on a string. Moles pegged out like leather kites. John played with Robert Hadman and George Pitts in a brass band (Anna's favourite music). It didn't help.

John published the fact that, like Mr Rawlings of Peterborough, he would supply 'Members in the Neighbourhood, with Bread at *Sixpence Farthing* the four pound loaf and Flour at a reduction of 2d per stone'. The advertisement didn't work, villagers patronised the bakers they knew. John took out a licence on a Werrington inn, the Wheat Sheaf. Then offered it for sale.

By April 1868 he was again put to the expense of inserting a notice in the newspaper: 'I, John Hadman, will not be answerable for any Debt or Debts my wife, Francis Charlotte Hadman, may contract after this date.' An unfortunate marriage, expectations dashed: disaster. Mrs Bunten thinks that John fell into a depression and killed himself. Melancholia drifts from the Fens like clammy autumn mists.

Young Robert Hadman, husband of Louisa Maria, prospered. He moved to the Cherry House Farm on the main road through Werrington: Church Street. The road on which Clare would have come, limping from Peterborough, for his collision with Patty. Perhaps it was the Wheat Sheaf he favoured? Robert would have been six years old at the time; his brother Henry, seven. They might have witnessed the scene, as they roamed the village, looking for sparrows to kill.

Robert managed cherry orchards. His thatched farm, the one I photographed on our walk to the church, was now a restaurant with a Routier badge. The orchards were on the far side of the road. Old Albert Plant recalled being sent as a boy to drive the cherry crop to Peterborough on his cart. 'Remember, lad; I've counted them,' stern Mr Hadman used to say. 'I'll know if you eat so much as one.' Peterborough was famous for its cherries.

It was a rare Hadman, bankruptcies and brass bands aside, who made it into newsprint: the *Peterborough Advertiser*. But Robert's funeral notice (of 1924) preceded the tributes accorded to his second son, William.

YESTERDAY

In the presence of a sympathetic gathering of mourners and friends, the remains of Mr. Robert Hadman, one of the most well-known and respected inhabitants of Werrington, who passed away on Sunday morning, after a short illness, were laid to rest in Werrington Churchyard yesterday (Thursday) afternoon. Deceased, who was 87 years of age, had taken a prominent part in the life of the district and held many public offices, which he relinquished a few years ago owing to failing eyesight.

He was the second son of the late Mr Robert Hadman, farmer, of Werrington . . . For many years Mr Hadman was a member of the Werrington Parish Council, and prior to the formation of the Parish Council, acted as Surveyor to the village. For sixty years he was a member of the Werrington Church Choir, and he possessed a very fine tenor voice . . . He was an original member of the old Greycoats, when he played the euphonium, and had vivid recollections of playing at the wedding of the present Marquis of Huntly to the first Marchioness over 50 years ago. He was in the Corps Band when they went to Bristol and secured a second place in a band contest . . . He was hon. treasurer of the Werrington Pig Club . . .

Highlights of the orchard-keeper's life are taken down by a jobbing hack, along with names of those who attended the service. Eight of his twelve children were present. 'Of the sons,' remarks the obituarist, 'William Hadman is a successful farmer at Glinton.' Alfred is the schoolmaster at Newborough. Percy has taken over the family farm. Hadmans, Tylers, Machins, Aspittles, Vergettes and Roses are well represented. The coffin is of plain English oak with brass fittings. The funeral arrangements are by Mr A. Stimson. If the Hadmans weren't related to the Stimsons, they were buried by them. And beside them. Generation after generation in the small churchyard of St John the Baptist.

And here the story seems to end. The older Robert came to Werrington, his sons stayed. Some of them kept pubs. One looked after cherry orchards. One tried to peddle tares. Beyond Anna's

great-great-grandfather, the thread was lost. The earliest census record places Robert in Washingley, a settlement on the ridge above Stilton, now excised from the map. Only the photographs in Mrs Bunten's book stay alive: unblinking eyes test our nerve. A conduit into a past that we can read, remake, but never experience.

Standing outside his property at 90 Church Street, Robert Hadman's pride is in being present, in this place. Trim white beard. Euphonium-player's moustache. Striped coat and matching waistcoat. Bow tie. Heavy watchchain. Savagely polished boots. A man of substance. The sleeves of his coat swallow working hands. Behind him, in the darkness of the window, is the faint outline of a watching woman. The white impression of a high collar and an unseen face.

On the same occasion, Robert's daughters are brought out. Strong-featured, tall: not a smile to muster between them. Women

who married butchers. Or became feared school-teachers. Anna identifies with the dark Caroline and the redbrick villa she built, on Church Street; its name still visible above the door: Carisville.

Mrs Bunten, keeper of images, is also a keeper of secrets. A twin. Her mother, so she says, had no idea that a brother was coming. The passion for collecting and collating Werrington family histories begins with her own. A mystery in her parentage, undiscussed until that moment, was revealed when she was told to look closely at the name-plate on her grandfather's coffin. She learnt that, as with the Clares and many other village families, there were children born out of wedlock. The name on the coffin, the blood she shared, was Stimson.

Peterborough

Peterborough confounds us, as it confounded Clare. The boy who walked from his Helpston cottage to the Glinton turnpike, the cathedral city; down to the river, for his hopeless excursion to Wisbech. And the troubled poet captured by the wife of a bishop. Peterborough is like a dying star, dragging in debris from the surrounding countryside, swallowing villages and villagers. We make several circuits of the asteroid belt, stop-starting, before we crack it: a way of reaching the car park of the Bull Hotel. (Convenient for library, museum and Queensgate Shopping Centre.)

Even in my bookdealing days Peterborough was an occasional visit, two low-key shops, modest prices, modest returns. *Driffs Guide* (*sic*), as tricky to negotiate as the Peterborough road system, ignores the town completely and, in later editions, dismisses its premier hutch, Old Soke Books, in a sentence: 'I'm sure the name of this shop is a mistake, he didn't look like an alcoholic to me.' A fact worth remarking in the provincial trade.

In more recent times, I received a list of Clare materials from the Peterborough poet and dealer Paul Green. I ordered the 1964 reissue of Frederick Martin's 1865 biography. Martin reports the tale of Clare being taken up by Mrs George Marsh, the German-born wife of the bishop; a lady of irresistible charity who did her best to anchor the poet to a writing desk, while macerating him in the society of the cathedral close. The long-suffering bishop was persuaded at one point to visit Clare's home. 'It was certainly not a little "Malapropos" that you could not ask your noble visitor to enter your cottage, in consequence of the door being lock'd against you,' Mrs Marsh chided. They had the misfortune to try Helpston on a day when Patty found her husband unmanageable: drunk as a bookman.

Walking, Martin suggests, soothed and repaired Clare. He was persuaded to leave the confinement of the Northborough cottage for short excursions, during which the melancholy poet allowed himself to be guided, Lear-like, by his daughters. 'Daily rambles continued for more than a month, Clare at last seemed almost recovered from his malady.' Repeated rituals form a circuit in the brain, a mapping confirmed and improved by each new day's stroll: the trivia of village life, the breath of the fields.

He pushed his circuits wider – heath, woods, road – until he found himself caught in the coils of Peterborough. (As Stamford was to Helpston, the destination of youth and ambition, so Peterborough was to Clare's Northborough exile: a symbol of alienation, hapless wandering, doctors and bishops.)

One day, when rambling about on the confines of the cathedral city, he met and was recognised by Mrs. Marsh. The good old lady was delighted to see her poet again, and insisted that he should make up for his former neglect by accompanying her at once, and staying for a few days at the episcopal mansion . . . To prevent her poet from running away again, [she] kept him constantly in her company. Conversing with him on all subjects, Mrs. Marsh at times thought his remarks rather singular; while his sudden swerving from one topic to another often astonished her not a little. But all this the good lady held to be perfectly natural in a poet and a man of genius.

Clare endured, until it came to the episode in the theatre. Provincial theatres are large events in small towns, social as much as artistic; a question of being seen, of patronising the culture. Joseph Merrick, the Elephant Man, was brought from his room at the London Hospital, to plays and performances. (Not knowing that he himself was the prime exhibit.) John Clare, the trophy of Mrs Marsh, was carried in triumph to a production of *The Merchant of Venice*. He stood up in the 'box reserved for the wife of the Lord Bishop', and yelled at Shylock: 'You villain, you murderous villain!' His final act of sanity: getting himself ejected from the theatre, the claustrophobia of the cathedral close. Returned to wife and family.

The next morning, Clare went back to Northborough, having received an intimation from Mrs. Marsh that it would be best he should go home at once. He wandered forth from the city in a dreamy mood, and lost his way before he had gone far. Some acquaintances found him sitting in a meadow, near the hamlet of Gunthorpe, and seeing his wild and haggard looks and strange manners, they took him by the arm and led him back to Peterborough.

Gunthorpe is found between Paston and Werrington, Hadman territory. Clare's collapse was a rehearsal for the fugue of escape from High Beach, the incident with the farm cart. Werrington seems to be a pivotal place, between the pull of Peterborough and seductive memories of Glinton spire and Mary Joyce: meadows of tares, pig sheds, future airfields. Hadmans who are not buried in Werrington are buried in Paston: George Edward and his wife, Emily, H. R. Hadman and Lavinia Hadman, Walter John, Jessie, James, Robert Henry, Robert Henry Ford, Edith Carrie, Edward.

Paul Green, a poet living on London Road, Peterborough, down which Clare marched, identifies with the myth. I asked him if, having grown up in the area, he knew of any Hadmans, and he replied:

My identification with Clare is very personal, and nurtured by my living (between the ages of three and seven) in the village of Marholm, some two or three miles from Helpston . . .

Early indigence in the Marholm and Helpston localities, then a later exposure to poetry, helped bring me to a very personal appreciation, and identification with Clare. He is not simply the local famous poet (with his name given to a pub and a library theatre), but an outsider symbol, or a figure of marginality that shows to what extent a person's origins can descend, without the need for expressive creativity being expunged . . .

When I attended school in Walton, there was a caretaker whose name might have been Hadman. My second sister, born after being rehoused and moved from Marholm, now lives in Whittlesey . . . One curious point here is that her husband's family owned a bungalow in the Eastfield district of Peterborough, which meant that for many years they were the next-door neighbour to Edward Storey. Before he went into adult education, Storey held a clerical position with Hotpoint, so would have worked in a similar profession, and the same office (probably a large one) as my father. Storey, as you know, turned into a Clare biographer, so there is a somewhat sophisticated and circuitous later connection.

Contemporary poets reiterate Clare's experience: and in doing so discover themselves. Myth becomes truth. Modernist 'open field poetics', as proposed by Charles Olson, defy the system of enclosures imposed on language by formalist reactionaries. Rip out hedges, fences, prohibitions, for a method of reading the world from horizon to horizon. No ceilings in time. No knowledge that may not be accessed and inserted. Such metaphors are wasted on Peterborough, a town without irony. How else could they boast of a John Clare pub, library and – theatre?

This is not a comfortable town to negotiate. The market element has been overwhelmed by a retail labyrinth, the Queensgate Shopping Centre: 'John Lewis, Marks & Spencer, Argos, Bhs, Boots, Waitrose, Virgin Megastore plus 100 other shops in a relaxed environment.' An arcade project owing more to Walt Disney than Walter Benjamin. Solitaries and reluctant groups stagger around the notional centre in search of a quorum, enough ciderheads to make up a mob.

I'd never before witnessed a feeding frenzy of the kind encouraged by an eat-till-you-burst-for-a-fiver Chinese restaurant. Genetically-modified birthday kids (English faces, pale and crumpled, on American bodies) take it in turns to stand under an ice-cream dispenser, mouths agape; visibly inflated on a teat of soft yellow slurry. Saturday-night dudes, cowboy boots and string ties, waddle in from the backwoods, to cruise trays of sticky batter-meats and fish balls. They compete to see how many circuits they can achieve before they are too swollen to get out of the chair. The room disappears into a dense flatus of incense, aftershave, sweet gravy, cola-wind and tobacco: sucked between mouthfuls as an appetite depressant, to make room for the next shovel-load of chemical swill.

Sated with remorseless good times, we retreat: windblown, rain-pelted, down parodically generous pedestrian precincts that advertise their total absence of content. A chainstore is peddling discounted first editions of J. G. Ballard's *Millennium People* for a couple of pounds; local scavengers are not agile enough to bend down to check the price ticket. The only sure method of finding your hotel, even when it is fifty yards away, is to call a cab. But that's impossible. Cabbies are too smart to risk picking anything off the streets at the weekend. They run a shuttle service from outlying villages to city-centre clubs, booze barns with a door policy barring customers wearing anything more elaborate than lip-piercings and Elastoplast. There is no transport when you need it, but scratch your ear, lift your knuckles from the paved highway, and a mini-cabber will bundle you into his vehicle with the alacrity of a Beirut kidnapper.

We had a number of items to check before we left town: the enclosure maps of Glinton in the Peterborough Library, the premises of the photographer who made card portraits of Anna's unknown relatives, the butcher's shop once operated by the family of Anna's first cousin, Judy Brown. But the real attraction, for me, was the 'small collection of ornamental snuffboxes' that Jonathan Bate says is 'still held by Peterborough Museum and Art Gallery Society'. The boxes were among the 'very few possessions' left at John Clare's death. Random gifts. Scarcely enough to fill a suitcase.

The library was no problem. I could have spent hours poring over maps, but I knew by this point that there were no Hadmans in Glinton before the early twentieth century. A short walk through the town demonstrated that the premises of Thomas Blackman, 'Artist Photographer, Miniature & Portrait Painter of St John Street', had vanished. The artist photographer ('portraits coloured to order') placed himself between the old cattle market and the cathedral, in the expectation of catching farmers. Anna's relative, the old gentleman with the snowy Shaker beard, is undergoing an ordeal, an ordeal of retention. His eyes have black holes at the centre of the irises, holes in a statue. The 'artistic' part of the transaction is discovered in a wispy loss of focus around the edges, leaving the rustic patriarch afloat: a very material spirit summoned at a seance. The old lady in her cane chair, caped like a widow, clutches a dead flower. She doesn't look at the camera, at us. She meditates on mortality, the uplifting text that will be cut into her gravestone.

BROWNS SPECIALITY MEATS are also defunct. The family firm has decamped to Stilton, on-line butchery, quality provisions for the carriage trade. Peterborough no longer sustains a connection between Hadman farmers and Hadman butchers, between relatives to north and south of the Nene. The market and the big agricultural shows were once the meeting place: business, gossip, society. Lawrie Hadman, her father's older brother, so Anna discovers, worked as a butcher in Whittlesey before he took up farming in Glinton. He trained in Chelmsford. We saw the photograph: arcades of meat, hooked herds, naked chickens, all-too-human pigs (like headless clients of the Chinese restaurant).

That leaves the museum and art gallery. Which is closed, while an exhibition is being hung. But I persist; I get somebody on the phone, discover the hour when we'll be allowed in. The grey stone building is forbidding, information is given out with some reluctance. Clare's pathetic goods have been imprisoned here, and can be viewed, if we insist on it, as part of a journey between one gallery and another. 'Tiny tots are welcome in our award-winning *Mini Museum*, while adults can get nostalgic in the *Period Shop*.'

The reason I'm so keen to view the snuffboxes is that Anna, who is not by temperament a collector or hoarder, makes an exception for small boxes. It began when we travelled together and I insisted on ducking into used-book shops 'for a few moments'. Which might stretch into hours: back rooms, cellars, circuitous conversations endured in procession towards improbable treasure. Anna hit the junk shops, usually in the same part of town, and trawled for curious boxes. Bone, brass, plastic. Round, square, oval.

Old Soke Books in Peterborough worked out well; alongside the books were a few curios, tins, figurines. Anna fell for a pair of wooden Chinese puzzle boxes. One had a sliding lid with a river scene: beached boat, four trees, distant snow-capped mountain. The boat was heaped with earth, a shape that duplicated the mountain. Inside the box were fifteen numbered squares; which, exploiting a single free space, could be manoeuvred into a correct sequence. The second, larger box was more interesting. It came from the same source: another river scene, in marquetry, on the lid. Two moored craft, one tree with two branches, one boat under sail, distant snow-capped mountain. The trick was to open the box by sliding various chequered panels.

Anna couldn't crack it. The bookman watched her struggle, then revealed the secret. A blindman had solved the mystery. I didn't ask why a blind person would be visiting a bookshop that didn't run to items in Braille. By touch, the puzzle was solved. Inside the box was another puzzle: a board divided into complex shapes that had to be fitted together.

Under some pressure, Anna lent the puzzle to a relative, who wanted to try it on a wealthy patron, a collector of such things: private press fine editions, games, watches, pens. The man died. The collection was dispersed. Anna's puzzle vanished. That is the fate of such objects. All puzzles are metaphors. Moves must be made blind, like the clicking of prayer beads, hand gestures, mudras: the purpose is to stretch time. Solutions are meaningless. Unthinking motions of the fingers are everything.

Clare's snuffboxes would offer a remote trace of the man's heat; hands rubbing against wood or brass. In Northampton, I had seen the books. This was more intimate: touch without premeditation, reflex gestures when the mind is elsewhere. Personal objects exposed for public exhibition, trophies of a city's self-satisfied display.

The term 'snuffbox' has a double meaning: Thanatos and Eros. Death and love. Wooden casket. Pudendum. Sniffing and snuffing. Clare relished such word play. In High Beach, stirred by prurient fantasies, taking on the Byronic rags of *Don Juan*, he pictured Lord Melbourne violating the 'snuffbox' of little Victoria, the new queen. He imagined himself, in Oedipal pride, as the queen's father: Ubu in madness. An asylum clown polishing the box which is both a receptacle for his own ashes and the gamey delta of his daughter's sexuality. (The daughter who has replaced him on the throne of England.)

When Lucia Joyce was treated by Jung, the Swiss analyst employed a woman called Cary Baynes, who had trained at the Johns Hopkins Medical School, to act as her companion. Lucia didn't respond to Jung. She found his insistence on remembering dreams a nuisance. Lucia preferred Baynes: who talked about leucocytes by their proper name. The beginning of transference occurred, so the companion decided, when Lucia presented her with a small hand-painted box.

Blood again. It was discovered that Lucia suffered from what Joyce called 'a superabundance of white corpostles'. 'Hers is not a disease at all,' he wrote to Giorgio, 'but a symptom.' Misdiagnosis and failure to attend to the obvious set Lucia on the path to Northampton. Undisclosed dreams. Dreams from which there was no escape.

Anna, when I first knew her, husbanded her energies; 'pale and interesting' was her number. That was what she had been told, amid the din of family life, and she went with it: rests after lunch, pints of stout to counter a supposed iron deficiency. Periods of Keatsian languor were justified by vague (and hopeless) medical opinion. All too soon, she would be running a classroom of cadet Hackney gangstas, a house, three children of her own; an improbable regime beginning at six in the morning with housework and concluding with a full family meal. There were, there had to be, periods of 'collapse'. Blood was tested and found to be deficient in red corpuscles. Platelets were counted at regular intervals. Pills prescribed. Then, much later, came a frightening episode, nightmarish, unexplained: darkness pressing too hard, difficulty in stepping outside. Fortunately, Anna's sister recognised the symptoms: thyroid. More pills, calm restored, condition managed. But it is very easy to see how the mechanics of blood, misread, lay a person, often a woman, open to barbaric treatment and physical abuse.

Tim Chilcott, introducing *John Clare: The Living Year, 1841*, speaks of 'tortured clutches at a sense of dissolving identity . . . counter-pointed against perceptions of complete clarity and ordinariness'. In these unpredictable shifts of perception lies the terror: visionary instants, unbidden voices. Dictation the scribe struggles to clarify.

'Cun-ys' and snuffboxes occupy Clare's High Beach satires: 'The snuff went here and the snuff went there.' Men are prisoners and women are ravished: 'All that map of childhood is overcast.' The spire of the forest church points straight to heaven. Clare sits in a clearing, waiting for gypsies, taking a pinch of snuff.

> Prince Albert goes to Germany & must he
> Leave the queens snuff box where all fools are strumming
> From addled eggs no chicken can be coming

I wrote to Peterborough Museum's 'Access Officer: Curator-Human History' enquiring after Clare's collection. 'Thank you for your letter,' she replied.

I'm afraid we have only the one snuffbox, which is on display. Also, I cannot find anything in our index that refers to Clare's walk from Epping Forest to Northborough . . . Public access to the manuscripts is tightly controlled and usually only academic researchers are able to utilise them in a useful way. We would require a reference from your academic affiliation for access to manuscripts. Two weeks' notice is also required for appointments.

Two weeks we don't have. I settle for Clare's rather sad display case. The solitary box sits alongside an open copy of *The Village Minstrel*. The ends have been rounded: it's a wooden book. 'Snuff-box which belonged to John Clare and was later owned by his relative John Clare Billing, and then passed to L. Tebbutt of Stamford,' says a typed card.

The wood is dark and highly polished. The lid slides open by way of an indentation in the shape of a human fingernail.

We retreat for the night to the Bull Hotel. What do we have to show for our Peterborough researches? Anna's sense of being draped with Werrington relatives: shrunken heads on her shoulders, fox masks. Names and dates from mildewed tombs. A family tree for John Clare supplied by Peter Moyse of the Clare Society. Six rolls of exposed film. And my instinct to move out, start walking: we must try to follow Clare's voyage down the Nene, from the town bridge to Wisbech.

Among the papers, spread across the executive-style desk, is the photocopy of a newspaper in smudged type. An obituary notice, for 'The Late Mr. William Rose of Glassmoor', published under the heading: 'Whittlesey Farmer's Funeral'. A note has been written in the margin: 'Father of Grandmother Hadman.'

Checking Clare's family tree, I made a potential discovery. On the line descended from the poet's daughter, Eliza Louisa, by way of another John Clare (Sefton), came a Rose. Dorothy Muriel, born 1926 and still alive, married a certain Eric Rose. Could Geoffrey Hadman's vaunted connection be made through his Glinton grandmother, Florence Rose?

The Roses, so the obituary made clear, lived to the south of the Nene, on the fringes of land recovered from Whittlesey Mere. We would investigate the district tomorrow as part of our river walk. William Rose, Anna's great-grandfather, was another farmer, another churchwarden (at the Angle Bridge Mission). Two hundred people attended his funeral: Roses, Hadmans, Robinsons, Reads, Rowells, Fountains. The coffin, of 'plain oak with brass furniture', was contracted to Messrs Rose and Son.

Whittlesey, Glassmoor: attractive names. I looked at the map, Whittlesey was a spider trapped between rivers, surrounded by Fens and dykes and ditches. A landscape in which, as Iris Murdoch wrote, 'it was a marvel to see at last something upright, to see a man'.

Whittlesey

A turn around the cathedral, former burial place of Mary Queen of Scots (dug up and removed to Westminster Abbey), glimpse of the Ramsey Psalter (Fenland illuminated manuscript): and out. Pause to admire the West Front: Lincolnshire limestone from Barnack. Detour around the private quarters of cathedral functionaries, a sequestered zone of gables, lanterns, eccentric roofs, odd windows, arches, weeds, diagonal shadows. And down to the river.

This is the best of Peterborough, sunken gardens, high walls; a view that combines river, town bridge and the triumphalism of the cathedral. A functioning Lido that puts to shame the decommissioned swimming baths and architectural vanities of Hackney (millions wasted on leisure centres too dangerous to use). A riverside theatre. And, at last, we are reunited with the Nene.

Wide, stately, steel-grey, the Nene is serious; you hear the thump and squawk of industry on the south bank, barges are moored. We go up on to the bridge that brings London Road, Clare's weary route, into the city.

when I told my story they clubbed together & threw me fivepence out of the cart I picked it up & called at a small public house near the bridge were I had two half pints of ale & twopenn'orth of bread & cheese when I had done I started quite refreshed only my feet was more crippled then ever & I could scarcely make a walk of it over the stones & being ashamed to sit down in the street I forced to keep on the move & got through Peterborough better then I expected

From the bridge, Clare could have looked down on the place where, as a youth, he took the boat to Wisbech. Craft are still tied up, alongside a sign: KEY FERRY RIVER TRIPS. But it is out of season and pleasure boats now head upstream, in the direction of Wansford and Fotheringhay. Names have been scratched on the grey parapet, above still water in which bare trees are reflected: MARV + HANA 4 EVER.

Everything is grey: sky, river, Anna's raincoat, the stone flag pavement on which you cross the bridge. Anna remembers her brother-in-law, Richard Ellis, saying how he'd taken a minesweeper down the Nene from Peterborough to Wisbech. 'Ah, Wisbech,' he mused. 'Never saw the crew so drunk. And the women . . .'

Some of the craft seem to have been abandoned; rust, debris, tough grass swallowing rudders. Others are still in business. Shaggy horses crop the verge: the kind that might once have towed passengers and cargoes to King's Lynn or Ely. We are the only walkers on a melancholy avenue of mature willows. Wet grey mud. A frenzy of contradictory directional arrows: the footprints of birds.

There are attractions to consider, possible detours: sewage farm and Flag Fen with its 'reconstructed roundhouses'. (Flag Fen, the Late Bronze Age Settlement, was an artificial island: rectangular huts, on a timber platform, floating in water. England's earliest prehistoric wheel, alderwood, was found on the site. Precursor of the coming Peterborough loop, motorway hell.) As ever, we are alone; quit the city and you enter a world of your own choosing; the silence of the river is broken by distant trains. It's possible, if you make a conscious effort, to hallucinate Clare's river journey; slow and steady momentum carrying a nervous boy, ill clothed as Werner Herzog's changeling time-traveller, Kaspar Hauser, towards a place of judgement. He moves, by this shift of surface, road to river, out of his element. Out of his country. Land vanishes behind steep banks. The world is sky. It's like being suddenly translated from poetry into a novel written by a stranger: into Kafka's *Amerika*. Terrible things happen. Told in a particular way, with a particular emphasis, they are comic. Experienced, they are painful. Everybody has a script, a street map of the town, you alone are uninformed: it is always the first day at a new school. Language you don't speak.

When we achieve something called 'Shanks Millennium Bridge' we have two choices: blow it up or march across. And since the far bank promises a 'Fen Causeway', a 'Roman Road' leading into Whittlesey, we cross. Good decision: everything changes. The old causeways, timbers laid over mud, were ladders into the unconscious, dream-tracks between turf islands that might at any moment be withdrawn. A broad sandy path, bordered by mutated thorns and savage bushes, navigates a bleak landscape of back rivers, sluices, thickets of teazel. And in the distance, as a marker, a great black cloud issues from a group of tall, slim chimneys.

This is much more like it, apocalypse, struggling nature asserting its potency in the face of feeble human threat; a major quarrying operation, noxious fumes, fountains of blood-red water pouring from blue-grey cliffs. What we are negotiating on our Roman road is the perimeter fence of the London Brick Company. Or, from another point of view, the streets of London in an as yet unrevealed form: buried in peat like the stone blocks of Ramsey Abbey. Here lies sleeping London: canal-side redevelopments, future estates of Thames Gateway, the Olympian hubris of Stratford East. Here is gouging, excavating, baking in furnaces. A procession of rattling trucks and lorries. Wounded red earth. Nitrous sulphide. A poison cloud of yellow-grey methane drifting over Whittlesey.

Naturally, I have to duck under the fence – TIPPING RUBBISH IS STRICTLY PROHIBITED – to experience the quarry; an epic of ravishment on the scale of the Rainham Marshes landfill site, on which is dumped most of London's waste: to smoulder, fume, shudder, slither towards the Thames. There is ambition in this enterprise, an energy equal to the period when London was torn up for the construction of railways. There is employment for discontinued farm-labourers, citizens of Whittlesey, its outlying bogs and hamlets. Clay pits are another form of heritage, self-supporting, coughing forth Barratt units, dormitories of the new inner-city suburbs, replacement estates (in mustard yellow) for Hackney and Bow.

I have to pick up one of the bricks from a pile of slag. Nice philtrum, lovely shape: Tate quality but damaged, chipped. Rose red. Spotted with moss. The clincher is that word cut into the skin: LONDON. A relic worth stuffing into my rucksack. London is where I'll carry it, chinking against my spine at every step; a constant reminder of its origin.

Whittlesey, friends, is a potential Dickens theme park, Coketown from *Hard Times*: pick up your brochure at the F. R. Leavis Human History Centre.

It was a town of red brick, or of brick that would have been red if the smoke and ashes had allowed it; but, as matters stood it was a town of unnatural red and black like the painted face of a savage. It was a town of machinery and tall chimneys, out of which interminable serpents of smoke trailed themselves for ever and ever, and never got uncoiled. It had a black canal in it, and a river that ran purple with ill-smelling dye.

Sounds right, but the Coketown of Dickens isn't here, it's closer to the other side of Anna's family, her Lancashire mother, birthplace in Blackpool, her Preston relatives. The London Brick Company is a surreal intervention in a flat land of rivers and dykes, a land that requires beacons for navigation. Glinton spire, Peterborough Cathedral, Whittlesey chimneys: markers for trainee jet pilots who will be over the Wash in seconds and wheeling away to Scotland in minutes.

Our walk started well, light rain diluting the methane, streaking us with yellow, and it improved with every mile we advanced on Whittlesey. The Roses, Anna's lost relatives, were worth chasing. They had found the perfect antidote to the subdued pastoral of Glinton and Werrington: those villages were drowned by development, Whittlesey had risen a few inches out of the peat. Its inhabitants, I imagined, would be cousins of H. P. Lovecraft's fish folk: part-human, part-animal, all alien.

'The Rose Of The World Was Dear Mary To Me': John Clare's Epping Forest lament. Mary Annabel Rose Hadman now understood that the Rose part of her name was no decorative addition, but a mark of family loyalty. The walk was a homecoming and she stepped out briskly, relishing immodest skies; unfenced, untidy, amphibian horizons.

For years, above my desk, I kept a yellow poster; the print of a poem in holograph by Charles Olson. It was dated from 1965 and designed to mimic the shape of a rose. A sentence twisted round on itself until it reached the centre of the mystery: 'This is the Rose of the World.'

Whittlesey, on the direct route between the island abbeys of Thorney and Ramsey, on the Fen causeway between Peterborough and March, is another rose; beaten flat, choked by fumes from the London Brick Company.

Something below us, beneath the pylons, catches my eye: a blue-white object trapped in the fork of a sapling. Something wet and grey planted in a naked patch of brown earth: chunks of broken brick as compost. Anna decides to stay on the path, while I slither down the rampart to investigate.

This is no bird, a bear. A winged bear arranged so that it clings to the branch. Two other creatures, part-dog, grey as slush, accompany the shaggy angel; they have been secured by pink ribbons. Two further bears have been strapped, like Calvary thieves, to the trunk. A sprig of holly. A small white cross. A wooden dagger. The single word: REMEMBRANCE. The tree of bears marks the spot where a child has died. But I have never come across such a renegade memorial. There is a bench of undersized bears in East Tilbury, but that is arranged in such a way that walkers on the river path can pause, take in the view, pay their respects. The view here, on this damp morning, is bleak: sodden fields, distant cathedral town, looming chimneys.

The map of Whittlesey suggests a museum, a cemetery, several churches: plenty of opportunity to search for relevant Roses. The funeral service for Anna's great-grandfather, William Rose, took place in February 1910, and was conducted by the vicar of St Mary's.

The road into town, long and straight, is austere and low level.

Whittlesey is like somewhere achieved, late in the day, in the middle of Ireland: breeze-block bungalows from catalogue, random houses with varieties of extravagant transport parked between front door and road. Clay pits give place to vegetable patches, narrow garden strips. Nobody is walking, nobody is out in the car. It's not actually raining, not much, but tarmac shines in a plaid of greys and grey-blues. Telegraph poles run all the way towards the centre, wherever that is. Out of nowhere, another of those Viking horses appears; a girl leading and a red-haired child in pink rubber boots perched on its back. 'North Dublin,' I said. 'Horses kept in the front room.'

The town is deserted, abandoned to through traffic (which is held by lights stuck on red). I note the window of the monumental mason: more bears. In granite-look, sculpted conglomerate. With a choice of colours: light grey or dark grey. Two roundhead bears with Wayne Rooney ears hold up blank books. Whittlesey is different and proud of it: Methodism, bear worship and a hopeful identity as an 'ancient market town'. Timber-framed houses ('preponderance of mellow buff brick') cheek by jowl with grease caffs, rag-pickers' dens, empty shops with potato sacks.

Agriculture and blue clay: the economy. Chips, buns, dank pubs: the fuel. Church or chapel: duty. The 'first and foremost of Whittlesey's sons' was Sir Harry Smith; also known, after his part in the Sikh Wars, as the 'Hero of Aliwal'. The town of Ladysmith, the brochure informs us, was named after his Spanish bride, Juana Maria De Los Dolores DeLeon. Sir Harry Smith sounds like the novel Conrad never quite got around to writing.

The brochure, after a section on 'Where to Eat' ('good choice of takeaways from Pizza, Kebabs and Burgers to traditional Fish and Chips'), suggests that researching 'Family History' has become the principal Fenland passion (easily done, around here, without leaving the house). Whittlesey Library, in Market Street, keeps parish registers (1654–1960) on microfilm.

We scoot down Broad Street and into Market Street: the Library is open. This is a proper, walk-in, civic amenity; books, information, rows of grey screens. We have William Rose (4 November 1844– 21 February 1910) as our starting point. We have a machine, some-body to show us how to use it, and rolls of microfilm. 'Roses?' the librarian says. 'Funny that, another woman was after them. Only last week.'

We'd better start cranking the handle, jumping the names, addresses, occupations of the dead. Census forms provide a column in which to make a mark if you're infirm, simple-minded or imbe-cile: discriminations of waterland lunacy. Not the Roses. There are dozens of them, farmers, publicans, go-getters with large families; sons to work the land, daughters to marry property (often a brother of the man with whom their sister went to the altar).

At the time of the 1881 census, William Rose was a farmer who also kept the Windmill Inn. He was thirty-six years old. His wife, Mary, was thirty-five. He had three daughters: Annie (thirteen), Florence (nine), Martha (one). And a son, William (seven). By 1891, the family had moved to 72 Benwick Road. (We check this out. The house is on the southern outskirts, close to Whittlesey Dike. The Roses are creeping closer to open Fens, the opportunity of acquiring land.) There are three more sons: Harry (ten), George (six) and another William (four). And a fourth daughter: Nellie (seven). The older William is described as a 'labourer', presumably on his father's farm.

Florence Rose, the second daughter, has left home. She is Anna's grandmother, the one who will marry William Hadman in 1902. Her photograph sits on our Hackney wall: posed in the garden of the Red House with her three children. Once, this was a period piece, sepia sentiment; now the figures are placed. Now Florence looks back at us. We know her as an elderly woman, bespectacled, flower in hat, walking down a street in Lancashire; visiting Geoffrey Hadman in Cleveleys. She keeps step with the much taller Miss Marsh, her younger son's landlady. Miss Marsh carries a wicker basket.

Piece by piece, a pattern is revealed: empty spaces have been left for Anna and her siblings. People disengage from place, place gets on very well without them. Every one of William Rose's children was born in Whittlesey. What happened to Florence? How did she come to Werrington? There were Roses in the village, we knew that, friends, fellow churchgoers, in the choir with the Hadmans and Stimsons. And there were meetings between farmers, from Werrington and Whittlesey, at Peterborough's Agricultural Fair.

The Roses, according to William's obituary, also had connections in Ramsey. Tributes were displayed from 'Mere House'. A Florence Emily Rose, born at Ramsey, is listed in Whittlesey's 1901 census; described as a 'milliner/worker', boarding at a property kept by Hannah Donnington in Almshouse Street. The other lodger was James Henry Parker, manager of a draper's shop. If this were a fiction, a novel by Thomas Hardy (or middle-period Wells), Parker would be a direct descendant of the mysterious John Donald Parker, Clare's grandfather. And Florence Rose would be the future Florence Hadman (the marriage to William taking place the following year). A boarding-house liaison? Manager and counter girl? Pregnancy, desertion; another drowning in the cattle trough?

I found a Parker grave, Thomas Parker (died 1923), in Werrington. (And more of them in Thorney.) Could we trace the wandering schoolmaster, on the road south – Glinton, Werrington, Whittlesey – scattering his bad seed? John Donald has vanished entirely. The Florence Emily Rose of Almshouse Street is not the future Florence Hadman. Our Catherine Cookson version implodes.

Great-grandfather William continues his push on Ramsey; every few years a new property, more land. He relocates to Glassmoor; now he is really out there, on the Middle Level, a muddy desert of thin, parallel strips. Rich soil recovered from the water. Whittlesey, so they tell us, was once an island surrounded by marshes: Whitel's Ey. Glass Moor is an extension of Whittlesey Mere. Looking at a map from 1786, we discover an inland sea, in the approximate shape of Australia, stretching from Stilton (in the west) to the Roses' future holdings. 'Bevills River' emerged from the Mere to run alongside Glassmoor House: the present Bevill's Leam. Coleridge and De Quincey could have saved themselves a lot of shoe-leather, the Mere was as impressive as anything in Cumbria. John Clare was quite right when he made his disparaging comment about the Thames: a puddle, a khaki trickle.

Edward Storey, in a note added to a reproduction of the 1786 map, quotes John Bodger, who produced the survey. The Mere, Bodger asserted, was 'the most spacious fresh water Lake in the Southern part of Great Britain ... Its surface is 1,570 square acres and the depth varies considerably.' The Mere is a considerable absence, out of which stones and treasures have emerged, including 'a silver censer and incense ship which were believed to have once been part of the silver of Ramsey Abbey'. Loss of water affects the microclimate of the empty land in the triangle between Whittlesey, March and Ramsey.

In 1851, hundreds of people converged on the Mere, with carts and baskets, to take advantage of the final drainage by the Appold Pump. They slither in mud, fighting over dying fish, all that is left of the original 'abundance of pike, eels, perch, carp, tench, bream, chubb, roach, dace and gudgeon'.

John Clare, in his journal (November 1824), writes that his friend Henderson, the Scottish head-gardener from Milton Park, sends news from Whittlesey:

discovered a new species of Fern a few days back growing among the bogs on Whittlesea Mere & our talks was of Ferns for the day he tells me there is 24 different species or more natives of England & Scotland one of the finest of the latter is calld the Maiden hair fern growing in rock clefts

My walk from Holme Fen, that evening when I left Anna in the car and went looking for the risen Ramsey stones, took on additional significance. The sheds around Engine Farm, and even that name, were worth investigating. Reading Storey's remarks, in the margin of the 1786 map, I understood why. The famous Appold Pump, used for the draining of the Mere (which as early as 1805 was losing its water levels), had been shown at the Great Exhibition. It was brought into use at Johnson's Point, below Bevill's Leam. Or: the area where Engine Farm is now to be found.

But Appold is also a street in Shoreditch, passing into the City of London, and as such is part of my sacred geography. Standing in Bunhill Fields, September 2004, I tried to explain the theory of drift to a San Francisco muralist who had picked up a commission on the corner of Hoxton Square. We were in the enclosure between the graves of John Bunyan, Daniel Defoe and William Blake: the energy lines of England run out from this spot. Bunyan used knowledge gained from his walks around and beyond Bedford to formulate a pedestrian parable. Defoe travelled Britain in the double identity of spy and reporter. Blake turned local geography into universal geography, his own religion forged from the dustiest of particulars. I repudiated the notion of Nicholas Hawksmoor – whose grooved obelisk at St Luke's, Old Street, we could see, in its alignment with Defoe's obelisk, and distant Christ Church, Spitalfields – as a member of an occult elite. London is a body kept alive, energised by complex lines and patterns that can be walked, built upon: celebrated or exploited. The reality is democratic, anyone can play. All it requires is open eyes and stout boots. Start moving and the path reveals itself.

In my 1987 novel, *White Chappell, Scarlet Tracings*, two of the characters (Brian Catling and myself, an episode borrowed from life) break into the roofless church of St Luke's; a true temple of the City. A site given over to self-seeded trees and wild shrubs, early light picking out blood-colours in shards of stained glass. We climb into the bell tower, witness sunrise as a form of alchemy, then wander, without premeditation, into the streets.

His spine resting on the buried bell. The bell within the obelisk. The cancelled bell that has been hidden from the world.

A flutter of birds against the window. Bird lime. Stench of old feathers.

We turn away, our prayers are made. Down into the face of the lion: Bunhill, Finsbury, Sun, Appold . . . the path of old stone.

All writing is made in a kind of trance. The Catling expedition to Ramsey happened at the wrong time. The 'buried' bell of St Luke's will reappear in the Fens, on an island: a memory that got ahead of itself. Appold's Pump circulates the blood of the heart. White stones break the surface of a peat sea.

'Beneath the mud,' Storey concludes, 'were also discovered the skulls of a wild boar and a wolf, remnants of a history some several years earlier. Now only the map reminds us of what was; the rest is in the imagination.'

We'd covered enough ground for one day. We would visit Whittlesey Museum, which kept very eccentric opening hours, then make our way back to Peterborough. Glassmoor was too large a step. Let it keep. The immediate challenge, in the cathedral city, is to find a restaurant that doesn't have an ambulance with winking lights waiting for overenthusiastic diners.

Straw Bear

Come, give me your great bears paw

James Joyce, *Finnegans Wake*

Step inside the museum, wait for your eyes to adjust to the dim light, and there it is: the photograph. The confirmation. Of all the weirdness that has attended our passage through this landscape. A man attached by a rope to an ambulant mound of mud and twigs. The man has the authentic heavy-browed Hadman frown, the gravity-obeying moustache. A battered top hat with fungal outgrowth bursting through the lid. Moleskin trousers with much of the mole still evident; greasy, free-standing. Heavy waistcoat and jacket (cut from an army blanket). And in this person's left hand what Catling took to be, when I showed him the postcard in Oxford, a brick. The professor knew nothing of Whittlesey and the brickworks, but he had the climate absolutely right: driver, rope, brick, bear. 'Pay up or I cut the bond, let the creature loose.' That's what they call the bear's attendants: keepers or drivers. Bear-walkers come, as I would discover, watching film of the winter ritual, in two types. The old fellow, flounced and feathered, only a little drunk in the morning, who minds the bear as he guides it from public house to public house. And the younger, fiercer man who drives the exhausted beast, with goads and tugs on the rope, as the sweating straw-thing staggers into evening. On the following morning, ash in their mouths, chastened rioters burn the bear, a damp bonfire in a bleak field.

The brick is a collecting box, a slit in its lid. 'Give us your pennies.' The Whittlesey Straw Bear Festival is a harvest ritual at the wrong time, an Eastern European folk revival in the wrong

place. Bears in this country would be an awesome phenomenon, harbingers of thieves and gypsies, the worst kind of travelling people. A vertical thing, like the chimneys and spires, dominating a flat land. John Clare, knowing and sympathising with medicine-show tricksters and wandering mountebanks (he had their blood in him), identified with the bear. Remember his remark about Stamford? About being 'dragged into it like a Bear & fidler to a wake'? Clare and his broken father, on the road to Milton Hall, in search of patronage: bear and driver.

Lucia Joyce, in her *Wake*, reached out for an untrustworthy paw (Americanised pa). She was haunted by a bear in Zurich Zoo. 'What sort of a God does that fellow have, do you think?' she asked Cary Baynes, her paid minder.

Hard winters, plough boys without employment. They use the bear as their weapon. One of them plays the part; he is tailored into straw. The others dance Whittlesey streets, demanding money to carry them through the winter months; money for drink. Against the threat of riot. Burnings. Straw bear or thatched roof: your choice. The custom settled on the Tuesday following Plough Monday (always the first Monday after Twelfth Night). In dark January, Christmas decorations put aside, gaunt men blacked up: to make sport of their grievances. They were, by tradition, the spirits of the returning dead: looking for warmth.

A boy with tightly twisted straw bands around his legs, arms, chest. Sticks, fastened to the shoulders, meet at a point over his head: rustic dunce, Klansman. Jon Pertwee as 'Worzel Gummidge', Barbara Euphan Todd's scarecrow brought to life, would be the English version; tamed for the juvenile market, toothless prankster. Turnip lantern. The Whittlesey bear was a crueller performance. The boy could see very little. He was pulled this way and that. All around him the noise of dancers and drunks; not morris men clapping sticks, but mudfaced Molly Gangs. Even now, in the film of the 1997 festival, shot by Roy Harrison, the Mollys are in evidence: New Road Molly, Old Hunts Molly, Gog Magog Molly, Old Glory Molly Gang, Seven Champions Molly, Mepal Molly Men, Handsome Molly, Pig Dyke Molly. Norwich Shitwitches. And, from Alan Moore's Northamptonshire, covens like the Kettering Witchmen: 'Dark and mysterious as their name suggests. With dances such as Wicker Man and Wild Hunt.' Faces part-white, part-black; feathered top hats, smoked glasses. 'Performances that are pagan in the extreme.' The burning recalls the sacrificial bulls of Knossos; Cretan farmers driving cattle through the flames, for purification, a rich harvest. But Whittlesey asserts its difference: scorched souls do not ascend to the Spiral Castle to await rebirth, they drown in black water.

Swaying drunks, reelers and stumblers in hobnailed boots. Afternoon dancers at the pub door, the Windmill Inn. Circling, crossing, clapping: for themselves, not for the watching crowds. Labourers with women's dresses over fieldwork jackets; bulging cord trousers, boots. Travestied gangs, Uncle Tom faces and white eyes, leaping and stamping over a prone figure with spread legs. The town gives itself up to riot and music-making. The beast, the bear in its pointy, penitent's cowl, is driven from pub to pub. 'It has become a German Bear custom to hug a lady from the crowd and fall backwards with her on top of the bear – only a kiss will release his grip!'

Whittlesey, decorous market town, old island, goes mad: urgent and uncomic intent. Some of the Molly Gangs look stern as Belfast Orange Men: hats, sashes, Masonic regalia. Melonhead Prods converted to voodoo, blacked-up, pounding the beat (like the head of a captured Taig): as terrible to imagine as Ian Paisley, drink taken, trying on his wife's frock. Or John Ford Indians capering around a burnt-out wagon, wearing the Sunday dresses of women they have raped and killed.

'Molly dancing,' so the Festival Programme claims, 'is by nature august.' Hobnailed dancers are accompanied through town by mobs of plough boys dressed in white shirts or smocks, cracking whips. 'It was said that if you did not contribute even one penny, you would find a furrow ploughed across your lawn by morning.'

The festival of the Straw Bear was halted in 1909, the year that William Hadman bought the Red House in Glinton. It had become too wild, said Whittlesey's police inspector; an excuse for 'cadging' and debauchery. Prison sentences were meted out to miscreants. After a 'breach' of seventy-one years, the Straw Bear re-emerged from his hide in 1980, in keeping with the spirit of the times: the advance of Molly-Lady, Margaret Thatcher, from neighbouring Grantham to Westminster. A back-country Shitwitch. A man-woman, heels and handbag, at the centre of power.

Frozen by the museum's bear photograph, I was caught by one of the keepers. But I wasn't finished yet. This monster was nothing like the yellow-gold, capering stook of recent times: this bear was a dredge of mud and slime, straight out of the water. A heap of blue clay rolled into town, picking up nests of twigs and brambles on its way. The Whittlesey bear was a negative, the dark contrary of its keeper; same height, same bulk, same soul. The brains of both were compressed, stored in the brick. The double act was a Fenland translation of Jekyll and Hyde. The bear *was* a hide, on the move: thing from the black lagoon. Its rope? An umbilical cord. Only Samuel Beckett got the relationship right: Lucky and Pozzo, strangers, arriving from nowhere, to deliver their lines and depart. The mute stack of the Whittlesey bear hoards his unpunctuated monologue, silence is absolute. As Beckett understood. Lucky, like John Clare, speaks in tongues.

The museum woman, a volunteer, not one of the professional curatorial types, doesn't quiz me; she knows just where my interests lie. Very soon she has me in a dark, interior chamber looking through yellow newspaper cuttings, bear reports. And after that, in an outhouse containing the most fearsome relics of the place: bits and pieces of redundant agricultural machinery, sacks, rags and objects that defy description. Such as? A lump of bone-coral, horned and holed, mounted on a rusty metal spike, which is itself attached to a severed hoof. Speculative title? 'Fenland Witchcraft Totem'.

Also to be found are military uniforms (relics of Sir Harry Smith), brick-making displays, faked schoolrooms, a mammoth tusk, a Woolly Rhinoceros leg bone, odd vertebrae donated by bison. A cabinet of mongrel curiosities like that displayed by John Tradescant in his Lambeth 'Ark'. The past is preserved as a series of fatal and non-fatal accidents: waxworks, blood-stained shirts, nicotine prints of demolished buildings and buried people.

Among the dim photographs on the carousel, I find William Rose's 1881 home, the Windmill Inn. An illustration from the Brothers Grimm: L-shaped, whitewashed, thatched (random windows peering out like asymmetrical eyes). The building is about to fall in on itself, taking its lost history into a blank white rectangle of photographic paper. There are two boys in the street. One braves the camera; the other, booted, creeps towards the mean slit of the pub's door. The boy is the right age, seven years old, for William (son of William and Mary Rose). His father, the innkeeper, also farmed forty-five acres, employing three men and seven boys. By the time he moved to Glassmoor, Anna's great-grandfather had one hundred and seventy acres and employed three men, one boy and a woman.

Tomorrow, before we return to London, we'll try to locate the Glassmoor house, to form a picture of where the Roses lived and worked: unencumbered space to set against busy clusters of Werrington Hadmans with their cherry orchards, brass bands, primitive airfields and books of dead sparrows.

Up to now, the Peterborough orbital motorway system, I've always enjoyed being in a car with Anna. We've had our disagreements, loaded with children, luggage, cats, it's true: the 'Do *you* want to drive?' moments, door held open, voices raised, minor sulks. But, on our own, cars were generally good times; out of Dublin to the West, empty roads, deserted beaches, lunches with rain beating against the windows, or unplanned expeditions to Wales, Cornwall, the Farne Islands. A chance to talk or share a companionable silence, shifting landscapes and somewhere strange to sleep at the end of the day. Frets dissolving, accidents of touch, unthreatening incidents on the way towards renewed intimacy.

Peterborough rescinds all that in seconds, human affection. The road system is designed to incubate conflict, induce rage. And it works. Before looking for the Rose farmhouse, on Glassmoor, I decided to make a short visit to Milton Hall. I noticed on the map that it was on the western rim of Peterborough, south of Marholm. It was flagged as a golf course, with lake and house at the centre of the park. After three days, driving and walking, Clare's geography was beginning to make sense: territory divided between Burghley House (Marquess of Exeter) and Milton Hall (Earl Fitzwilliam), with anything left squabbled over by various bishoprics and Cambridge colleges. After the enclosures, tenant farmers accumulated spare strips; they intermarried, thrived. Cottagers moved up or went under: diversification (butchery, pubs, baker shops) or submersion (suicide). Cattle (and farm-workers) drifted down from the hills behind Stilton to summer pastures, the edge of the Fens: the dynamic we find in the Rose family. A new property every five years, a new child every two; more land, more animals. Further and further out from Peterborough, from Whittlesey.

As with any orbital loop, the easy option is to keep going, round and round Peterborough, into highway reverie: block buildings of a certain height, the same hoardings, blue-and-white traffic signs that come too late. The Werrington turn is always missed. It isn't what it looks like. You have to anticipate the move, suppress logic: they have closed the ramp. So try another circuit.

Milton Park was tricky, slip roads are exactly like other slip roads. We make several foiled attempts, suburban sprawl; then hit, by accident, a wet lane down which Clare might have walked. It's not much more than three and a half miles from Helpston, the familiar tramp to visit Henderson and Artis: to collect a dole from the toffs. Patronising advice, coins for the pocket. Before handing over newly minted copies of books whose pages will never be cut.

We abandon the car and go into the fields, soft, featureless, with that sense Clare knew better than anyone: invisible eyes, watchers. Gamekeepers. Green-keepers. Farmers who own and control un-worked paddocks of grey-brown mud. Thistle crops. Spiders' webs.

The Hall, as seen from the road, remains a prospect, a remote view. Gates are secure. Until, at last, and very wet, we come across something like a permitted footpath into the woods. We know we're on the right track when we find the signpost chopped down and chucked into the bushes. When we emerge, yet again, on a golf course.

Beware of foresters. We learnt, from the pile of Werrington obituaries, that Anna's grandfather began here. Before he tried farming, acquired land in Glinton, he was employed at Milton Hall. As forester, responsible for these woods, he was of equal status with Clare's friends, Henderson and Artis. Subtle plantings, that now screen us from the golf course, had been supervised by William Hadman.

It's early, raining hard; the only golfers are young, keen, tolerant of our intrusion on a public path that brushes against expensively tended grass. I carry on until I'm up against a hedge, a ditch, with clear sight of house and lake. A long, grey, limestone barrack with regular windows and the smack of isolation hospital: the usual sinister/benevolent institution you always find in English parkland. Clare's nerve, approaching such a place, must have been strong. The walk through the gates of the General Lunatic Asylum in Northampton would have been a homecoming.

Morbid speculations were soon confirmed. A friend, the artist Keggie Carew, told me that we'd missed her own visit to Milton Hall by a few days. She been taken there on a coach, with her father, who was attending an SOE (Special Operations Executive) reunion: the sixtieth anniversary of their country-house stay. The old boy, one of eighteen rugged and independent survivors, had been based at the Hall in the spring of 1944: pre-invasion of Normandy. Like all spare property, spacious, secluded, out of the public gaze, the Fitzwilliam estate had been requisitioned by the military: code-breaking, interrogation, small-arms training. Never was so much fun had by so few, the time of their lives for brave pipe-smokers and bright young things from good families.

Milton Hall housed a unit called the Jedburghs, known as the 'Jeds', who were parachuted into France before, or immediately after, D-Day: 'Operation Neptune'. Each group was supposed to feature British, American and French members, who would liaise with the French Resistance (over whom they had no authority). Two gents (officers) and one non-commissioned chappie to operate the radio. Their target was the 2nd SS Panzer *Das Reich* Division.

Keggie's father was later occupied in the Middle East and Burma. The Milton House mob were intelligent, driven, often crazy individuals who sat around playing chess, reading Chinese poetry, inventing diversions. And shooting at walls. The chips and splinters I'd put down to Cromwell, and the English Civil War, belonged to Keggie's dad and his mates. Here they stand, lean, prop themselves up: a coloured photograph in *The Times*. A fine bunch of white-bearded, eye-patched pirates enjoying the sunshine.

*

Getting from Milton Hall to Whittlesey should have been a matter of no great consequence; Anna with the map, my eyes fixed on the road. But we were soon undone by identical roundabouts, road signs blocked by high-sided, deep-freeze trucks: paranoia about being suckered again by Peterborough and its ever-shifting centre.

The turn was missed. I shouted. Anna threw the map out of the window. We rehearsed, in moody silence, old grievances. How could I have spent so many years with this person who told me to take a right (meaning left), two minutes *after* we'd passed the slip road? Thereby condemning us to crawl into Peterborough and over the Town Bridge. By the time we reached Whittlesey, property, goods, children had been divided (without speech); the Clare project was abandoned and those tare-peddling, sparrow-murdering peasants, the Hadmans, could be left to rot in the obscurity of a Fenland midden from which they should never have been extracted. Our improbable alliance had been wrong from the start. Now it was revoked, done with, abjured. No more drives, no more memories.

I scribbled down a couple of lines of Orson Welles dialogue from the video of *The Third Man*. He's on the Big Wheel with Joseph Cotten, contemplating murder. 'The dead are happier dead,' he says. 'They don't miss much here.' Then the Harry Lime character doodles a name in the condensation on the window: ANNA. Capitalised. A heart. Arrow through it. Absurd gesture, I thought. Women in these romances are always called Anna. Like flatlands daughters. The oldest son of the Glassmoor farmer, William Rose, whose house we were searching for, was another William. He married a woman from the neighbouring village of Doddington, her name was Anna. (The name of John Clare's first child.) In 1901 they were living with William's father at 73 Glassmoor. ('Anna was; Livia is and Plurabelle's to be.' James Joyce.)

The picture, coming off the Ramsey road, is so haunting that our quarrel is suspended. Every move is a shot from the film Chris Petit never made; darker, gloomier, wetter than *Radio On*. This is the true version of his abortive second feature, *An Unsuitable Job for a Woman*. He took on P. D. James for the setting, sluices, long straight roads with telegraph posts: only to be stuck, overcrewed and impotent, in a riverside studio and a Berkshire gravel pit.

The top of the windscreen has a bluish filter that applies mascara to a dead sky; road and water (Bevill's Leam) are parallel lines, divided by a narrow strip of grass. Fields are flat with occasional wooded clumps, huts, houses. Telegraph poles lean out. A broken white line vanishes into the sodden distance. Anna is, immediately, at home. Revived by the minimalism of the tonal range: green to grey. Mildew, mud, puddled tarmac.

We get out of the car and walk up the drive towards the property that Anna wants, so badly, to be her ancestral home. 'Glassmoor House', it says. 'C. E. W. Saunders'. This is the house that Anna has fantasised as a retreat from Hackney. Featureless fields. Dark canal: outflow from Whittlesey Mere. A mature and managed garden: fir, laurel, yew, box. Family mansion smothered in creeper: blue door, porch, bay windows. There have been additions and revisions, but this, in essence, is a farmhouse of the period of the Hadman property in Glinton. An oasis of civility and good living made against the indifference of the surrounding agricultural land, with its unavoidable assertions of pig and slurry and steaming vegetable matter.

Anna hovers at the top of the drive, I march directly to the blue door. I want to confront these Roses, now. I want to move on. Our wanderings have brought us to a place that Anna is prepared to acknowledge as a potential conclusion: 'I could live here. I *have* lived here. The Roses thrived. I belong in the landscape which has meant most to me.'

I ring, I rattle. Nobody at home. Nothing resolved. We return to the car and to London. I can't decide what the next move should be: or if I have written myself into another cul-de-sac. Another set of open-ended parentheses.

Ramsey

Two phone calls.

Anna, exploiting our recent membership of the John Clare Society, made contact with Eric Rose. Mr Rose was married to Dorothy Muriel Stokes, Clare's great-great-granddaughter. Anna's researches among her Rose relatives turned up an Eric, and she became quite excited, thinking that the link her father claimed was about to be proved.

Mr Rose is elderly and not to be drawn out. He has no knowledge of Whittlesey, Ramsey or Glassmoor. He refuses to surrender an address. He has no interest in adding peripheral members to an already complex family tree. There are too many Roses, and not a few thorns, dressing the ground: Peterborough into Norfolk, into Suffolk, and as far afield as Dorset. The Hadmans, breeding more modestly, never strayed more than a mile or two from the shores of the Mere. It began to look as if Stilton was their frontier; peasant-labourers in the hills to the west, go-getting farmers and butchers in the flatlands to the east. Clare territory, without a doubt, but we could discover no blood relatives. Just endless, frustrating hints: Beryl Clare (born 1938), another great-great-granddaughter of the poet, married Douglas Harrison. Nellie Rose, sister of Florence (Anna's grandmother), also married a Mr Harrison. Roses and Clares both allied themselves with Reads. At such a distance, we are all part of one great family whose only ambition is to put as much mileage as possible between itself and any dubious third and fourth cousins. (Particularly those who make importunate phone calls.)

A second ring: Professor Catling from Oxford. He has been cruising the Net and come up with a narrowboat, available, if we make an immediate booking, at the weekend. Ship out from March on the Middle Level, down the Nene (Old Course) to Ramsey; and then, if we have sufficient time, and haven't come to grief on a low bridge, round to Whittlesey and Peterborough. By slow and secret backwaters. Sounds good. Do it. Make the call.

Anna, overhearing this conversation, offers to join the crew: a first. Catling boat trips, after early experiences out of Norwich, are usually avoided. Especially when they head down the Thames, out to sea, with competitively drunk, drugged or deranged skippers: Hunter S. Thompson awaydays. (No insurance, no charts, one life-jacket – childsized – shared between five large adults.) But the thought of going by water into Rose country is a temptation not to be resisted.

Much food, in Anna's generous fashion (cook in expectation of the entire family, plus friends and lovers, appearing at your table), has been loaded into the car when Catling demands a Tesco's pit stop in Huntingdon. He's working his own interpretation of the Atkins diet and presents a more svelte and compact figure than the Wellesian cigar-chomper of my Oxford visit. This is nothing new, the man has always been a shape-shifter; an ability that stands him

in good stead as a certified performance artist. One day: fabulously bouffant, silver-minted. And the next? Cropped like Magwitch. One day, full-cargoed, under sail; the next, hunched, shuffling, Sherlock Holmes overplaying the vagrant. The range, by his reckoning, runs from early Charles Laughton to eye-patched John Wayne being winched on to his horse. A preternatural ability to swerve, on the beat, from clubbed pathos to diabolic intensity.

This is a very forgiving diet: high protein, no carbohydrates (to speak of), exceptions made for five-star restaurants. Essentially, it involves stocking up on yards of Cambridgeshire bacon, fish bits, lamb; no poncing about with green stuff. Skewer the lot, stuff them with garlic, cook slowly. And meanwhile keep the Blood Marys coming by the pitcher. That was Catling's spin on Atkins: no whisky, not the first day out, but steady vodka (the reformed drinker's friend); the day's vegetable intake coming from tomato juice, spiced with tabasco, Lea & Perrins, lime and a fistful of ice-cubes. Tremendous self-discipline; he'd lost half a stone in a couple of weeks and looked nothing like Nigel Lawson (that absence, that empty suit). To keep up his strength, between jugs, Catling padded his loose jacket with cellophane packets of sliced corn beef.

The March boatyard is a live-and-let-live, take-us-as-you-find-us operation; keys, tour of the craft – fridge, double-bunk, TV, hot shower, Calor gas – and cast off. Boat-builder Harold Fox's son-in-law lets Catling grab the tiller (narrowboats are virtually indestructible, if you don't smoke in bed, or chop up the deck for a barbecue). 'River cruiser, is it? Out on the Thames?' says the boatman, as Brian fumbles the gears. But the professor compensates by making an immaculate U-turn, sweeping us back upstream towards the yard.

'Where you heading for then?'

'Ramsey.'

Silence.

'Ram-sey?'

'Ramsey.'

'Any special reason like?'

Nobody, in the history of Fox's Yard, has admitted to Ramsey as a voluntary destination.

'Nice pub, Outwell way. Some folk reckon on Cambridge.'

'Ramsey. Family.'

'Ramsey, right then.'

Anna, instantaneously, is a figurehead at the prow, hand on hat. Catling manages the craft with insouciant command: the first Bloody Mary, first Toscani cigar (black as a camel's toenail). The pace is seductive, a brisk walk. The engine purrs. We lie on the surface of things, fields and farms hidden behind earth banks. We drift, drift downstream towards Ramsey.

'Where are you going?' shouts a dog-walker.

'Ram-sey.'

'Ramsey. Oh. Good luck then.'

Promised rain holds off; clouds are pressing, agitated. Pylons and radio masts are our event horizon. Concrete bunkers, overgrown, have a forlorn freight: distressed history. The engine thuds softly. Hours pass without register. Anna's sense of well-being is palpable. I take over the tiller and Brian manoeuvres his way around the outside of the boat to join her in the bows. They are very old friends. He's been coming to our house since his student days. He is our daughter Farne's godfather. Now, in the suspension, the steady rhythm of the narrowboat's progress down the old Nene, there is confirmation that this is the right, the only possible place to be. Mile by mile, river-time unpicks the Clare walk; a ballast of unnecessary facts is quietly offloaded. Being on water is entering the dream; junking futile quests, letting go.

The Nene thickens, surface slime tangles itself around the blades of the propeller, but doesn't slow our progress; nobody has travelled this way in months. We don't pass another boat. No humans, a mile out of March, walk the river bank. Coming free of green sludge, cloudscapes are reflected in a vitreous carpet. Broken bridges are ruined craft, no farm-worker goes near them. 'Cock-up bridges,' they say: humped memorials to the ancient causeway system.

As pale sun breaks through, the golden hour, we arrive at Benwick; a hamlet backed into a bend of the river, between Rose farmland and Ramsey Mere. We make fast in the local version of a bayou: drooping willows, creepers, rickety dock, burial ground (everything but the alligators).

Prismatic shafts splinter heavy foliage. The Benwick church has gone, pulled down, leaving nothing but a brick altar in a field of nettles: 'Site of the Parish Church of St Mary the Virgin, 1850–1980.' Gravestones diminish into an allotment patch, before the open fields begin. Dead Roses are here too: Thomas William Brittan Rose, son of William and Louisa, died 27 January 1909, aged twenty-two years. Henry William Brittan Rose, his brother, died 14 June 1912, aged twenty-three years.

We moor for the night, a mile or two shy of Ramsey, beside a *Waiting for Godot* tree; a skeletal black stump on which perch cormorants, pretending to be vultures. Catling cooks a notable feast, skewered fish and bacon, complemented by Anna's chicken. Much wine. Crimson sunset. A crash into dreamless sleep (the voyage is the dream) interrupted by my screams as I wake to spasms of cramp, which hurl me, swearing, to the floor. The twisting and lifting of narrowboat life isn't doing much for my back, but a companionable torment is a small price to pay for the gain in mental space: fresh night air, stars, when I sit out on deck, to watch the cormorants watching us.

Dawn skies squeeze us closer to the water, which is smooth and ripple-free. Catling, bacon-and-egg breakfast cooked and eaten, nurses a mug of coffee as he pilots the narrowboat through the mean outskirts of Ramsey. And all the time, our channel tightens. There would be no possibility now of another nifty U-turn: passing the marina, we have no choice but to carry on as far as this ditch, the High Lode, will take us. Catling doesn't drive cars, never has (there are women for that), but the slow-moving, go-with-the-drift waterworld of the Middle Level suits him very well. Let it happen, it is inevitable. The narrowboat has the kind of valves, flanges, nozzles and teats that he likes. A firm turn of the key. The engine coughs and obliges.

There are Catlings listed on the census forms at Whittlesey Library, huggers of the river bank: watermen, rooters of vegetables. There were always two sorts of folk on the Middle Level between Nene and Ouse: farmers, jealous of their recently acquired land, and river rats (lightermen, demi-pirates, water gypsies). They fought, bare-knuckled, with sticks and clubs, ferociously. Horses, bred to tow barges and flat-bottomed craft, were no respecters of towpaths. (There were no towpaths until they created them.) The horses were as strong as the men. They learnt to come on and off boats. If necessary, they went into the canals to drag their burdens. They jumped obstructions. When river gangs, hauling corn and malt, arrived at a Fen pub, miles from a village, they drank it dry. It was a famous night for the farmer/publican if they didn't burn the place down. 'Conspicuous conviviality' the books call it.

Whittlesey families, servicing the brickworks, using the Mere as a connection between Nene and Ouse, included the Hemmaways, Boons and Gores. Three of the Gores are recorded as attending the funeral of Anna's great-grandfather, William Rose. Among recorded floral tributes, most sent by relatives, is a wreath from 'Mrs Gore and family'.

The Roses, it appears, lived on the hinge of the dispute between riparian interests and watermen. Their land was always bordered by a canal or a river. Sons picked up property, where and when they could, between Ramsey and Whittlesey. The beer they brewed was drunk by watermen as much as by farm-labourers. They emerged as an established family in the golden century of water transport, 1750–1850, before railways took over. It was a self-reliant, low-church (revised pagan) way of life: women ferrying horses, across leams or drains, by punting with long poles known as 'quants'. Men scuttling lighters to make improvised dams. Boys healing a breach in the dyke with tarpaulin. Stupendous acts of porterage: the dragging of craft across every natural obstacle. Cargoes carried in bundles on the head. The Roses must have been a strong-necked crowd: wide in the shoulder, bowed in the leg.

Our narrowboat is a forty-six-footer, the Ramsey channel brushes against our ribs. Anna has woken, not surprisingly, with a cracking headache. I can feel the aftermath of the cramp in my calf. But our skipper is jaunty, convinced that we'll find somewhere to moor. And he's right: nobody has attempted it in recent times, but there is an industrial dock, turning space, in a town where industry seems, at best, inactive.

We come ashore, the ground is none too steady; it is still recovering from the shock of emerging from the black waters. The abbey church, for centuries, was a yellow-grey ghost reached by ladders laid over the mud.

Near-rain, a mongrel atmosphere of air and water (for the benefit of those who breathe through their gills), has evolved as Ramsey's microclimate: it sluices you in liquefied stonedust. Energy and heat are sucked from mammals, so that only the most determined pilgrims get away.

To keep up stamina, I buy a loaf in the shape of a wreath; it is so heavy that, used as a life-belt, it would take you straight to the bottom of the river. Catling buys a bottle of whisky, a large one. More corned beef. More everything. Sherry to improve the Bloody Marys. Chops, spring onions. The only way to carry all this stuff to the church, so I decide, is in a bag: a blue plastic laundry bag with very short straps. This, from the Ramsey equivalent of Prada, at £1.99.

The spirit of the town is located, by Catling, in a shop that specialises in reptiles. He's fond of reptiles and used to spend much of his time sending out stick-insects, locusts packed in cotton wool. Lizards, he's fond of those too. So he is delighted to discover a Golden Python from Burma, the pride of Ramsey, its unacknowl-edged totem and oracle. The beast slumbers in a vast tank, waiting for supplicants with troublesome requests. Its head, so Catling reports, rests in a dog's water bowl. What happened to the dog he doesn't say.

We recognise the grass, the wall; the church, the burial ground. It hasn't changed in the years since we arrived here, on the burn, in search of that elusive 'key'. 'Ramsey holds the key.' (And holds it close to the chest.) But this time we have voyaged, unhurried, by water. We have meditated for many slow hours on our destination: desultory conversation, mixing of Bloody Marys, horizon-chasing. Apart from the clinking laundry-bag burden, I'm ready. It's now or never.

My earlier stupidity, cobwebs over the eyes, was astonishing. All that was required, Anna and Brian holding back, swaying in the porch, not sure if they should return immediately to the boat, was a brisk walk down the north side of the parish church of St Thomas à Becket. A careful reading of stained-glass windows. The answer was so obvious, so literal, we must have been ashamed to recognise it in our hunger for signs and portents. It's not the Ackroydian 'Resurgam' on the outside of the south wall of the chancel. Prebendary Robins, who died in 1673, requested that this word/symbol be cut into a stone near his grave. Nor is it the fish-shaped recess above the round-headed lancets on the east wall. Revelation comes with the window in which a yellow-bearded Saxon warrior, out of a superhero comic, is gripping a very large key in his right hand: 'Gift of the Ailwyn Lodge of Freemasons No. 3535, AD 1912.' An open book floats between twin Masonic pillars: golden compasses, golden pentacle. The window, dedicated to the memory of James Sanderson Sergeant (20 September 1823–13 April 1882), has been subscribed by a clutch of Masons from St Leonards-on-Sea.

The golden key dangles like an open-ended rebuke. The warrior's left hand crosses his breast. There are wands and tassels: standard elements of mystical geometry. And rich colours: scarlet, green, midnight blue. The shape of the man, in the jigsaw of glass slivers, makes a vertical map. Lead rivers, islands of sand. Whittlesey Mere as a portion of brilliant red cloth.

I can see *where* the key is, the riddling message, but I have no idea what it means (beyond the path the key seems to indicate, across the graveyard, to a bricked-up door in the abbey wall). I am as dull as ever – until I notice the opposite window, the south wall: St Etheldreda. A tall, handsome woman, big haired Pre-Raphaelite, holds another key: silver against a gold background. The teeth of the original Masonic key are closed, they point to the east. Etheldreda points to the west. She has a crown, a crozier; a model of the church rests on her right hand. Her left hand, crossing the breast, steadies the model. The saint is wrapped in a long scarlet cloak. Red flowers decorate the grass at her slippered feet. They should be roses.

'The unbelieving husband shall be saved by the believing wife.' Announces a banner behind Etheldreda's head. Let that be my key. Anna, on our first expedition, was the missing element. The brandishing of phallic toys, keys too clumsy for any lock, has now been countered by a justified sense of place. By the witnessing of my wife: the lost half I have pursued, so blindly, for so many miles. The quarrel of the road has long since been resolved. The Ramsey window is a coloured mirror. My belief in unbelief is tested afresh. My belief in the potency of Anna's memory is confirmed. All those months ago, walking from Stilton to Glinton, I was drawn to try Hardy's *Tess of the D'Urbervilles*: a warning against genealogical truffling. Alec D'Urberville, with his faked pedigree, has something to say to Tess: 'The unbelieving husband is sanctified by the wife and the unbelieving wife is sanctified by the husband.'

Etheldreda is the daughter of the chieftain of the East Angles: King Anna. She is honoured, liturgically, as a twice-married virgin. Her first husband died, marriage unconsummated, after three years. Released from the vows of a second marriage, she took the veil: to live in retirement on the Isle of Ely. But the pious Etheldreda is not the woman in the window: a lush artist's model, smothered in flowers, playing her part in a Golden Dawn ritual. Beneath her, a troop of monks and bishops labour with blocks of masonry: the mislaid Ramsey stones returning from the Mere. Flying and drowning, in the suspension of stained glass, are indistinguishable.

*

The church of St Thomas is thought to have been built as a hospital or gatehouse for the Benedictine Abbey. Its buildings were converted to accommodate pilgrims. Abbey lands, after the Dissolution, were sold to Sir Richard Williams, the great-grandfather of Oliver Cromwell. Tumbled stones were used to build or extend Cambridge colleges: Caius, King's, Trinity.

I spoke the word aloud: 'Caius'. Keys. The connection with Cambridge, Renchi Bicknell's childhood, is reaffirmed. Trips of my own, poetry initiations. Renchi is devouring, so he explains when I visit Glastonbury, a book about visionary journeys: *Dark Figures in the Desired Country: Blake's Illustrations to The Pilgrim's Progress* by Gerda S. Norvig. Who demonstrates how Blake converts Bunyan's Interpreter into a 'key figure'. 'He literally "holds the key" . . . to the next room of the dream.' A real key, or bunch of keys, is the pertinent metaphor. The confirmation, I now realise, that we are on the right track, in the right place.

We wander across Abbey Green to the Gatehouse, which is late fifteenth century; an accidental fragment from which the rest must be assumed or invented. A sepulchral figure, thought to be Earl Ailwyn (of stained-glass fame), floats in a cage. He has been granted three-dimensional reality, then starved to essence. The effigy is imprisoned within the ribs of an upturned boat. A hatchet-carved intensity of gaze burns off accidental tourists. Here, Catling acknowledges, is a major item of sculpture: beyond representation, beyond pious devotion. Spirit in stone: angry and vital. The setting is as important as the thing itself. A standing figure laid on its back, caught in a man-trap, placed in a tower with a blind set of stairs. Worn steps leading to another bricked-up doorway.

A circuit of the church grounds, gravestones, memorials, is undertaken, without much conviction, before our return to the river. By now, we appreciate churchyard etiquette, stately pace, soft rain, bare trees; one burial site dissolving into the next. Ramsey is grander than the others, it trades on its association with the church and the walls of the abbey: curtains of trailing willow, well-nourished parasites. Urns with rams' heads, curled horns.

Angels with folded arms. Clusters of submerged Roses. Ramsey is the fountainhead of the family. Where one Rose is found, we know, there will be others. We have William, son of Daniel and Ann Rose, who died on 6 October 1842. And another William Rose. We have his wife, Hannah. The Hannah part was botched by the stonemason and had to be recut. Beneath this revision, the earlier attempt is still visible: an obliterated Anna. Beyond the Rose reservation, more obscurely, set against the wall and swallowed in ivy, is a solitary stone. A family connection?

The Christian name, Daniel, can be read without strain, but the date is almost erased – perhaps 1830? The surname, lichen padding the indents of cut letters, is clear enough. A name we have never come across in this country, SINCLAIR.

Was he Jewish, or part-Jewish, this Daniel in the den of Roses? I read everything I can find about fetches, doppelgängers, spectral twins: honouring a misplaced Scottish heritage. I had to track down *The Double*, a novel by the Portuguese author José Saramago. The plot, with winks at Sterne and Dostoevsky, is playful. A history teacher notices a bit-part actor playing a hotel receptionist in a video. The man has his face. The receding hair, the moustache he wore five years ago, when the film was made. By a tedious process of elimination, labouring through all the other tapes from the production company responsible for the first film, he discovers the name of the actor, his double: Daniel Santa-Clara. Daniel Sinclair. Driven to conclude an insane quest, the history man fixes the jobbing actor's real name: Claro. Clare. The literal translation of Saramago's Portuguese title is 'The Duplicated Man'.

The Cherry House

Tomorrow, Sunday, will be Anna's birthday. By the time we come through Ashline Lock in Whittlesey, she is asleep (recovering from Ramsey), so I take Brian ashore to show him the Straw Bear photograph, the 'Witchcraft Totem'. The museum is closed, the town deserted: apart from kids hanging about on the grass outside the Leisure Centre, putting on time until the next burning.

We found a pub with a bear sign and tried some peat-black beer, treacly and reviving. Pumped straight from the Mere, Brian reckoned. Whittlesey is a grander place than Ramsey, even where the architecture is heritaged or allowed to devolve into empty squares and traffic islands: ghosts are busy, money made from water and clay. Contiguous memories are of flooding and horse-drawn fire engines.

The rain relents; we nudge our craft through a leafy area known as the 'Bower'. Overhanging greenery reminds Catling of the Oxford backwaters. This was where Whittlesey courting couples came. 'A trysting place,' says the caption on the postcard. Was it favoured by Anna's relatives, the Roses? There is a photograph, from the late-Victorian era, three men in a boat, facing the camera, while two girls – sisters? – watch from the bank.

As we pass the brickworks, King's Dyke takes on the romance of Jean Vigo's film, *L'Atalante*; liminal land. Beasts in wild paddocks between road and canal. Sheds, shacks, caravans. Illegitimate fishermen. Thickets for lurkers and sex pests. Black plastic fronds flapping on razorwire. A monster hoarding: CARPETS 4 LESS. I know what I should do for the birthday: book a table for lunch at the Cherry House Restaurant in Werrington, former home of Anna's great-grandfather, Robert Hadman. But this is no easy matter: first, we have to moor in Peterborough, which means passing through Stanground Lock ('attended, 24-hour notice required'); and then, a sterner challenge, I have to figure out how to use Anna's mobile, while Brian keeps her busy by asking for a fresh Bloody Mary pitcher.

It works. I find the number in an old notebook. (We tried to get to the Cherry House when we stayed at the Bull Hotel, booked out for weeks.) I hit buttons, phone icons, until a connection is achieved. We can have a table, as soon as they open, at twelve-thirty. It's going to be tight. We have the lock to negotiate, on our way back; so that we can reach the outskirts of March by nightfall, to return the narrowboat to Fox's Yard first thing on Monday morning.

There is nowhere to moor, housing estates, broken parks, until we reach the Stanground Lock: a cottage with a steeply terraced garden. Brian and Anna try the cottage while I tie up the boat. They knock, hear nothing. They knock again, are on the point of walking away, when the door opens. An old lady. 'It was like a fairy story,' Anna said. The old lady thought the whole thing very amusing, that anyone should want to sail through, at this hour, to Peterborough. It was no simple operation, the lock; a booking would have to be made for nine o'clock the following morning. Meanwhile, we could stay where we were; we could make fast at the dock.

Catling got to work on the Ramsey chops, the sherry-enhanced Blood Marys (with whisky chasers). We kept the hatches open, to clear the smoke: watching rain fall like grapeshot on oily water.

The lock-keeper, keen gardener, reluctant custodian of the waterways, pressed a button, cranked away, to let us escape. He resented his wife's generosity, accepting this early booking. 'You can come through at three o'clock,' he warned. 'After that we're closed for the night.'

The great doors of Stanground Lock open, like Traitor's Gate, to a stunning prospect of the city. Peterborough, achieved by water, is a vision. The limestone cliff of the cathedral rises over reed beds, pylons; it travels with us as we curve into the broad Nene, under a road bridge, to tie up on the town embankment. Ancient liberties

can be assumed from the presence of rough sleepers in pup tents and on tartan rugs. From craft moored, without charge, against the cathedral meadows.

It was only when we found ourselves drudging around pedestrian precincts, steel-shuttered shopping malls, that our spirits flagged. The cathedral was roped off, busy with choirs. Anna started to make noises about supermarkets and stocking up for the evening, our final meal. The obvious solution was to suggest coffee and biscuits in the Bull Hotel, knowing that this leisurely process would allow me to book a cab for the ride to Werrington.

Brushing off crumbs, suggesting another look at the family butcher shop, Anna steps into the street. She points to the direction she thinks we ought to take. A smart taxi screeches to a halt. 'Sorry,' Anna says. Believing that her arm movement has summoned a cruising predator, desperate for custom. We are sliding northward through suburbs before she guesses the destination: Werrington. The cabbie gets us there, easy when you know the orbital system, in under ten minutes. He agrees to collect us, in plenty of time to make the return voyage to Stanground Lock: a nervous Indian with eyes full of blood.

The Cherry House, under the thatch and whitewash, is very good. Coming off water, out of Ramsey, we present a challenge to any respectable establishment. Anna's fine: serviceable blouse (pattern of roses), neat linen jacket. I have to fudge an eccentric fisherman look, distressed grey shirt under multi-pocketed waist-coat. Mud-crusted boots, coming apart, are tucked out of sight beneath my chair. A contortion I sustain while we order glasses of celebratory champagne. Professor Catling's uniform (his children won't be seen in his company when he sports it) is a Hawaiian shirt; worn, loose, outside the trousers. A scarlet-and-black, martial-arts interpretation of William Blake's 'The Great Red Dragon and the Woman Clothed with the Sun'. Given his luxuriant silver barnet, back-river tan, dark glasses, trimmed bulk, he looks like a porn star moonlighting as a hitman.

The other Cherry House punters are soft-spoken, recessive, not quite sure if they should be doing this on a Sunday. The rest of the town and most of the surrounding countryside are in church, singing and shaking: affirming. I wanted, very much, to make a second tour of St John the Baptist, Norman doorway and chancel arch, but it was out of the question. Morning service was massively subscribed, earth-shudderingly popular: it went on for hours. From time to time, people left; they scuttled away for sustenance, while the main event continued. Many returned, reinvigorated, to add volume to the joyful choir.

Wine, excellent. Food, delicious. (Goat's cheese, followed by salmon, for me. Red beef for the other two, Catling limiting himself to one slab of Yorkshire pudding.) Setting, disconcerting: low ceilings, heavy Regency drapes across cottage windows. Good linen, candles. Chatting to the young woman who serves us, we discover that she has come to Werrington from York (reversing Dick Turpin's journey). Her surname is Horseman. Her grandfather was mayor of that city: too young to have passed sentence on the highwayman. Ms Horseman is friendly and attractive. 'Perfect teeth,' says Catling. She listens, without yawning, to my account of Anna's connection with the building, old Robert Hadman. Then goes off to find early photographs, fields and orchards. She tells us that the Cherry House is a fine place to work, apart from the poltergeist. When she is clearing away, on her own, glasses fly through the air, cutlery jangles, plates smash, doors slam, windows rattle.

Back on the water, after this memorable meal, after the lock-keeper's daughter has waved us through, we're ready to chance the Twenty Foot River with its obstacle course of low and very low bridges. The man in the boatyard at March, in his laid-back fashion, advised against it: 'If the water's high, you'll stick fast. Your decision, boys. We'll come out and cut you free.' Our passage, between Whittlesey and Angle Bridge, was like Flanders: banks dressed with poppies, gun-emplacements peeping from a carmine curtain. A memorial to battles that had not yet been fought.

We decided to branch off, before taking the Twenty Foot River, to make a run at Bevill's Leam. The Leam was a conduit to drained Whittlesey Mere. Glassmoor House, Anna's fantasy home, faced the Leam – and was reachable, if we risked being unable to turn the boat, by water. Catling, cocky now, thought he could manage reverse gear. Hubris induced by quality champagne with a corned-beef chaser.

Loud print at both ends of our craft. Catling's Hawaiian flames and dragons at the tiller. Anna's roses (travelling expectantly to-wards other Roses) at the prow. Dark clouds, darker water. Furled poplars. An overgrown bank: edge emphasised by a stain of river scum. The Leam, a narrow trench when we stood safely on the road outside Glassmoor House, appeared, at water level, broad and deep. Very straight. Carrying the eye to that notch in the horizon where the entrance to Whittlesey Mere would once have been located. This detour, I concede, will give my narrative some sort of closure. The elements are in place: time of day, wind roughing up water, birthday lunch in the old Hadman home.

We pass under a bridge, steep banks cancel fields and solitary houses. The notch in the horizon draws us on. If we reach it, we will fall off the end of the known world. We will enter 'Three Miles Up', a ghost story by Robert Aickman; the one in which a narrowboat sails on and on, to the beginning of the primal lake. Bevill's Leam is the only certain way of accessing Whittlesey Mere. But you have to be dead to do it. Aickman's canal 'immediately broadened . . . a sheet, an infinity, of water stretched ahead; oily, silent, and still, as far as the eye could see, with no country edging it, nothing but water to the low grey sky above it'.

We stopped talking and remained in our separate positions on the boat: tiller, prow, roof. 'Navigable,' says the Middle Level chart, 'but not as a through route.' Beyond Tebbits Bridge, you sail into John Bodger's 1786 description of 'the Beautiful Fishery of Whittlesea Mere and of Such Navigable Rivers with which it has communication'. Bevill's River enters the north-east corner of the inland sea. Other access points were allocated to powerful local interests. 'Doomsday Book,' writes Bodger, 'mentions that the Abbot of Ramsey had one Boatsgate.'

Sluggish currents of submerged memory float us to another place. I jump on to the bank, drive in the metal spikes, make fast. We have come alongside Glassmoor House: riverborne invaders. From the property, we can't be seen. Sunlight breaks through cloud cover, late-afternoon shadows of box and yew: we march up the drive.

Dog. Dogs. Large and black: alert to our trespass. A woman emerges from the shrubbery.

'Yes?'

That paper-cutting uppercrust voice. Coveted property under siege from three windblown, over-lunched strangers. Nameless and without family. One of whom, a silver-crusted type in dark glasses, is wearing the kind of shirt that is favoured, in this part of the world, for target practice. Dogs paw the ground.

'We think my wife's family' – I should have said people – 'once lived here. The Roses.'

'Actually, my husband's *people*, the Saunders, built the house. They've been around for a hundred years or so. I'll fetch him out.'

And, actually, yes; Mrs Saunders is gracious about our intrusion. Mr Saunders, visible through the bay window, manifests to deal with uninvited guests, a possible extension of his private party. He is ruddy, copiously cardigan'd; a seasoned extension of belly.

'Rose?' he said. 'Old George? Good lord, he didn't live *here*. George kept a pub, down by the bridge, the Wheatsheaf. The entire road is Glassmoor, actually. We don't have numbers. George Rose in Glassmoor House? Good lord.'

Anna's illusions were visibly shattered. Catling swayed on his heels. Mr Saunders, recognising a fellow spirit, was all for coming aboard and casting anchor.

'Arrive by water? Good show. Sun over yardarm? I'm very tempted to come along with you chaps.'

George Rose, it appears, was a farmer; and not quite, in the formal sense, a gentleman. Decent fellow, of course. Goes without saying. Salt of. Worked his land and ran, with the help of his wife, a waterside pub: the Wheatsheaf. 'You'll spot a plaque on the wall as you sail past.' The pub was strategically sited at Angle Bridge, catching boats, crews and horses, travelling in all directions; on the dyke between Peterborough, Whittlesey and March, or the Leam which, as it flowed under the bridge, became the Twenty Foot River. There were stables for horses. Home-brewed beer for the men. George Rose also kept pigs.

The property was no longer with the family, Mr Saunders thought. Building work in progress, but we should be able to have a good poke around, undisturbed. So that became the revision of our plan: ivy-covered house lost, publicans and working farmers still to be found: we would drive back, tomorrow, on our way to London. This evening, nothing to lose, we would risk the Twenty Foot River, circle around White Moor, and return to the Nene, a mile or two above March.

This evening passage, under a red sunset, is the most otherworldly of them all. The TV aerial has to be taken down so that we can scrape under the third bridge; if it rains again, and the water level rises, we're going to find ourselves wedged, stuck fast. We are cruising, quietly, at walking speed, through a sanctuary: bird life is affronted. Herons, with their prehistoric bloodline, are disdainful; badly articulated umbrella-forms wishing us hence. Arctic terns divebomb the pilot, regroup, come again as a second wave. Swans, imperious and sharing a mutual dislike with Professor Catling ('I hate those bastards'), are troubled by the boat. They hammer and slap, strain to lift off, leaving a trail of watery footprints in their wake. Then they settle, shrugging white coats, until the narrowboat, keeping its distance, comes alongside. The process begins again. One wretched bird, fisherman's hook caught in its mouth, line tangled through its wing, cannot fly; it panics, thrashes water; refuses to allow us to get ahead, get away.

The lowest bridge takes the skin from my knuckles. I have to release the tiller as we chug under it. Eventually, light fading, we make the turn towards the Nene. A sewage farm. An encampment of travellers. Scrap-metal traders in bivouacs made from surplus stock. They watch from salvaged perches, music amplified over the quiet river; they wait patiently for our first mistake.

We tie up between a radio mast and a few scrawny trees: our final feast, the last pitchers of a drink that complements the fiery sky. Polished wood shimmers in virtual flame. The boat hook is striped with colours that precisely match Professor Catling's shirt: red, yellow, black.

Laws of the universe, as they apply to time, space, magnetism, respect for living things, are different here. Fenland rivers undo us, challenging previously held convictions. In 1838, Samuel Birley Rowbotham conducted an experiment on a six-mile stretch of the Old Bedford Level, in order to prove that the earth was flat. He assumed that the world's curvature, if it existed, would be revealed by observations made with a telescope: barges, at a sufficient distance, should become invisible. They would drop over the lip, out of sight. Ignorant of refraction caused by the air, Rowbotham's results satisfied him. Case proven. He was wise in his choice of location. On the Old Bedford Level, the world *is* flat. Barges vanish.

Reforgetting

People vanish. Then reappear, centuries later, with stories to tell. Drowned faces, six miles off, are more detailed, easier to remember, than those of the people at the other end of your narrowboat. (When viewed through the wrong end of a tumbler of Catling's tipple.)

Such madness doesn't go away. In 1904, Elizabeth Anne Mould Williams (Lady Blount) took up Rowbotham's cause: planist philosophy. She led an expedition to the Levels, hiring a photographer (with telephoto lens) who was instructed to capture white sheets hung from distant bridges, two feet above the water. If the bottom of the sheets remained in shot, the world was flat. The prints proved satisfactory. The earth, out here, where we were moored, remains flat. And goes on for ever.

The Wheatsheaf

J. H. Prynne, talking about Charles Olson's *Maximus IV, V, VI*, identified the essential movement of that epic, and by implication all epics, as a 'homecoming'. The poem was 'a noble arc' of light and language; moving, from river to shore to ocean to void, in a curve: 'which is love'. The quality we must bring to this country, against the void of the drained Mere. And our own drowned memories.

Angle Corner enjoys a strategic position. You can see exactly why the Roses shifted from Whittlesey and settled out here. Reedy canals intersect with back rivers. Obscure farms have names such as 'Wype Doles'. Transport abandoned, we look around us, trying to identify the curve of love in a territory occupied by flat-earthers. A stone bridge. Green-gold crops beaten down by the rains of a poor summer. Flattened fields offering evidence of alien invasion (by capital, by robotic technologies). The scale and quality of emptiness unsettles Londoners: all the ground between Highbury Corner and the Angel, King's Cross and Primrose Hill, under cultivation. Unpeopled. A few bushes, low trees, on the horizon. Telegraph poles. The forensic glint of water. Scarlet poppies follow the dyke back into Whittlesey: an illuminated flight path.

Road signs are fiction: Burnt House, Turves, Benwick (our riverside burial ground). The compact redbrick house – twin bay windows, narrow door, wheatsheaf symbol – commands a broad prospect: ground rises, a few feet above the bridge, before the road runs away across Glassmoor towards Benwick.

I wouldn't say the red house was abandoned, as Mr Saunders suggested: in limbo. The Wheatsheaf has been re-roofed with tiles, given the replacement-window treatment (fake Mediterranean shutters). It is being prepared for sale, although no builders, that morning, are in evidence. This moment of hesitation on Angle Bridge is as close as we have come to a living Rose relative, a building with a working history: alongside the house is a large barn with marks or bites along the boards. Anna feels that it is her duty to knock at the door, before we invade house or barn.

I was standing off, to one side, when she took the two or three steps from gate to door. I had lined up a nice shot, in which road and canal would be reflected in the window, when Anna knocked. When she stepped smartly back. There would be nobody at home. The warmth of the Roses, even I knew, had long since dissipated. The Wheatsheaf was an old property waiting for a very new buyer, land speculator.

The Chinese man, undershirt, tracksuit trousers, took us by surprise. As we surprised him. The stance was challenging. He blocked access, swaying on the balls of his bare feet, looking up and down the road: searching for black cars, white vans, blue uniforms. He stared, wild-eyed, as Anna muttered something about George Rose. She was a foot taller than the tightly sprung man with his panic stance: one of the original family returned to demand her inheritance.

I imagined all manner of improbable scenarios, based on Sax Rohmer and the yellow press (the Morecambe drownings were fresh in my mind). Work gangs concealed in the barn? A pipeline for smuggling illegal immigrants? White slavery, dope? But it was the Chinese householder who was being inconvenienced; doorstepped, peered at, interrogated by three large occidentals in shabby clothes. Riffraff with cameras and an incomprehensible tale of lost ancestors. We backed off. With difficulty, I stopped myself from bowing. The door was slammed. The man watched us from the window as we climbed back into the car.

That should have been the end of it. Victory for the flat-earthers, nothing connects with nothing. We'd followed the trail from Glinton to Werrington, Whittlesey to Ramsey. We'd travelled on foot and by water. The Roses had been tracked from faded obituary notices to microfilms in Whittlesey Library, address by address, to a defunct waterside pub. Which was now in Chinese possession. There was a book to be written. It was time for me to let go. In life, neat resolutions are rarely possible.

We spread out maps to pick a route back to the A1. I felt quite nostalgic about rejoining John Clare's road, following him south to London. Clare begins his 'Autobiographical Fragments' by knocking off his antecedents in a single paragraph. His forefathers were part of him, a part best understood by re-remembering his own life. Whatever any man achieves, it will continue, this complex interweaving of place and personality; that which is given and that which is stubbornly reconfigured.

I cannot trace my name to any remote period a century & a half is the utmost & in this I have found no great ancestors to boast in the breed – all I can make out is that they were Gardeners Parish Clerks & fiddlers & from these has sprung a large family of the name still increasing were kindred has forgotten its claims & 2nd & 3rd cousins are worn out

A young woman with a wriggling child in her arms raps on our window. She has come from the farm beside the Wheatsheaf and has witnessed our confrontation with Mr Chan. Even when there is nobody to be seen, eyes are on you: taking your measure. Hands on telephones. Dogs on chains. Shotguns in cupboards.

She gives us that name, Chan, but has no information to offer on the current status of the former inn. She knew the Roses. And the Turners who lived in the Wheatsheaf in more recent times. And how the Roses and the Turners were related. William Rose, Anna's great-grandfather, farmed on Glassmoor. His final property was a short distance down the road, in the direction of Benwick: Delavals Farm. We had not been far from the mark when we tried the Saunders house, the two farms were back to back: one faced Bevill's Leam, and the other faced the road (former track) across the Fens.

George A. Rose, who kept the Wheatsheaf, was William's son. George had two daughters, Mary and Edith; who married, according to the custom of the place, two brothers, the Turners. Norman Turner, the son of the younger Rose girl, Edith, lived in a bungalow in Doddington, a few miles down the road. The Turners, this woman thought, farmed somewhere this side of Benwick. If we went to Doddington, we were sure to find them; not far from the hospital, a neat property, set back from the main street. A name like – 'The Hollies'?

Once again we are standing outside a strange house, ringing a bell, waiting for a face we won't recognise; a person whose very existence was unknown twenty minutes ago. We'd managed conversations in driveways and at garden gates, but we had never been let inside. Until now. A blonde lady, of middle height, wearing a plum-coloured jersey, listened attentively to our tale. Then invited us in for tea. 'We're related, sort of cousins,' she said; treating Anna, at once, as one of the family. Carol Turner, wife of Norman. Daughter-in-law of the former Edith Rose.

Carol apologised for the state of her immaculate property, as we scuffed Fenland mud into a Welcome mat. Even the home improvements were being improved; everything, by our standards, was new and bright. Deep carpets. Big television. Polished wood. Video shelves. Conservatory. Shaved lawn. Caught on the hop, by unaccredited genealogists from London, Carol whipped up tea and biscuits; before producing family albums, the fruits of her research. She was the other person who had been looking into the Roses in Whittlesey Library: working her way towards Anna. As Anna advanced, by fits and starts, on her.

The history of the Wheatsheaf was soon revealed. Old William Rose, keeper of the Windmill Inn, came out of town on to Glassmoor: Delavals Farm. A sizeable property that was later managed by his oldest son, another William – who married, inevitably, another Anna. Florence, his second daughter, married William Hadman of Glinton: the farmer and forester who launched our journey across the Fens.

Old William's third son, George Rose, developed a fancy for the

Wheatsheaf, when he walked past it on his way to school. He vowed one day to own the property. And in the fashion of the Roses, determined folk, canny with cash, he succeeded. He kept the pub and farmed thirty-five acres. The pub part of the operation was closed down in the Twenties. 'The Irish,' Carol thinks. Rivermen were always a rough lot, good drinkers, but when the Irish came it was too much. Better to acquire more fields than to sweep up broken glass and mend windows. The Roses were restless. They bought land, rented it out, bought more, diversified into whatever was going.

George, getting old, retreated into Whittlesey: 13 Bread Street. Michael Turner, son of Mary, first cousin of Carol's husband, Norman, took the Wheatsheaf. He didn't run it as a pub, he kept pigs. Hundreds of them. The barn alongside the house had originally been for the horses who pulled cargo boats: the 'Horse Water Shed' it was called.

Norman and Carol bought the Wheatsheaf in 1987. Norman still farmed, but the house and much of the land had been sold. It was the 'Horse Water Shed' that caused the problem for the present occupant, Mr Chan. Chan decided to wholesale ducks and other feathered delicacies for the restaurant trade. He packed them into the Wheatsheaf barn. The scoring we had noticed, at ground level, had been caused by rats. Rats gnawed through wood and feasted on food laid out for the ducks. Hence, Mr Chan's suspicion of cameras. There had been an episode, before Christmas, a prosecution by the RSPCA. It made a big stir on local television. Our unannounced arrival would have been seen, by the former duck-breeder, as a fresh intrusion by muck-raking journalists. It was far worse: we wanted the dirt on generation after generation of blameless (and quietly forgotten) working people.

'Do you recognise anyone?' Carol handed Anna the album.

'My grandmother.'

The photograph is dated, 7 June 1937: members of the Rose family at the wedding of Mary Rose and Ernest Turner. Standing on the right of the group (as we look at it) is Florence Hadman: pearls, flowers on hat, fur-trim at cuffs. This is the bespectacled face we know from the 1938 passport portrait. Hats for the ladies, shoulders drooping under a heft of dead fox. The farmers, silverhaired and trim, have the look of late Charles Chaplin: tight suits, eyes narrowed against the light. Self-confident. Established. On their own turf.

But it is the older photographs, weddings as remote as episodes out of D. H. Lawrence (even Hardy), that justify our quest. Anna can find, in the young girls attending these festivities, her own daughters: the spirit and the features. A rapid dissolve in which bone structure, attitude and temperament undergo minimal shifts and adjustments. They live in us, the old ones, and we have a duty to honour their presence. There are no clean slates. Forgathered, posed, the Roses offer themselves to us in their most public and performed aspect. 'The wedding of a daughter of William and Mary Rose of Glassmoor,' says the caption. That is all we know. William had nine children, five daughters. Anna thinks that the young woman in a straw boater, sitting in the front row, a baby in her lap, is Florence Hadman, her grandmother. With her first child, Mary. The aunt with whom she stayed at Balcony House in Glinton. The one whose husband cleaned the tar from her sandals.

'We think old William had a wooden leg,' Carol tells us, passing another photograph: 'William and Mary, with their children, at Glassmoor.' Here is a patriarch to set beside Robert Hadman of Werrington (when he posed with his daughters, in front of the creepered wall). William Rose is solid, moustached. He has the now familiar trick: raised eyebrow. The photographer had better know his business. Beyond all the fuss, there is enduring pride in the family as a unit: scrub off the pig shit, show the world what we are worth. Watchchains. Bow ties. Dresses with pinched waists and puffed shoulders. The Roses in their place.

There is also a study of the Wheatsheaf, as it was, before Mr Chan. A brick building square to the road. 'TAP ROOM', it says, on the parlour window. Above the door, and beneath the Wheatsheaf plaque, is the licence of George A. Rose. In the window of the tap room, arms on hips like a Greek vase, is a woman, looking straight back at us.

Carol contacted Michael Turner, Norman's cousin; the son of the other Rose sister, Mary. After the Wheatsheaf, Michael moved back into Whittlesey. A spotless bungalow tucked away off New Road: two German motors out front, fountains and statuary in the garden, at the rear. Everything, it appeared, fresh from catalogue. Newly released from its polythene.

Michael's wife, Pat, was a broadband genealogist, with files and photographs to display. These were generous people, offering hospitality to strangers, providing us with anecdotal evidence to flesh out speculative biographies. They brought the particulars of Whittlesey and Glassmoor to life.

Anna talked to Pat. Michael showed me his porcelain cabinet: prizefighters, hounds, figurines that cost thousands of pounds. A splendid collection. The striking photograph Michael produced was of a semicircle of tractors, out on the Fens. His father with new machines and the men who worked them. Like Russian collectivists on the steppes. But what Michael remembers, most sharply, is the fact that his father never accompanied him on his return to boarding school in Norwich; a function left to his uncle.

Whittlesey, through Michael's stories, is repopulated, no longer a town of ghosts and shadows. After the pig farm, he went into catering, a fish and chip shop. He cleared serious money, he told me how much, over the Straw Bear Festival: gallons of deep-fat cod, buckets of potato wedges, to soak up the beer. Later, he sold the premises as a Chinese restaurant. One of his great pleasures was to cruise the Middle Level in his boat; a short haul in agreeable company, pub lunch and afternoon snooze.

The potentialities of Whittlesey and Werrington – Roses met Hadmans at Peterborough Agricultural Fair – were what Anna's father turned his back on. That life was too inviting. The landscape swallowed you: tiny figures, at the mercy of the weather, labour under immense skies. Getting away, Oxford, Lancashire, private plane, property in Kenya, manor house in Rutland, required an active suspension of memory. 'My father never talked about his grandparents or any of the Roses,' Anna said. But Michael Turner knew Geoffrey's brother, Lawrie, very well. 'Lawrie and Madge? Oh yes. I visited their house in Glinton. Lawrie was a butcher in Whittlesey before he took up farming.'

There was a moment when Michael's family could have acquired the Saunders farm. 'You met Ted Saunders? Tall, red-faced gentleman? Well George Rose worked his land when Ted was away, the army.' Arable farming: sugar beet, potatoes. Anna's Glassmoor fantasy might have been realised, for the price of a few thousand pounds; Delavals Farm stretching to Bevill's Leam. £15,000 was the asking price. Half was available, in cash; the rest had been lent to a friend and couldn't be repaid in time. It passed. One branch of the family, socially restless, lost sight of the others, the ones who stayed within the gravitational field of Whittlesey Mere. Escape brought its rewards, but also its penalties: nostalgia, admitted or suppressed, for this melancholy land. The challenge of squeezing a living out of sodden fields and black water.

PRE-REMEMBERED

The road he had travelled had disappeared, and all that remained was the little space on which his feet were standing. He was dreaming and he did not know it.

José Saramago, *The Double*

Helpston

Property is on the move everywhere, it's like a madness; villages disappear, survivors are rattled, provoked by real-estate promos masquerading as documentaries. Helpston is not immune, Helpston is off-highway. The only marketable commodity is the 'Northamptonshire Peasant Poet'. Helpston is no longer in Northamptonshire. The only peasants are waxworks in heritage museums: waiting for the Black Death (as seen on television).

The Clare Society (in conjunction with Peterborough City Council) has produced a map of the poet's Helpston; a flattering sketch, based on the William Hilton portrait, decorates its cover. Returned to Stilton, the Bell Hotel, for a final push, we are spending one afternoon in Helpston, walking the John Clare trail. At 16 Woodgate, we re-encounter 'Clare's Cottage'. It is dazzlingly white, gorgeously thatched, and pegged with yellow-and-red boards provided by estate agents, Dickens Watts & Dade, of Cross Street, Peterborough. 'Viewing Strictly By Appointment Only.' £475,000. Tom Raworth's 1971 poem, 'Helpston £9,850', has come to fruition (in everything except price). The cottage has endured every indignity, from Bill Brandt's theatrical mists to soft-sell digital portraiture. Now it has been forcibly inducted into the Peterborough conurbation.

The walk, mapped out by the Clare Society, is pleasant; it's like scrolling effortlessly through deposits of memory rescued from numerous Clare biographies. I pose Anna, disguised by dark glasses, outside 'Bachelor's Hall', where the poet caroused with the Billings brothers. Pointing has been renewed, window frames freshly painted; there is a burglar alarm in the place where the old fire-insurance plaque would once have been sited.

We follow the trail into Royce Wood, quilted silence, a sudden eros of woody scents: the illusion of invisibility. The wood is a release from village life (eyes, twitching curtains). One element in Clare's work is much clearer now, the way a walk disperses social noise, drops into private meditation: the rhythm of the country, as it climbs, shifts from limestone to clay. And is randomly punctuated by roads, divided by rivers.

We hit Torpel Way at a point that carries us to the right, uphill, in the direction of Ailsworth and Castor Highlands. A fruitful error. I decided, quite arbitrarily, to get away from traffic, to take to the fields (another footpath sign left in a ditch). We made an easy descent, seeing the village, seeing how Helpston sat in its dish; the sweep of the horizon so different from its neighbours, Glinton and Northborough. That short move, to the new cottage, was a banishment the poet couldn't endure. The wooded hills around Helpston offered Clare the possibility of walking out, as the whim took him, into quite distinct topographies, productive of contrary moods: light and shade, good humour or slow-footed, sodden melancholy. Drowning or flying.

Anna has to be held by the ankles, before she lifts from the ground: the view across broad fields, divided by ancient oaks, is an instantaneous transfusion. A coming-into-herself. A recognition. Stands of poplars. A path skirting the edge of Oxey Wood. Knowing little of Clare's habits, she searches for orchids. There have been dreams and she tells me about them.

She is at home, her childhood place in the Blackpool suburbs, the familiar bed. 'If I opened my eyes, I would be there.' Her brother William and her younger sister, Susa, safe in their rooms. Robert's room, she worries, is a bathroom. Where will he sleep?

The babble of a party, it keeps her awake. They are downstairs in the salon (yes, that's what her father called it). They are waiting, out of place, Hadmans and Roses; the troublesome dead of Werrington and Whittlesey. In period costume, the clothes of their time. They have been brought back, diverted from the static cling of sepia photographs by the irritation of our gaze. They mill about this awkward room; people of the Peterborough fringe transported to Lancashire. Like wartime aliens to the Isle of Man. 'They want

to be organised,' Anna said. 'It's our fault. They came in a depu-
tation. They asked for coffee.'

I noticed Anna's horoscope in the paper and wrote it down: 'If
they start to form a semicircle around you – run towards the open
end. The horizon calls.'

From Oxey Wood, it is all horizon. Heavy cloud, shadows of
oaks; village and road as a pale mirage among remote thickets and
hedges. All our themes, our quests, are being resolved (or discontinued) at one time. A visible demonstration of the boundaries of
Clare's early poetry. And of Anna's emotional investment in this
landscape. The trail of the oldest Hadman we could trace brought us
back to Stilton. Information was coming now, faster than we could
cope with it. Two books I had been searching for were suddenly
available: the 'lost' poems written by Anna's father and the original
manuscript notebook of John Clare's 'Journey out of Essex'.

Thinking perhaps of Sylvia Plath, Anna remembered her father's
missing collection as *Ariel*. Which suited me very well, being the
name that Shelley wanted to give to the yacht on which he was
drowned, the *Don Juan*. But memory is fickle. I read Geoffrey
Hadman's poems on visits to Anna's mother, in her converted
cottage in a Rutland village, near Uppingham. I imagined specific
references to Clare's geography. There were none, apart from a
short lyric invoking Glinton.

> I faintly hear you,
> Lovely bells of lonely Deeping –
> Softly, softly, far-off pealing,
> Across waste water

The poems were handwritten, a black serif calligraphy, with red
titles and initial letters: clear as print. The collection was called
Spirit's Expense. (Shakespeare again, *Sonnets*. 'The expense of spirit
in a waste of shame/ Is lust in action.') It was astonishing that the
book reappeared just as I was struggling to tie up the loose ends of
my narrative. Anna contacted her brothers, her sister, none of them

knew where their father's poems had gone. I fell under suspicion, for allowing the handsome volume to be swept away, with the rest of the library, to an Uppingham dealer. I knew this wasn't the case. My memory might be full of holes, but books are never forgotten. The poems sat on the reserved pile, to be removed by the family, before the dealer arrived.

Spirit's Expense turned up in a box of diaries, papers, rings that had belonged to Anna's mother. Her sister, in Cumbria, had it in her safekeeping. And now Anna could handle this unique folio, read it with fresh eyes. Neat symmetry: thirty-one poems published in 1941, when the author was thirty-one (thirty-second birthday in July). Fine paper with watermark of J. Green & Son. Vellum and calf. Gilt lettering on spine. The production was the gift, as Anna understood it, of her father's glamorous London friend whose limp Judy Hadman had imitated.

Twenty-Five Poems, by Dylan Thomas, was published in 1936. He was five years younger than Anna's father. David Gascoyne's *Man's Life is This Meat* also appeared in 1936. He was seven years younger. Auden published *The Double Man* and *New Year Letter* in 1941. He was two years older than Geoffrey Hadman and would have been a contemporary at Oxford. Stephen Spender, also at Oxford, was two months younger. Eliot published *The Dry Salvages* in 1941. *Little Gidding* appeared the following year. 'Here, the intersection of the timeless moment/ Is England and nowhere. Never and always.'

Geoffrey Hadman's verse, privately published, is not of that order; a casual reader would place the collection well before the First War, with Brooke and the Georgians, or with Housman (who is directly invoked). The language is archaic, ripe with 'e'en were' and 'say nay'. It is a long way from the colloquial vigour and sharp-eyed specifics of Clare. Clare's poetry is his existence. The verse in this extravagantly bound folio is a gentlemanly exercise, the exhibition of technical facility; a manageable neurosis of memory and regret, abdicated love, anticipation of death. But it would be unfair to form a critical judgement of a volume that was never offered to the public.

One of the surprises is a poem addressed to 'lovely Annabel'. It was written and published two years before Anna was born. She has no idea who the addressee is, or if she existed as anything beyond an echo of Poe; but here might be the clue to that name which was never quite her own: Mary Annabel Rose. The Mary was understood, her Hadman aunt. The Rose part was found in Whittlesey. The Annabel drifted as seven lines in a book of verse, published in an edition of one. In this poem, if anywhere, was a reflection of Clare: the way he dedicated a 'moment's rapture' to the unknown Anna who carried his first daughter's name.

It was good that the book had been recovered, but I was no nearer to any real connection with Clare. Clare operated, like all great poets, in an active present, in which deep images from the past continued to assault him. Time is plural, form a convenience. Sonnets are bent to suit his purpose. Imitations are exercises, contrived, when times are hard, to turn poetry to cash.

The poem in which Geoffrey Hadman comes closest to the place where we are walking, from Oxey Wood to Maxham's Green Lane, is called 'Clouds'. I realise now what the poem actually is: a meditation on flight. The cross-country trip, Blackpool to Glinton, in the Auster. The poet is looking down on the clouds.

> White wisps of spirit
> Fading into space,
> Paling the blue infinity of sky,
> Writhing, twisting, ghostly cirrus!
> Frozen souls of the dead,
> Purified in purgatory.

English fields are masked by 'blankets of grey stratus'. The pilot's reverie is convalescent, drifting from 'morphia to nostalgia'. As cloud cover breaks, 'shafts of washed, golden light' pick out 'pinnacles and spires' of a cathedral: 'convolute in pure white'. Peterborough is a cloud castle. The vision, based on experience, does approach Clare; his dream of Helpston Church, the Day of

Judgement. At last, in the memory of flight, Geoffrey Hadman's elective relationship with the Helpston peasant, with this landscape, is explored and justified.

Sidney Keyes, another Oxford man, was killed in action: Tunisia, 1943. His 'Garland for John Clare' claims that there is only ever one poet, possessed by different voices, operating under various disguises (Shakespeare, Chatterton, Byron). One poet for each place. 'But sometimes I remember,' Keyes writes, 'the time that I was John Clare, and you unborn.'

We started early, this final push, driving to Huntingdon, the County Record Office, to trawl for Hadmans. We shared the task, dividing up materials relating to territory we were about to explore, the hills behind Stilton. Very soon, I was at a table with pouches of parchment; waxy, yellow, nibbled by rats. The ink held. Many of those married, christened, buried were lost: Hadman or Hadenham, parish clerks were never sure of the spelling. The givers of information may well have been illiterate. I worked back, magnifying glass to document, as far as 1680. To no great effect.

I noted: Elizabeth Jane, daughter of Richard and Sarah Hadman, baptised in 1857. And her brother, William George, baptised in 1859. Richard Hadman is described as a 'labourer'. Then there was William Hadman, who died in 1887, aged eighty-four. And Mary Ann Hadman, who died in August 1893, aged eighty-nine. At Holme. That caught my eye: the last Hadman recorded in Huntingdon was living in a village on the edge of Whittlesey Mere; the place where we had gone searching for the posts that marked the drop in the land. Holme River was the south-western entrance to the Mere, as Bevill's Leam was the entrance in the north-east.

All these Hadmans came from one place, Caldecote. Caldecote? Caldecote barely exists, it is less than a village; it's a memory smear on the (2.5 inches to the mile) Pathfinder map. A farm, a wood. A motte and bailey castle. Caldecote is tucked against Washingley, on rising ground beyond Stilton. Washingley, we knew, was where Anna's great-great-grandfather, Robert Hadman (1808–63), later of

Werrington, began. Washingley was as far as our trail went: a deleted village, a present farm (with fish ponds and earthworks).

In Huntingdon, I discovered the Washingley Estate Map from 1833; hand-coloured, precise, financial returns laid out like poems. In 1803 the estate brought in £2,138. In 1824: £2,141. No increase in real terms. A farmhouse with garden produced £12–3s–17 in annual rent. The kennels adjoining the pleasure ground produced £35–0s–11. Tenant farmers were named: Jasper Perkins, Robert Peake, William Handbury. As were the more humble cottagers, the keeper of a public house. Not one Hadman. They were beneath the level that produced revenue for the estate. They laboured.

We were no closer to Anna's great-great-grandfather, the Robert Hadman who made the break, eight miles to Werrington. We decided to move on at once to Northampton. Anna would hit the record office in Wootton Hall Park, while I went back to the library to view John Clare's notebook with the 'Journey out of Essex'. I had the required letter from my publisher, access was promised.

I can't believe the generosity, the trust, of the Clare keepers, but Northampton has that quality: it draws you in, it keeps you. Locals know (even when they're wrong) the history of their town, and they talk about it, with affection but no particular respect. There could be no better place to shelter Clare or his memorials. In Northampton, he was a tolerated presence, adding lustre to the stone. The alcove in All Saints' Church still has a 'reserved for mad poet' aspect; loose citizens muse, nurse a can, but soon shuffle off. That seat is too hot. The alcove clamps like a wired helmet offering a vertical blow-dry.

I want to say, 'Don't do it. Don't risk your precious relic.' This man has the dealing virus in his blood. I picture the entry in a catalogue: 'Poet's holograph.' One of one. The notebook is kept in an archival box: 'John Clare Poems, 1841'. The driven year at High Beach when he worked on split Byronic narratives, 'Don Juan', 'Child Harold'; on biblical paraphrases. Before the escape. A torrent of words in smudged blocks. His furies demanded that he took to the road: to recover himself, to catch up with his wandering spirit, to shake off Byron's clammy grip. Byron had already been carried north. The club-footed aristocrat liked to put up at the Bell in Stilton, where Clare would come close to losing his nerve: 'He shams.'

Urgent prose cuts against seizures of poetry: so that 'I wandered many a weary mile / Love in my heart was burning' confronts the entry about the 'wide awake hat'. Script slants to a wind from the east, ruffling Whittlesey Mere. Paper is precious. Every inch of space is exploited. Clare wrote in Northborough, after the road, unpunctuated paragraphs: the voices caught him. He sweated and trembled, pushing his nib across the page, mapping memory before it was lost.

The last sentence of that journey, as I had seen it reproduced by Eric Robinson in *John Clare by Himself*, was chilling:

Returned home out of Essex and found no Mary – her and her family are as nothing to me now though she herself was once the dearest of all – 'and how can I forget

Quotation marks opened, never to close. Now, using my magnifying glass, I see that the published transcription is incorrect, quotation marks *do* seal Clare's challenge to his readers. That we should learn how to forget. To let him go. Leaving poetry as its own legend.

It was raining, the shower caught me as I hurried from the library to my pre-arranged meeting with Alan Moore. We would pay our respects to Lucia Joyce at Kingsthorpe Cemetery. Asking after cabs in Northampton minimarts produced blank astonishment: nothing to be had, ten minutes from the centre, nothing but novelty stores, tabloid newspapers, cigarettes, cut-price CDs, used leather.

When hail bounced from the tarmac, my quest took on a certain urgency. I spotted a cab, parked up, tattooed driver doing his best to look like an unemployed getaway specialist, a redundant blagger.

He was, he said, on a job, waiting for a client – but, bugger that, cash is cash, jump in.

'What do you do then?'

'Writer.'

'Thought so. Always tell, I can. Had solicitors. From London. Had writers. Never wrong, me.'

What soon became obvious, on our short run to the cemetery, was that cabbies are messengers. In Northampton, time on their hands, they are also local historians.

'Clare? I was in the John Clare School. Music now. I went there, that school. It was all right.'

Cabbies are the chorus, hurrying a narrative along. No curiosity about what I write, or about my business with Alan Moore. 'Know *him*? Seen his picture, like, in the paper.' Plenty of curiosity about the town: Romans, Thomas à Becket, Clare, shoes. 'Good luck then.' He scratches a nose that is too flat to pick. It looks as if he tried to get out of the cab, in a hurry, forgetting there's a windscreen in the way.

I'm early and have time, in the rain, to locate Lucia Joyce's gravestone, before Alan arrives at the gate. The cemetery is built on a hill, in parkland, an extension of the golf course. It is arranged with the usual avenues and planted with a variety of trees and shrubs. I shelter under a chestnut. There are dozens of Haddons here, but no Hadmans. Haddon is the (old) Northamptonshire village that I walked through, with Renchi and Chris Petit, on the last leg of our journey out of Essex. Haddon is close to Stilton, to Washingley and Caldecote. I'm convinced that this is how the family name emerged, out of place: William (or Robert) of Haddon. Haddon-man, Hadman.

Before I make the turn, up the slope to where Lucia is buried, I find a nice marker, the grave of a certain Finnegan. James Joyce would have enjoyed that. Lucia might be less happy, the pain of her involvement with *Work in Progress*, before it became *Finnegans Wake*, is still active; provoking critical theories about incest, actual or metaphorical.

Alan, unprotected against the rain, stick in hand, arrives at the gate. I guide him to the grave. The red Aberdeen granite stone for the daughter of James Joyce, more years in Northampton than Paris, is stark.

LUCIA ANNA JOYCE. Trieste 1907. Northampton 1982.

She was two years older than Anna's father. She is left here, surrounded by Haddons and other Northamptonshire families, without a cluster of relatives; grounded in a far country, part of an alien history.

As we walk back, sodden, to Alan's house, he broaches a relativist's General Theory of Northampton, loosely based on some late pronouncement by Stephen Hawking. The town, it seems, is a black hole from which only 'mangled information' can escape. And that, Alan acknowledges, is his lifelong task: to de-mangle (and interpret) Northampton's cuneiform script. Its codex of madness and possession. Old magick is the new physics.

Lucia, aged seventy-three, frail, gaunt, was visited at St Andrew's by Dominique Maroger, a childhood friend. Maroger was shocked by the appearance of a woman she had not seen for fifty years. Lucia, she reported, was 'a medicated shadow'.

They took tea. Carol Loeb Shloss, in her biography of Lucia Joyce, tells us that the interior spaces of the hospital, its halls, were 'the portals to the Heart of Darkness'. 'The guarded doors, the knitting women, the unspoken horrors.' There was a lift Lucia feared and hated. St Andrew's was the Marienbad of Middle England; well-connected neurasthenics in formal wear playing bridge. The sedated and the forgotten, in their pre-posthumous limbo, obedient to social rituals. And otherwise consigned to silence.

'I mangle language,' whispered Lucia, 'because I never have anyone to talk to.'

At a fork in the road, we come on a monument, a pillar whose particular history Alan cannot recall. He knows about the witches hanged in the park on the other side of the road, but not this: a plinth of cut stone, a cube, a cannon ball. An inscription: V.R.I. The pillar must, I surmised, mark young Queen Victoria's triumphant procession through Northampton, perhaps the point where she left town.

I remembered Clare's 1841 notebook. 'The man whose daughter is now the queen of England is sitting on a stone heap on the high way to . . .' Highway to somewhere. I couldn't make out the destination. Smudged script was too taxing for my increasingly blurred vision.

John Clare, supposed lunatic, peasant poet, and William Wordsworth, ex-radical, Tory laureate, were both in Northampton to witness the royal progress. They never met.

As I step into the road, to photograph Moore, who is always game, ready to strike a mad-eyed stare, another figure invades the frame. Another stick. It's one of those lovely accidents: two men of the town, absorbed in their own affairs, cross paths. Moore, blinking, eyes shut. The native blindman in the bright yellow jacket (wise precaution), his dark glasses out of Chris Marker's *La Jetée*. Rogue trajectories intersect for the one and only time. Souls jump, make their bloodless exchange; return to shocked bodies. Clare could have done more with the incident, the accidental transmigration. I come away with a snapshot. This must be what Alan means about 'mangled information'. It is there but we don't see it. Without an adequate key, a tedious volume of explanation, photographs mean nothing.

Stilton

This is a sleeping country. To the casual eye, it remains unpeopled; but they are following us out of Stilton, close on our heels, the ones Anna has summoned. No spectral presences clamour around the bed at the Bell Inn. They accompany us on our walk to Fotheringhay, tapping our shoulders if we take the wrong path.

For years, Anna spoke of Fotheringhay as the saddest place in England. There is something about the setting that goes beyond the execution of Mary Stuart: its position on the Nene, a quality of afternoon light. A landscape in mourning. She was always telling me I should go there, but I never did. I remembered her recommendation every time I passed the road sign, but I was in too much of a hurry, books or projects.

Now, crossing the main street at Stilton, we felt a pressure lifted. The materials for the Clare book were in place, I could start a primitive assembly. Anna spent a fruitful afternoon in the Northamptonshire Record Office and couldn't say enough about the efficiency and friendliness of the staff. And I was beginning to think, with rumours of celebrity genealogical truffle-hunts on TV, that it was time to take up a new hobby: collecting yellow-and-blue murder and assault notices (adverts) in Hackney. When a subject is presented by Bill Oddie or Alan Titchmarsh, it is time to duck out.

We had carried the Hadmans as far as we could, to a period before the birth of John Clare. Anna discovered that her great-great-grandfather, Robert Hadman, was the youngest of four children. The first of them, Elizabeth, was baptised in 1794 (one year after the birth of Clare). The second son, William, married the Mary Ann who died in the village of Holme: the old lady I had already listed in the Huntingdon County Record Office. Mary Ann was illegitimate. Her father was unrecorded. Her mother, Jane Bunning, had the child baptised in 1809. If a link was to be projected with Clare, here it was: some wandering schoolmaster or fiddler, another John Donald Parker, passing through. His name is not known and can't be known.

Recorded Hadmans stay close to the Washingley Estate. Caldecote Hadmans, the ones I had found, were descendants of William and Mary Ann. In Anna's direct line, the Robert Hadman who moved from Washingley to Werrington was the son of Richard Hadman (1768–1822). Richard married Elizabeth Hill (1767–1813) in the church at Lutton. Folksworth, Washingley, Caldecote, Lutton, a scatter of farms, within a couple of miles of each other, took care of the entire Hadman lineage. We could visit what was left of these settlements in a morning, then come down off the hills and into Fotheringhay.

The walk, to Stilton Church, was precisely the one undertaken, four years earlier, with Renchi and Chris Petit. Back then, we got it wrong, giving ourselves many needless miles. At the fork, seduced by an avenue of tall trees, we took the left-hand path and spent a long morning wading through corn, accompanying dogs; with the feeling that we were trespassing, we would be turned off. Now, by contrast, the route to Folksworth is direct, but less inviting. A meadow. A dew pond. No cattle: Anna is nervous of cattle. A view back, across country, across the A1, to the smoking chimneys of Whittlesey. The Mere, in its pomp, approached within two miles of Stilton. Fields are so wet they look burnt: ash-brown stubble, corrugated mud picked out with flints and stones.

Folksworth has a village pond, suicide trough, and bright new houses (convenient for Peterborough commuters). Not much to detain us, no churchyard to prospect for stray Hadmans. The path twists, through farms and woods, to the next duck pond. Low jumps for schooling horses. One or two curious beasts, hopeful of apples.

Everything drains towards Washingley and Caldecote. I repeat those names, under my breath, like a mantra. 'Medieval Village of

Washingley (site of)', says the map. Because there is nothing left, nothing visible. Earthworks. Fish ponds. Our walk has the smack of an official ramble, it is good for us. There are things to be noticed and appreciated.

Sheep. Hundreds of them.

Anna can cope with sheep, their vulgar curiosity, dark brown heads rotating to follow her movements as she clambers over a stile. And down towards Manor Farm, the Washingley ponds. They bleat like the tide. (In Hastings, Anna has been dreaming about an ocean of sheep.)

Coming off the Folksworth to Lutton road, turning back towards Stilton, we cross the path of that first blundering attempt to pick up John Clare's traces. Cereal crops have survived the weather, bound and compressed wheels of straw look as if they have been assembled for a ritual vehicle of enormous size. The English surrealism of Paul Nash, washed-out colour, military detritus, is deployed, quoted, as the keynote of the Washingley Estate.

A light so pure that it is unreal: diagonal paths, skull-faced sheep, a building with a central tower like a decommissioned concentration camp. We make for that, after detouring to inspect the ponds and the supposed motte and bailey castle.

PRIVATE FISHING. SYNDICATE MEMBERS ONLY. KEEP TO MARKED FOOTPATHS. PLEASE LEAVE NO LITTER. THANK YOU.

The syndicated pond is achieved after a woodland trawl on permitted paths: dark water hidden by close-planted bushes and drooping trees. A wooden bench, from which red paint has peeled, waits for those who feel the need to sit and stare at ruffled water. It has a name, this bench, stamped on a yellow lozenge (like a number plate): CECIL.

The redbrick building with the sinister clocktower turns out to be a set of stables, the kind used for training racehorses. But there are no horses, the multiple green doors are shut. One animal occupies all this space, pressing itself against the wall, a donkey: a beast like Robert Bresson's 'Balthazar', from one of my favourite films, *Au Hasard, Balthazar*. I try to photograph the animal, but my camera won't do it, too far away. Donkeys gave stoicism a good name. The creature doesn't move, doesn't solicit our attention, or come trotting over like a horse. It's there because it's there, our witnessing of the saintly beast confers no blessing on the walk. (Heresy requires as large a leap of faith as any other doctrine.) Bresson's Balthazar, I recall, dies among a field of sheep, during a smuggling expedition.

A gravel road, between pollarded trees (no taller than Anna's head), leads down to a farm. To Caldecote. A small church excised from the Ordnance Survey map. Anna spotted, with magnifying glass, the ghost of a cross, on the large-scale Pathfinder: her faith is justified. This is the church where the ur-Hadmans, traced through Huntingdon records, are buried.

Except that it isn't a church, not now. At one time, Caldecote Church, placed between two manor farms, must have served the Washingley Estate. It is a private house, very much occupied, revamped. Dormer windows cut into the weathered tiles of the roof. Creeper encouraged around the porch. Garden furniture of a playfully rustic kind (wood teased to look like bone). Lots of yellow gravel. Nobody to be seen. The rules of the fairy story have to be obeyed. But humans have stepped out of the frame: a wooden recliner with a backrest that can be set in position, like a deckchair, by a series of notches. And on the grass, beside the recliner, a recently abandoned wrap or bathing suit, as brightly coloured as Professor Catling's Hawaiian shirt.

Vegetation threatens to overwhelm the church, swallow it up. The garden is under control, cut back; greenery will swamp the drive, climb the walls, leaving no trace of the former building. The graves and monuments have already disappeared. We will never find the burial place of the Washingley Hadmans.

Before we come away, to follow the path that will skirt Caldecote

Wood and bring us to Lutton, I try to get close to the church. I want a photograph from the east end. This manoeuvre involves my forcing a path through a tangled wood, clambering on a strategic stone: a gravestone. All the crosses and memorials of Caldecote have been removed to a thicket of thorn and ivy. There are stones arranged in straight lines and solitary slabs thatched with roots and creepers. Inscriptions are erased. Names sandpapered into obscurity. Centuries of memory have leached away; biographical details dripped into earth. Hadmans are here, but we can't find them. We were lucky to find the church, the replanted burial plot, hidden in the trees. I'm happy with Caldecote as the resolution of the small part of the story that I have been allowed to tell. Families emerge, thrive, vanish. They take their name from the ground they work and they give it back: blank grey stone, soon to be absorbed by nature.

Caldecote, struck from the official record, is a significant node; ancient paths branch off, uphill to Washingley, or across the fields to Lutton. Painted on a sliced cross-section of tree, like the cattle baron's ranch in a western, is the name of the property.

F. FOUNTAIN & SON. MANOR FARM. CALDECOTE. NEAR STILTON.

The name is familiar. I remember where I have seen it before: Delavals Farm, out on Glassmoor, land that once belonged to Anna's great-grandfather, William Rose. Fountain was the link. He owned the Caldecote farm that stood beside the church where the most distant Hadmans were buried: in the place where they had been recorded as 'labourers'. And he, or a namesake, also owned the Rose farm on Glassmoor. When we got back to Stilton, to the Bell Inn, I checked my files for the William Rose obituary. And there it was: 'Amongst friends in the Church and at the grave were noticed: F. Fountain.' A floral tribute was received, 'With deepest sympathy', from Mr & Mrs C. Fountain.

Whittlesey Mere, as described by John Bodger, stretched from the edge of Glassmoor to Caldecote; below Stilton, keeping out the water, was 'Caldecote Dike'. The aptly named F. Fountain owned property on both banks, properties that linked the two branches of Anna's tribe, the Roses and the Hadmans. The Mere, in my private reconfiguration of the land on either side of the Great North Road, became a swamp of ghosts: like Paul Nash's *Totes Meer*. This painting from 1941, the year of Geoffrey Hadman's poems, depicts an inland sea made from crashed aeroplanes. Sea of death. A blue-grey scene that marries flying and drowning.

Aircraft snub-nosed in Kentish cornfields. Gathered as scrap at the Cowley dump. Bruised silver with meat traces; crushed, wrinkled. Nash approached his painting through a series of photographs. In 1940 he visited Cowley to log wrecked German aircraft against a thinly wooded skyline.

Roger Cardinal, in a Nash monograph, describes *Totes Meer* as 'a lifeless metallic sea, a displaced arena of death set amid an otherwise pastoral English setting . . . a charnel house for winged creatures, a graveyard for birds'. He goes on to quote the writer Lance Sieveking, a trained pilot, who praised Nash: 'for his genius at evoking the sensations of flight despite never having gone up in a plane'.

The path to Lutton was clear, a solitary oak, then a series of white feedbags hung from branches to mark our way along the edge of the wood. They swayed and flapped in the breeze. There were no problems until we came to the BEWARE OF THE BULL notice. 'I'm not going into that field,' Anna said. As I blustered: this was an old trick. A right-of-way sign proved my point. 'Farmers always try to put you off with the bull thing.' And, since the alternative led to barbed-wire and unfordable ditches, Anna reluctantly agreed to follow the designated track.

We almost made it. A lane at the end of the field would let us out, a lane that ran south towards Little Gidding. The lane had a name: Bullock Road. And then I saw them, through a gap in the hedge, in a parallel field. A herd of white bullocks. Grazing. Or standing. Mostly standing, ears pricked. It was a large gap, a corridor. Anna had unpleasant childhood memories of bullocks. Perhaps she wouldn't notice them, their malign whiteness.

She froze. The worst had happened. The herd sniffed her panic. No point in retreating. We stepped it out. But the herd had our measure, they galloped in an idiot mob: stampede. Minor revenge before (or after) they were castrated, dehorned, carted off to the deep-freeze. There was another gap, we discovered, at the end of the field nearest to the road. This farmer was a sadist. The bulls swung through the distant gap and thundered straight at us.

I pushed Anna into the hedge and put myself in front of her, pretending I knew what I was doing. The animals were as dumb as they were blind; they charged straight past us, pulled up short and stood, snorting and stamping, denied their fun.

By which time, we were over the fence and in the lane. This must be the place Peter Ashley called 'Moonshine Gap': where Washingley drovers brought cattle down from the hills on their way to summer grazing in Glinton. I thought of James Stewart and Walter Brennan driving a herd to the Yukon in *The Far Country*. Classic American sentiment: the dream of saving money to buy that ranch in Wyoming. Bad things happen. It was Stewart's masochistic postwar period, on location with Anthony Mann, a sequence of savage landscape westerns.

Lutton was in reach, across fields, by a path that was increasingly English, increasingly remote from the A1: pylons on the horizon, oak avenues casting shadows over grey-brown corn. The village was caught in a deeper warp than any of the others (once you walked past the factory farm with the group of Balkans chattering at the gate). Lutton looked and behaved like one of those Salisbury Plain settlements taken over by the military during the Second World War and never returned. A church that can be visited once a year. A fake street laid out for the convenience of tank invasion.

The church is on a grassy mound. And it's open. We move

inside: a cool, musty retreat. This is where Richard Hadman, Anna's great-great-great-grandfather, married Elizabeth Hill, on 4 August 1788. Five years before the birth of John Clare. One year before the French Revolution.

For Anna, it was the end of her journey: the precise location where a tangible event had taken place, a marriage. This couple, Richard and Elizabeth, at twenty and twenty-one, were two years younger than we had been when we married, in 1967, a few miles up the A1, in Market Overton. (Breakfast taken, we headed straight back to London; and, on that afternoon, to Ireland.)

Anna stayed quietly at the back of the church. Later she told me that she had experienced a strong sense of a couple, standing before the altar. A sturdy figure in brown and his much shorter bride, who was wearing a long cream dress: Richard and Elizabeth. Anna witnessed an event that she was directing, the fall of light in a dim church.

I poked about, drawn by the sight of an American flag, the dazzle of the Stars and Stripes making a considerable noise in that drugged space. A coffin-altar had been set up, draped with the Pop Art flag, dressed with two silver bombers, on black plinths, inside bell jars. Two documents – PLEASE DO NOT MOVE – were placed in front of the bell jars: remembrance books for the wartime dead. The wall behind the shrine showed evidence of restoration work, or an erased mural. There was a stone effigy, a sleeper with curls, open eyes and a nose as flat as the Northampton cabbie.

And so we came, over the hills, to Warmington. Hedge sparrows fussed in the dirt. We walked faster, sweated, ran, to reach the only pub before the dreaded two-o'clock cut-off for food. Then wondered why we'd bothered; a heavy swill of battered cod and mushy peas sat on the belly as we bridged the Nene and strolled the last miles to Fotheringhay.

Anna was right, this conical mound (reminiscent of a less bald Beckton Alp) incubated melancholy; from its summit, achieved by a worn path, the Nene ox-bowed and twisted. Pleasure boats moored alongside, but excursionists didn't visit the ruins or the church; they picnicked on the bank. What was left of Mary Stuart's prison was a shadowprint, a freeze in the stone, a crop of giant thistles. (Like Scottish V-signs knitted with frost-bitten, purple fingers.)

One chunk of the original castle is itself imprisoned by black, painted, thistle-crowned bars.

IN MEMORY OF

MARY STUART, QUEEN OF SCOTS,

BEHEADED IN THE GREAT HALL

OF FOTHERINGHAY CASTLE

8TH FEBRUARY 1586/7

Fotheringhay, birthplace of Richard III, is an unlucky place; strategically sited, on a bend in the river, between Northampton and Peterborough (where dead queens are taken to lie in state). Dark clouds press on the mound. Invisible jets play chicken at the edge of the stratosphere. Their screams bounce off the hills, reverberate across the killing ground.

Mary Stuart was kept prisoner for sixteen years, moved from house to house, watched, confined, until she came here. For the black ritual of execution. Judges and witnesses lodged in the village and the surrounding farms. Mary arrived in Fotheringhay, 25 September 1586, accompanied by two gentlemen: Sir Amyas Paulet and Sir Thomas Gorges. Gorges was a name with roots in the area. John Clare's great-grandfather, another John Clare, married Alice Gorge in 1724. Their daughter, yet another Alice, had a child, born out of wedlock, with John Donald Parker. This was Parker Clare, father of the poet.

A cold prison, in the damp season, up against the Nene; Mary suffered badly from rheumatism and lack of exercise. She had to be supported to the block. The climate has not improved. We decided to call a cab to take us back to Stilton and, while we waited, we made a circuit of the church.

It seems that Mary Stuart was another versifier, a stopped poet, whose work at a time of crisis prefigured other writers of this country. 'In my end is my beginning,' she wrote, anticipating the Eliot of *Little Gidding*. 'What am I, alas, what purpose has my life?' shares its tone with another poem of confinement, Clare's most frequently anthologised piece, the Northampton elegy: 'I am – yet what I am, none cares or knows.'

The summoned cab-driver broke our mood. He made it appear as if he had been parked in Fotheringhay for months, waiting impatiently for us to complete our pedantic progress; when, all along, he had the story we needed.

'Got a metal plate in my leg,' he announced as he crashed the gears. 'Had to retire after twenty years in the job.'

And what, I had to ask, was that?

'London Brick Company, Whittlesey.'

He knew Bow, knew Hackney, all my haunts. He'd driven there with loads of bricks, mile after mile, up and down the A1; he was intimate with every greasy spoon. He lived in Ramsey Heights.

We had to laugh at this.

That Ramsey, an inch or two out of water, should have such a district. A traffic island was a considerable protuberance in the town of the Golden Python. Ramsey Heights, when I checked the map, was the depressed area we had come through in the narrowboat.

Not much had been said before the driver announced that he would offer us 'a bit of a tour, no charge – no hurry, now, to get back to the office'. Hadman business done, we were game. We saw fields that we had walked that morning flash past; he drove as if he knew there would be no other vehicles in the narrow back lanes. And he was right.

After Polebrook, I lost all sense of direction; the light was going and our man wanted to come off-road, into the woods. A private estate. He used to drive up here, so he said, with a cricketer. Nice bloke, unmarried; not a care in the world. The landowner allowed the villagers to play on his delightful pitch. The cabbie got to know the cricketer pretty well, picked him up most weekends; and, on these jaunts to scattered grounds, he learnt about the country too. 'Only thirty-six, he was,' the driver said, 'when he hanged himself. Military-medium bowler. They were quite upset, his mates. Who is going to open from Derek's end now?'

We weren't sorry to emerge on open road. We were ready for a bath and dinner.

'One more place to see.'

Line of poplars. Lowering sky. The cabbie with the plate in his leg limps around to open Anna's door. In the twilight, looking across a long, bare field to the pink horizon, we recognise a special place. We are standing on a section of antique grey-top; a preserved and maintained runway that stops abruptly at the edge of the grass. Flight aborted. Go close and you notice tyre tracks, the scorch of black rubber. And just where tarmac gives way to agricultural land: three sculpted shapes. Two slabs (stone tables). One glossy black triangle set on a plinth (in which a phantom bomber has been carved: 1943–1945).

I make the connection with the memorial in Lutton Church. The black pyramid, dressed with various symbols, honours THE 351st BOMBARDMENT GROUP (HEAVY). Men who: FLEW COMBAT MISSIONS FROM THIS AIRFIELD OVER OCCUPIED EUROPE.

Witnessing fly-pasts in Victoria Park (Hackney), formations of Second War veterans grumbling towards Buckingham Palace for some forgotten anniversary, Anna would always shed a tear. Even on television, bombers over London, sweeping down the Mall, were worth a sniff. The cabbie had brought us back to the war years, the period of our birth: before memory. A great shaft of light breaking through low cloud, illuminating sheds and barns that once were hangars, made old fears palpable. There was no film left in my camera. The vision, rapid movement of the eye, runway to lift-off, was therefore more intense. It wouldn't be recorded. Without the false corroboration of photographic record, memory is absolute. Outside time.

The second black slab, a catafalque with no corpse, was more provocative than the pyramid. Text in gold letters:

IN MEMORY OF LT. GENERAL JAMES T. STEWART, 1921–1980,
USAF COMMANDING OFFICER OF 508th SQ. 351st BOMB GROUP
WHO FLEW 60 COMBAT MISSIONS AGAINST THE ENEMY FROM
THIS AIRFIELD 1943–1945.

Jimmy Stewart. I'd clocked photographs in the biographies, cap on the slant, hands in pocket, posed outside an English hut. The lopsided look he'd perfected, sun too bright for the eyes. He suffered badly from the English cold, sniffled his way through two long winters. A visit to London was too much effort to contemplate. He preferred to spend time away from the base on a rented boat. The experiences of these years, flights over Germany, put iron into the Anthony Mann westerns. After Audie Murphy, Stewart was the most decorated military man in Hollywood. Clark Gable, so the cabbie told us, was in the next village. He turned up at local hops in a tailored uniform; fingering his thin moustache, flashing false teeth. He danced with the driver's mother.

Flying had been Stewart's passion from his earliest days in California: he took Katharine Hepburn up, just once, before going to work on *The Philadelphia Story*. He kept a plane on a private airfield. In later life, when he became a housebound recluse, deaf and solitary, his daughters recalled that he never read anything in his life except film scripts and flight magazines. Stewart was a convinced Republican, uneasy with ethnic minorities, a strong supporter of Nixon and Reagan. His last trip before retirement from the Air Force Reserve was to South-east Asia. He accompanied a bombing mission to the Cambodian border. His stepson, Ronald, died on a reconnaissance patrol in the Quang Tri province.

The light is almost gone. But I can make out the contents of the hinged glass box, the strangest element of this wartime memorial. A map pinned to the backboard: Polebrook and the airfield. A posy assembled from Stilton fields, ears of corn reduced to yellow dust.

A red cushion, stitched with white flowers, on which sits a blue 'Visitors Book' and a comic strip of battle, signed by the flight crew. The comic obscures the thing in the corner, a Whittlesey bear in a scarlet jersey. A flying bear, a mascot, safely returned from its raid on enemy territory.

We had achieved a satisfactory conclusion. Now I could let the story go. Daniel Sinclair of Ramsey, a person with an unknown life, a gravestone, had been absorbed into the invented Daniel Santa-Clara of José Saramago's novel. My obsession with doubles, doubled narratives, was brought at last to ground. Jimmy Stewart, freed from the fixed trajectory of Anthony Mann's westerns, from landscape, was named in gold letters on a black slab; an altar overlooking the yellow, evening fields of Middle England.

But I was wrong. You may have realised, as Michael Moorcock did, when he read an early proof of my book, that I had the wrong James Stewart. The actor had commanded a squadron, flown bombing raids over Germany, but not from here. His base was on the far side of the A1, closer to the sea. Stewart was born in 1908. Lieutenant-General James T. Stewart was fourteen years old when his namesake made his movie debut in *The Murder Man*. Both flyers, both in England at the same time. Our mysterious taxi driver, bringing us to his favourite shrine, vividly recalled those local legends, Stewart and Clark Gable. Figures who had stepped down from the screen to attend dances and church fêtes. Mike Goldmark, the gallery owner from Uppingham, told me that he once lived in Polebrook Lodge, Stewart's wartime home. We remember what we want to remember and forge our own autobiographies. The Clare I found will not be your John Clare, nor the poet Geoffrey Hadman claimed as a relative. The track we travelled, coming from London, is no longer Clare's Great North Road. Through error, perhaps, we arrive at a richer truth: in the telling is the tale. The trance of writing is the author's only defence against the world. He sleepwalks between assignments, between welcoming ghosts, looking out for the next prompt, the next milestone hidden in the grass.

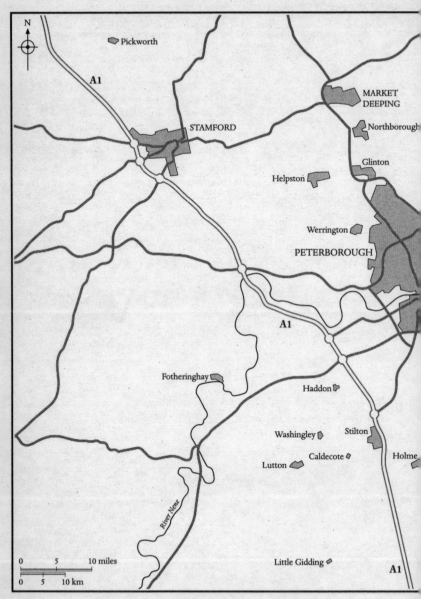

Edge of the Orison: Peterborough's gravitational field

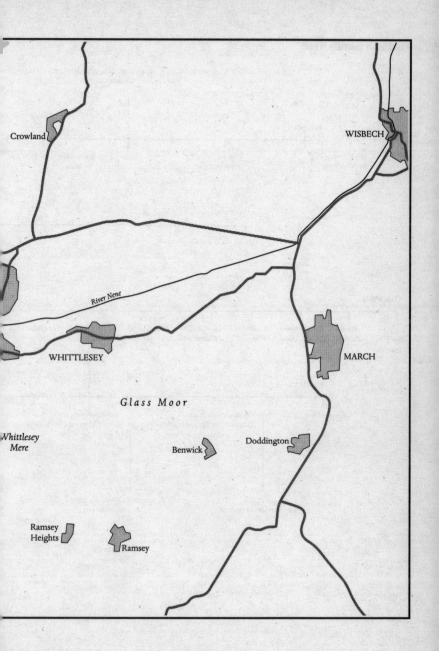

Hadman Family Tree

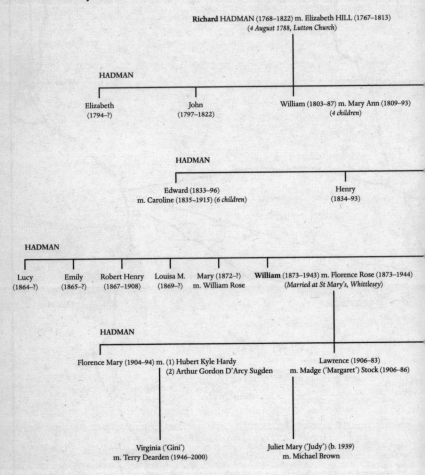

Richard HADMAN (1768–1822) m. Elizabeth HILL (1767–1813)
(4 August 1788, Lutton Church)

HADMAN

Elizabeth (1794–?)   John (1797–1822)   William (1803–87) m. Mary Ann (1809–93) *(4 children)*

HADMAN

Edward (1833–96)
m. Caroline (1835–1915) *(6 children)*   Henry (1834–93)

HADMAN

Lucy (1864–?)   Emily (1865–?)   Robert Henry (1867–1908)   Louisa M. (1869–?)   Mary (1872–?) m. William Rose   **William** (1873–1943) m. Florence Rose (1873–1944) *(Married at St Mary's, Whittlesey)*

HADMAN

Florence Mary (1904–94) m. (1) Hubert Kyle Hardy
(2) Arthur Gordon D'Arcy Sugden   Lawrence (1906–83)
m. Madge ('Margaret') Stock (1906–86)

Virginia ('Gini')
m. Terry Dearden (1946–2000)   Juliet Mary ('Judy') (b. 1939)
m. Michael Brown

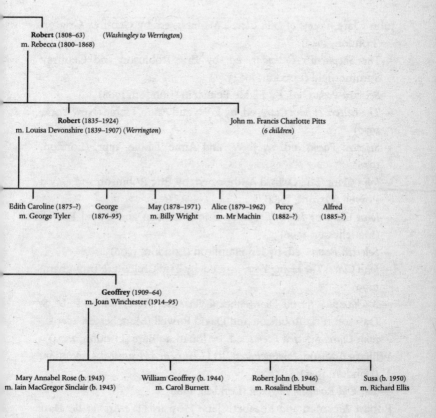

Robert (1808–63)   (*Washingley to Werrington*)
m. Rebecca (1800–1868)

Robert (1835–1924)   John m. Francis Charlotte Pitts
m. Louisa Devonshire (1839–1907) (*Werrington*)   (*6 children*)

Edith Caroline (1875–?)   George   May (1878–1971)   Alice (1879–1962)   Percy   Alfred
m. George Tyler   (1876–95)   m. Billy Wright   m. Mr Machin   (1882–?)   (1885–?)

Geoffrey (1909–64)
m. Joan Winchester (1914–95)

Mary Annabel Rose (b. 1943)   William Geoffrey (b. 1944)   Robert John (b. 1946)   Susa (b. 1950)
m. Iain MacGregor Sinclair (b. 1943)   m. Carol Burnett   m. Rosalind Ebbutt   m. Richard Ellis

367

Further Reading

John Clare, *Poems of John Clare's Madness*, ed. by Geoffrey Grigson (London, 1949)

—*The Shepherd's Calendar*, ed. by Eric Robinson and Geoffrey Summerfield (London, 1964)

—*Selected Poems*, ed. by Elaine Feinstein (London, 1968)

—*The Letters of John Clare*, ed. by J. W. and Anne Tibble (New York, 1970)

—*Selected Poems*, ed. by J. W. and Anne Tibble, repr. (London, 1976)

—*John Clare*, The Oxford Authors, ed. by Eric Robinson and David Powell (Oxford, 1984)

—*John Clare by Himself*, ed. by Eric Robinson and David Powell (Manchester, 1996)

—*Selected Poems*, ed. by Ian Hamilton (London, 1996)

—*John Clare: The Living Year, 1841*, ed. by Tim Chilcott (Nottingham, 1999)

—*A Champion for the Poor (Political Verse and Prose)*, ed. by P. M. S. Dawson, Eric Robinson and David Powell (Manchester, 2000)

—*John Clare, Selected Poems*, ed. by Jonathan Bate (London, 2004)

William Addison, *Epping Forest, Its Literary and Historical Associations* (London, 1945)

—*The Old Roads of England* (London, 1980)

Robert Aickman and Elizabeth Jane Howard, *We Are for the Dark* (London, 1951)

Jean-Philippe Antoine, Gertrud Koch and Luc Lang, *Gerhard Richter* (Paris, 1995)

John Ashbery, *Other Traditions* (Cambridge, Mass., 2000)

Peter Astley, *Comings and Goings* (London, 2002)

Deirdre Bair, *Samuel Beckett: A Biography* (London, 1978)

B. C. Barker-Benfield, *Shelley's Guitar (A Bicentenary Exhibition)* (Bodleian Library, Oxford, 1992)

John Barrell, *The Idea of Landscape and the Sense of Place (1730–1840): An Approach to the Poetry of John Clare* (Cambridge, 1972)

Jonathan Bate, *John Clare: A Biography* (London, 2003)

Samuel Beckett, *Endgame* (London, 1958)

Henry Bett, *English Legends* (London, 1950)

Renchi Bicknell, *Michael and Mary Dreaming (A Walk along the Michael and Mary Lines . . .)* (Alton, n.d. [1998])

Ronald Blythe, *Talking about John Clare* (Nottingham, 1999)

Edward Bond, *The Fool* (London, 1976)

Marilyn Brakhage, 'Stan Brakhage: Last Drawings', from *Square One (No. 2)*, ed. by Jennifer Dunbar Dorn, et al. (Denver, Colo., 2004)

Bill Brandt, *Literary Britain*, new edn (London, 1984)

Judith Bunten and Alfred Savage, *Werrington through the Ages: A History in Photographs* (Werrington, 1987)

Edward North Buxton, *Epping Forest*, 7th edn rev. (London, 1905)

Roger Cardinal, *The Landscape Vision of Paul Nash* (London, 1989)

Brian Catling, *Large Ghost* (Cambridge, 2001)

William Cobbett, *Rural Rides*, new edn with notes by Pitt Cobbett (London, 1885)

Stephen Coote, *Byron, The Making of a Myth* (London, 1988)

Thomas De Quincey, *The Collected Writings*, vol. III, ed. by David Masson (Edinburgh, 1890)

Donald Dewey, *James Stewart: A Biography* (London, 1997)

Edward Dowden, *The Life of Percy Bysshe Shelley* (London, 1886)

T. S. Eliot, *Four Quartets* (London, 1959)

Elaine Feinstein, *Ted Hughes: The Life of a Poet* (New York, 2001)

Robert Gittings, *John Keats* (London, 1968)

Geoffrey Hadman, *Spirit's Expense*, privately published (London, 1941)

Thomas Hardy, *Tess of the D'Urbervilles*, repr. (London, 1957)

Michael Hastings, *Calico* (London, 2004)

Richard Holmes, *Shelley: The Pursuit* (London, 1974)

H. J. K. Jenkins, *Along the Nene* (Exeter, 1991)

James Joyce, *Finnegans Wake*, 3rd edn (London, 1964)

James Knowlson, *Damned to Fame: The Life of Samuel Beckett* (London, 1996)

Howard C. Levis, ed., *Bladud of Bath. The British King Who Tried to Fly*, repr. (Bath, 1973)

John Mackintosh, *A Song of Summer* (Kirkcaldy, 2001)

Brenda Maddox, *Nora: A Biography of Nora Joyce* (London, 1988)

Charles Mapleston, *A Painter in Search of a Poet (Rigby Graham & John Clare)* (Uppingham, 1992)

E. W. Martin, *The Secret People (English Village Life after 1750)* (London, 1954)

Frederick W. Martin, *The Life of John Clare*, 2nd edn (London, 1964)

Gary Spencer Millidge, ed., *Alan Moore: Portrait of an Extraordinary Gentleman* (Quebec, Canada, 2003)

G. E. Mingay, *Rural Life in Victorian England* (London, 1976)

Alan Moore, *Voice of the Fire* (London, 1996)

Henrietta Moraes, *Henrietta* (London, 1994)

Gerda S. Norvig, *Dark Figures in the Desired Country: Blake's Illustrations to The Pilgrim's Progress* (Berkeley, Ca., 1993)

Christopher Petit, *Robinson* (London, 1993)

Tom Raworth, *Moving* (London, 1971)

Herbert Read, *Paul Nash* (London, 1944)

Gerhard Richter, *The Daily Practice of Painting* (London, 1995)

William St Clair, *Trelawny: The Incurable Romantic* (London, 1977)

José Saramago, *The Double* (London, 2004)

Will Self, *How the Dead Live* (London, 2000)

James Sharpe, *Dick Turpin: The Myth of the English Highwayman* (London, 2004)

Carol Loeb Shloss, *Lucia Joyce: To Dance in the Wake* (New York, 2003)

Iain Sinclair, *White Chappell, Scarlet Tracings* (Uppingham, 1987)

—*Flesh Eggs & Scalp Metal: Selected Poems (1970–1987)* (London, 1989)

—*London Orbital: A Walk around the M25* (London, 2002)

Edward Storey, *A Right to Song (The Life of John Clare)* (London, 1982)

C. E. Street, *Earthstars: The Visionary Landscape* (London, 2000)

Kim Taplin, *The English Path*, 2nd edn rev. (Sudbury, Suffolk, 2000)

James Thomson, *The Seasons*, pocket edn (London, 1838)

J. W. and Anne Tibble, *John Clare: His Life & Poetry* (London, 1956)

Izaak Walton, *The Compleat Angler*, Wordsworth Classics, reissue (Ware, Hertfordshire, 1996)

Bernard T. Ward, *Lawrence of Arabia & Pole Hill, Chingford*, repr. (Chingford, 1987)

Colin Watson, *Snobbery with Violence* (London, 1971)

June Wilson, *Green Shadows: The Life of John Clare* (London, 1951)

Simon Winchester, *The Map That Changed the World* (London, 2001)

Acknowledgements

One aspect of the story belongs to Anna Sinclair; her company on the expeditions, her memories. What I have presented in terms of Hadman family history is my version of Anna's telling, the episodes I asked her to recall. In points of detail, these will not be the memories of her brothers and sister. But I thank them for additional facts and other prompts, challenges and provocations. Susa Ellis retrieved her father's privately published poems at the optimum moment. Bill Hadman alerted me to the King's Cross war memorial and the Hadman who sailed on the *Titanic*. Anna's cousins, Gini Dearden and Juliet (Judy) Brown, provided much useful information. The Rose family connections – Norman and Carol Turner of Doddington, Michael and Pat Turner of Whittlesey – gave time and hospitality to importunate strangers. They treated Anna, at once, as a long-lost relative.

Out on the road, Renchi Bicknell's presence was, as ever, relished: always nudging the Hunter S. Thompson scenario in the direction of John Bunyan (all tracks lead to Bedford). Chris Petit's pertinent eye was valued as much as his measured asides: a necessary counterbalance to overheated rhetoric. In their contrary fashion, these men are true poets of the English landscape: ghost roads, river roads and motorway service stations. Both the paintings and the narrative of Emma Matthews haunted our walk.

The project would have stumbled without injections of blood/ treacle/gunpowder from Brian Catling in Oxford and Alan Moore in Northampton. Moore has pulled off that nice conceit of converting the stubbornly local into the universal: hill town as rock in celestial ocean. Without Catling's narrowboat, memory traces would have vanished for ever into the black depths of Whittlesey Mere.

For guidance and for valuable documentary evidence about Glinton and Werrington, I would like to thank Judith Bunten, Val Hetzel, Veronica Smith, Val Watkinson. Paul Green and Peter Astley gave me the benefit of their knowledge: sidebars on Peterborough, Ramsey, Engine Farm.

B. C. Barker-Benfield of the Bodleian Library in Oxford and the staffs of the Northampton Central Library, the Northamptonshire Record Office at Wootton Hall Park, the County Record Office in Huntingdon, the Peterborough Library, were courteous and helpful towards a resolutely unfocused and non-academic project.

Transcripts of Clare's 'Journey out of Essex' and other relevant materials were made from notebooks, ledgers and microfilm, in Northampton Library. But any invasion of the life and work of the Helpston poet's autobiographical writings must acknowledge the pioneering scholarship of Eric Robinson, the diligent decrypting of close-woven texts. Jonathan Bate's Clare biography is a definitive achievement against which earlier accounts must be checked. John Barrell's meditations on landscape, enclosures and open-field poetics were an inspiration.

For books, deeds, advice I would also like to thank: Vanessa Bicknell, Keggie Carew, Jennifer Dunbar Dorn, Melinda Gebbie, Mike Goldmark, Rigby Graham, Kevin Jackson, Juliette Mitchell, Peter Moyse (of the John Clare Society), John Richard Parker, Simon Prosser, Tom Raworth, Revd George Rogers, Paul Smith, Paddy Summerfield.

A version of the chapter entitled 'Ouse' was published, in a very different form, as a 'Diary' piece in the *London Review of Books*.

The Clare portrait, used as a frontispiece is reproduced by permission of Northampton Libraries & Information Service. The Shelley Memorial photograph is by Paddy Summerfield and is reproduced with his permission. The Straw Bear portrait is taken from the photographic collection of the Warburg Institute. Other photographs are by Iain Sinclair, or borrowed from Hadman and Rose family archives.

Index

IAIN SINCLAIR

LONDON ORBITAL

Encircling London like a noose, the M25 is a road to nowhere, but when Iain Sinclair sets out to walk this asphalt loop – keeping within the 'acoustic footprints' – he is determined to find out where the journey will lead him. Stumbling upon converted asylums, industrial and retail parks, ring-fenced government institutions and lost villages, Sinclair discovers a Britain of the fringes, a landscape consumed by developers. *London Orbital* charts this extraordinary trek and round trip of the soul, revealing the country as you've never seen it before.

'Erudite, ingenious, exhilarating, involving, unpredictable, enchanting … as a Hobson-Jobson to the quirks of a hidden England you feared had vanished it's unbeatable' *Spectator*

'Lucid, accessible, inventive, witty' *Independent*

'A journey into the heart of darkness and a fascinating snapshot of who we are, lit by Sinclair's vivid prose. I'm sure it will be read fifty years from now' *Observer*

IAIN SINCLAIR

DINING ON STONES

Andrew Norton, poet, visionary and hack, is handed a mysterious package that sees him quit London and head out along the A13 on an as yet undefined quest. Holing up in a roadside hotel, unable to make sense of his search, he is haunted by ghosts: of the dead and the not-so dead; demanding wives and ex-wives; East End gangsters; even competing versions of himself. Shifting from Hackney to Hastings and all places in-between, while dissecting a man's fractured psyche piece by piece, *Dining on Stones* is a puzzle and a quest – for both writer and reader.

'Spectacular: the work of a man with the power to see things as they are, and magnify that vision with a clarity that is at once hallucinatory and forensic' *Independent on Sunday*

'Brilliant, startlingly insightful. A fiercely original and distinctive writer' *Financial Times*

'Sinclair breathes wondrous life into monstrous, man-made landscapes. He has now excelled his previous efforts to tread where other writers fear to … *Dining on Stones* [is the] bastard son of *London Orbital*' *The Times Literary Supplement*

He just wanted a decent book to read ...

Not too much to ask, is it? It was in 1935 when Allen Lane, Managing
Director of Bodley Head Publishers, stood on a platform at Exeter railway
station looking for something good to read on his journey back to London.
His choice was limited to popular magazines and poor-quality paperbacks –
the same choice faced every day by the vast majority of readers, few of
whom could afford hardbacks. Lane's disappointment and subsequent anger
at the range of books generally available led him to found a company – and
change the world.

*'We believed in the existence in this country of a vast reading public for intelligent
books at a low price, and staked everything on it'*
Sir Allen Lane, 1902–1970, founder of Penguin Books

The quality paperback had arrived – and not just in bookshops. Lane was
adamant that his Penguins should appear in chain stores and tobacconists,
and should cost no more than a packet of cigarettes.

Reading habits (and cigarette prices) have changed since 1935, but
Penguin still believes in publishing the best books for everybody to
enjoy. We still believe that good design costs no more than bad design,
and we still believe that quality books published passionately and responsibly
make the world a better place.

So wherever you see the little bird – whether it's on a piece of
prize-winning literary fiction or a celebrity autobiography, political tour
de force or historical masterpiece, a serial-killer thriller, reference book,
world classic or a piece of pure escapism – you can bet that it represents
the very best that the genre has to offer.

Whatever you like to read – trust Penguin.